T0215445

API Marketplace Engineering

Design, Build, and Run a Platform for External Developers

Rennay Dorasamy

Apress®

API Marketplace Engineering: Design, Build, and Run a Platform for
External Developers

Rennay Dorasamy
Johannesburg, Gauteng, South Africa

ISBN-13 (pbk): 978-1-4842-7312-8   ISBN-13 (electronic): 978-1-4842-7313-5
https://doi.org/10.1007/978-1-4842-7313-5

Copyright © 2022 by Rennay Dorasamy

This work is subject to copyright. All rights are reserved by the Publisher, whether the whole or part of the material is concerned, specifically the rights of translation, reprinting, reuse of illustrations, recitation, broadcasting, reproduction on microfilms or in any other physical way, and transmission or information storage and retrieval, electronic adaptation, computer software, or by similar or dissimilar methodology now known or hereafter developed.

Trademarked names, logos, and images may appear in this book. Rather than use a trademark symbol with every occurrence of a trademarked name, logo, or image we use the names, logos, and images only in an editorial fashion and to the benefit of the trademark owner, with no intention of infringement of the trademark.

The use in this publication of trade names, trademarks, service marks, and similar terms, even if they are not identified as such, is not to be taken as an expression of opinion as to whether or not they are subject to proprietary rights.

While the advice and information in this book are believed to be true and accurate at the date of publication, neither the authors nor the editors nor the publisher can accept any legal responsibility for any errors or omissions that may be made. The publisher makes no warranty, express or implied, with respect to the material contained herein.

Managing Director, Apress Media LLC: Welmoed Spahr
Acquisitions Editor: Jonathan Gennick
Development Editor: Laura Berendson
Coordinating Editor: Jill Balzano

Cover image designed by Freepik (www.freepik.com)

Distributed to the book trade worldwide by Springer Science+Business Media LLC, 1 New York Plaza, Suite 4600, New York, NY 10004. Phone 1-800-SPRINGER, fax (201) 348-4505, e-mail orders-ny@springer-sbm.com, or visit www.springeronline.com. Apress Media, LLC is a California LLC and the sole member (owner) is Springer Science + Business Media Finance Inc (SSBM Finance Inc). SSBM Finance Inc is a **Delaware** corporation.

For information on translations, please e-mail booktranslations@springernature.com; for reprint, paperback, or audio rights, please e-mail bookpermissions@springernature.com.

Apress titles may be purchased in bulk for academic, corporate, or promotional use. eBook versions and licenses are also available for most titles. For more information, reference our Print and eBook Bulk Sales web page at http://www.apress.com/bulk-sales.

Any source code or other supplementary material referenced by the author in this book is available to readers on GitHub via the book's product page, located at www.apress.com/9781484273128. For more detailed information, please visit http://www.apress.com/source-code.

Printed on acid-free paper

For Dineshree, Kerisha, and Nicalen

Table of Contents

About the Author

Rennay Dorasamy has spent the last 20 years in various technology roles, ranging from architecture to development to operations, across a number of industries. He has worked in telecoms, with the government, and most recently in financial services. He has considerable hands-on integration experience working on middleware platforms from C-based messaging to Java Enterprise Edition. He is experienced in both core enterprise and digital contexts. As a full-stack engineer, he is intimately familiar with technologies such as containerization, cloud, and serverless technology for building and deploying mission-critical solutions. He is currently the Engineering Lead of an API Marketplace implementation, the first of its kind in financial services on the African continent.

About the Technical Reviewer

Robert Stackowiak is an independent consultant, adjunct instructor at Loyola University of Chicago, and author. He formerly was a Data and Artificial Intelligence Architect at the Microsoft Technology Center in Chicago and, prior to that, worked at Oracle for 20 years and led teams supporting North America focused on data warehousing and Big Data. Bob has also spoken at numerous industry conferences internationally. His books include *Design Thinking in Software and AI Projects* (Apress), *Azure Internet of Things Revealed* (Apress), *Remaining Relevant in Your Tech Career: When Change Is the Only Constant* (Apress), *Architecting the Industrial Internet* (Packt Publishing), *Big Data and the Internet of Things: Enterprise Architecture for a New Age* (Apress), *Oracle Big Data Handbook* (Oracle Press), *Oracle Essentials* (O'Reilly Media), and *Professional Oracle Programming* (Wiley Publishing). You can follow him on Twitter at @rstackow and/or read his articles and posts on LinkedIn.

Acknowledgments

First and foremost, this would not have been possible without God – from inception to completion. I would like to thank my wife and the nucleus of my power core, Dineshree, for her love and support during this project. Most importantly, for her unwavering understanding and patience when I set out on these crazy conquests. It means more to me than she will ever know. To my children – Kerisha and Nicalen – I am sincerely sorry if this book took away time that I should have been spending with you. I hope that the result makes you proud. The sagely advice, motivation, and counsel from my good friend, Asif Hamza, encouraged me to continually set the bar higher.

The African proverb that it takes a village to raise a child rings true, and I have been able to take on a project of this magnitude with a lifetime of encouragement, support, and belief from my family – Mannie, Ronnie, Kamala, Savanthala, Viverge, Tanya, Ethan, Neshica, Kerushen, Nishen, Kershnee, Alena, Ayla, Lawrence, Daisy, and Shivaal – and friends – Ajay, Nafisa, Zara, Rayyan, Bilal, Brett, Jairaj, Jason, JJ, Kiren, Mark, Paul "PCB," Rajesh, Sree, Srinath, Tony, Trevlyn, Vish, Walter, Warren, Waseem, and William (Mr. Magic).

To my fearless crewmates from the Starship Enterprise – Jacque Coetzee (Captain Kirk), Amjid "AJ" Ali (Mr. Spock), Kevin Kalil (Dr. McCoy), and Gareth Hiepner (Uhura) – it has been both an honor and a privilege to serve as the Head of Engineering (Scotty). I consider myself lucky as it is not often you get to work with like-minded people *and* people you really like. Special mention to our previous Product Owner, Shiv Rajah, who played a key role in our evolution.

Building the platform also afforded me the opportunity of working with a multinational team with a wealth of knowledge and experience, some of whom I have never met in person – all whom I consider lifelong friends: Philip Anderson, Shafaat Ali Yasir, my intercontinental brothers Ravi Shah (Mr. Open Banking) and Amit Pareek (API Connect Master), the indomitable Lakshmi Basireddy (Guardian of Quality), Miguel de Barros, Kaushik Lala, Dr. Ferdinand Damon, Donald Sepeng, Brightly Mphahlele, Mthobisi Kunene, Monika Vadlapudi, David Napo, Anvitha Swarangi,

ACKNOWLEDGMENTS

Sathya Perumalsamy, Deepika Chalpe, Deepika Jain, Ummair Asghar, Charles Swart, Dingane Hlaluka, Hina Kanwal, Olivier Mulmann, Shahanoor Ahmed, Priya Singh, Sahiti Nedunuri, Chenchaiah Sudulagunta, Louw Fouche, Ndoda Keswa, and Elizabeth Congdon.

I am also extremely proud to be working in an organization with seasoned veterans across several enterprise capabilities, who have been pivotal to the implementation of our Marketplace. API Gateway: Tiaan Mouton, Andries Marx, Nkomo Magolo, Lance Moore. Identity: Ashley Govender, Danie Weideman, Willie Visagie, Bhavna Yerpude, Heidi Van Zyl, SW Engelbrecht. Quality Assurance: Oagile Nthutang, Kamil Maharaj, Manesh Hari, Azeez Salawu, Criscelda Mogane. DevOps: Jaco Greyling, Steve Breyer-Menke, Marcus Talken, Darren George, Wayne Turner, Adam Aucamp. Architecture: Nico Basson, Paul Sing, Adele Jones, Bruce Barker, Ryan Mulholland, Gerard de Jong, Gys Le Roux, Louis Werth, Lourens Labuschange. Project Management: Gerhard Rabie, Annalinde Singh, Neziwe Manaka, Cyrilise Palmer, Jo Thindwa. Product: Shirley Malope, Serisha Iyer, Charles Phillips, Warren Tromp. Infrastructure: Jan Jacobs, Tumelo Malete, George Phage, Maanda Ambani. External: Pieter Myburgh, Lovemore Nalube, Dylan Youens, George Nel, Hardus van der Berg, Akash Shaha, Loyiso Matymza, Damon Vrkoc, Kabelo Mokwana, Henry Oertel. Forensics: Justin Fairhurst. Business Analysis: Tshepo Mekgoe, Kerassa Pillay, Pravesh Mungaldave. Information Security: Phillip Gerber, Tian Gerber, Enzlin Burts. Network Security: Andre Jansen, Jared Camberg, Iaan Botha. Change and Release: Amanda Kopolo, Patiwe Singapi, Stephanie van Ross, Cecil Loots, Marty Dada, Liesl Moss.

To the Apress team – Jonathan Gennick, Jill Balzano, Robert Stackowiak, Laura Berendson, and Welmoed Spahr – I cannot thank you enough for this opportunity of a lifetime. It is uncanny – although we are continents apart, I have continually felt your guidance and presence throughout the process.

Last, but not least, special thanks to Marco Vidulich and Ray Naicker for their leadership and uncanny ability to see around corners and the courage and resolute conviction to pioneer unchartered territory to build what has become Africa's leading API Marketplace.

Introduction

An API Marketplace is a key enabler for any organization with a goal of establishing a platform business. Due to its purpose as a digital channel between third-party developers and the enterprise, it is a delicate balancing act. Allowing access to internal services and capability – with fine-grained control. Innovative products and solutions – subject to organizational governance. Blindingly fast agile delivery – in accordance with enterprise standards of quality. Liberation and democratization of customer data – with consent. Planet-scale architectures on cutting-edge technology – with enterprise grade reliability.

The basic premise of an API Marketplace is openness. Continuing in this spirit, the intention of this book is to document the journey our implementation has been on, for many years now – to share our experience, learnings, pitfalls, and solutions with Engineering teams that are about to set out, or that may already be on a similar quest. The approaches and solutions discussed have evolved over time and are in a continual state of optimization. It is my sincere hope that it will accelerate other implementations and further enhancements of those platforms will also be shared to catalyze adoption of the practice.

Primarily intended for a technical audience, this book provides a view of an API Marketplace from different perspectives. As a point of departure, I identify the vision and goal of an API Marketplace – essentially the problem it solves (*why?*), the approach (*how?*), and the roles needed (*who?*). I then take a detailed look at the global wave of regulation sweeping over the Financial Services industry, which is also likely to occur in other sectors – such as Telecommunications and Health. The purpose is to understand the drivers for regulation and various responses from different territories to help you define the identity and roadmap of your platform.

A new digital channel brings a new audience, and in my chapter on Consumption, I discuss strategies to help both business and technical users understand and access the platform. In the chapter on Monetization, I discuss the nucleus of our implementation – the *API Marketplace flywheel*, as we call it – which has afforded our implementation self-sustainability. I also discuss the various technical elements in detail which are needed to support various billing approaches – some established, some evolutionary, some revolutionary.

Building an API Marketplace requires a change of mindset regarding Platform Architecture, API Design, and Delivery, and in these chapters, we dive into the detail of our approach – both past and present. A Sandbox environment is a critical element of any Marketplace implementation, and I propose strategies to handle various types of scenarios and consumers. Possibly the most demanding, but also the most exciting and dynamic, stage of an API product in its lifecycle is in an operational context. I provide an honest account of our experience, both good and bad, enablers, and practices to provide enterprise-level support for our implementation.

To navigate this book, I would suggest starting with Chapter 1, which sets the context for an API Marketplace, then diving into the chapter which most aligns to your area of interest.

- If you are still researching or deciding to build an API Marketplace, start with *Regulation*, then *Monetization*.

- Product Owners should start with *Consumption* and *Monetization*.

- Platform teams should start with *Platform Architecture*, then understand the *Sandbox* requirement and the execution context of *Operations*.

- Delivery Leads and Development teams should start with *API Design*, then *Development, Sandbox, Operations*, then circle back to *Consumption*.

CHAPTER 1

API Engineering

An API Marketplace is a platform for an organization to share internal services with third-party developers. The Application Programming Interface (API) is the mechanism used to achieve the access. Capability is packaged into different products – for example, to access customer data or to send messages on a GSM network. Much like a real-world Marketplace, this is the rendezvous point between the organization (seller) and third party (buyer) where the products are advertised and consumed.

Some API Marketplace initiatives start out of necessity – to meet regulatory compliance – some to play catch-up with competitors, while others are purely evolutionary. Ours started with a Vision. The aim was to empower third-party providers to harness the capability of our enterprise to better serve the needs of our customers. The altruistic view is that it results in a positive outcome for all participants. A win for the organization – revenue through increased consumption. A win for our customers – improved service through innovation. And importantly, a win for a third party – the ability to leverage established organizational capability to build a new product or service.

As pioneers in our market, even country, we were not bound with the shackles of project deadlines, or to meet regulatory timelines, and did not have competitors nipping at our heels. From the outset, we were acutely aware that an API Marketplace is a tremendous and rare opportunity to build a new digital channel to work with external parties, but the initiative needed to sustain itself and to generate revenue. We were fortunate to be given a blank slate and the latitude to make technology decisions which were outside the standard convention of the organization. Our key learning is that the foundational elements of the Marketplace are Technology, Process, and most importantly – People.

In this chapter, we start with the enabling technology element, the API, the capabilities it can afford, and ways in which large organizations have successfully used it. We then discuss the API Marketplace process, its purpose, and operation relative to the greater organization. We then move on to the people element and discuss the key roles which underpin an API Marketplace implementation.

© Rennay Dorasamy 2022
R. Dorasamy, *API Marketplace Engineering*, https://doi.org/10.1007/978-1-4842-7313-5_1

APIs in Action

Every night, before I go to bed, I walk up to one of the many Amazon Echo devices scattered around my home and casually whisper *"Alexa, Goodnight."* The TV, Audio Visual (AV) equipment, and lights turn off, and Alexa whispers a sweet message bidding me goodnight. One day, I will hopefully have a smart lock which will join that routine. To the layman, this may seem easy to achieve – however, this is integration engineering at its finest. It is simple, reliable, and easy to use. And it is all underpinned by APIs.

The words I spoke to Alexa were sent to a speech recognition service which converted the speech to text. Thereafter a Natural Language Understanding (NLU) service converted the text to an Alexa intent. The intent triggered smart home skills which interface to my universal remote and light automation via APIs. For this seemingly simple request, it triggered a wave of activity that probably spanned continents. Let us zero in on the light automation piece of this scenario.

For the light automation, there is a hardware relay which responds to a radio signal to either switch to an "on" or "off" state. To achieve this, the manufacturer created a transmitter and a receiver. So, instead of using the traditional light switch, which is physically embedded in the wall, I can send the request from a mobile transmitter. The manufacturer also provided the capability to initiate the request using a mobile device. To be honest, this was one of the key requirements for my selection of this specific relay – as being able to turn lights on and off remotely, especially when friends are over, is every techie's dream. However, what really clinched the deal for me was an arbitrary reference to an API on a lonely link in the corner of the product documentation.

The API allows direct software integration via HTTP to the relays without using the manufacturer's proprietary hardware interface. By exposing the API, the potential of the relay increased significantly. Trigger events are not limited to the remote transmitter or even the mobile application. It could be linked to sensors which determine the level of light, motion, or occupancy. It could also be linked to external services like Amazon Alexa or Google Assistant – and triggered by voice command. Possibilities are endless, and the humble relay which is hidden away in an electrical duct is now a meaningful contributor in a greater ecosystem.

And the pivotal component, which makes that ecosystem possible, is an API.

What Makes APIs So Special?

Although the lighting scenario might seem particularly intriguing and many might be inspired by the ability to turn off a light using software, the hardcore engineer reading this might not be so easily impressed. After all, the "interfacing" capability may have been available for years, and if you peel off the packaging and reveal the underlying circuit board, there may be jumpers on the board which allow this capability by simply applying a current to PIN#1. APIs? Big deal.

Although the lighting scenario is possible and it can be argued, it has been possible for *years*, there is only a small subset of people who have the technical acumen and ability to achieve it. Of this, there is even a smaller subset with the will to apply currents to pins on circuit boards. I can painfully recall wanting to turn on a lava lamp at the end of an automated build many years ago to indicate the build had failed but was not able to as I could not easily make the jump from software to hardware back then.

Like any democratizing technology, APIs allow access to the masses. APIs do this by being easy to consume, technology agnostic, and well documented. APIs have been modelled purposefully using constructs such as HTTP which underpin communication of the Internet. The use of a neutral platform allows different technology on either side of the interface. Although this may seem trivial, integration between systems has either been strictly proprietary, or attempts to make it neutral have been significantly complex. Anyone who has worked with Common Object Request Broker Architecture (CORBA) will relate that setting up client and server communications is no easy task.

JavaScript Object Notation (JSON) is also a pivotal component of this movement. It offers a lightweight mechanism to exchange data. Its predecessors such as Simple Object Access Protocol (SOAP) have attempted to achieve this through Extensible Markup Language (XML) for years. However, JSON is far more malleable and forgiving. The key element is that it is *human*-readable. Again, the hardcore engineer in the corner of the room, sipping on his cup of black coffee, is probably muttering that XML is *human*-readable too. The difference is *simplicity* – from first-hand experience, scanning through a list of key-value pairs is far easier than trying to keep track of opening and closing XML tags with embedded values.

One of my favorite stories is the Tower of Babel. The part that I really gravitated to was that people spoke a common language and understood each other. This presented *enormous* potential. Although there have been incredible advances over the centuries due to individual contributions from the likes of Newton and Einstein, we can achieve more through collaboration and sharing information. Again, the underlying premise is

3

the *ease* of the communication. It should be natural as speaking and APIs are a firm step in that direction.

Websites and mobile applications have revolutionized how we consume information. User Interface (UI) and User Experience (UX) define the navigation and flow of an interface. APIs are a key enabler of front ends and allow the clear separation between UI and logic.

Connectedness, Sharing, and Survival

Undoubtedly, the Internet has enabled an unprecedented level of connectedness. I cannot imagine how generations before us sat patiently waiting without updates, while their significant others were delayed in shopping queues. Or driving around without a GPS-enabled app, only armed with a paper map, trying to find street names or having to ask strangers for directions. With the first wave of the Internet outside academia, organizations established presence by having a website. Today, almost every organization needs a website and without one, identity and trust cannot be established.

This slowly evolved from a "contact us" form to full blown e-commerce capabilities which allowed end users to interact directly with suppliers. Smart phones have also enabled applications which allow direct interaction between end consumer and provider. Thankfully, due to the low price point of devices and the widespread availability of mobile data, large percentages of the world's population are now connected. This has also given rise to a wave of sharing.

Services such as Airbnb allow people to rent out a spare room or an entire home. Ride sharing services like Uber and Lyft are super simple to use and are constantly innovating with options such as low-cost trips and package delivery. This has enabled a paradigm shift as it could allow people to not make long-term investments in property and motor vehicles. Future generations may not need a driver's license as it may be more economical and practical to use ridesharing than owning a car.

From an industry perspective, the lines between organizations are blurring. One of the most successful mobile money services in East Africa is run by a telecommunications company. Healthcare providers have also entered the banking fray and are providing financial services. Banks have not rested on their laurels and are now offering telecoms services as Mobile Virtual Network Operators (MVNO).

Although movements into new industries are possible, it is far more difficult for established organizations to achieve this. However, collaboration and partnership are another route which could help established organizations to transition. Although it might seem "counter-survival," working with startups and potential disruptors could be the mechanism that allows an organization to survive. The adage of "*if you can't beat them, join them*" rings true, and many organizations are now partnering with startups and participating in bootcamps to incubate new, fresh perspectives. In much the same way as it seems unfathomable today for an organization to not have a website or a mobile application, not having an API for consumption will be viewed the same way in the future.

An API Manifesto

APIs are not new. The concept has been around for years and has been used internally within enterprises to achieve integration between applications. In 2002, Jeff Bezos issued an API Mandate, sometimes referred to as the "API Manifesto," which reads as follows:

All teams will henceforth expose their data and functionality through service interfaces.

- Teams must communicate with each other through these interfaces.

- There will be no other form of inter-process communication allowed: no direct linking, no direct reads of another team's data store, no shared-memory model, no backdoors whatsoever. The only communication allowed is via service interface calls over the network.

- It doesn't matter what technology you use.

- All service interfaces, without exception, must be designed from the ground up to be externalize-able. That is to say, the team must plan and design to be able to expose the interface to developers in the outside world. No exceptions.

- The mandate closed with: Anyone who doesn't do this will be fired. Thank you; have a nice day!

Any organization with a decent integration strategy reading through this may not be too concerned. After all, middleware is meant to achieve all the above – abstraction, clean interfaces. However, the words from the manifesto "*developers in the outside world*" is a game-changer.

Opening your organization to external consumers is likely to cause more than a little nervousness across the spectrum. Architects may not be keen on sharing their hallowed common data model with external developers. Development teams may put on a brave face but are probably thinking about the skeletons they've been keeping in the closet under the label of "technical debt." Spare a thought for the operations team who were probably looking around for the crew from candid camera. Remember, back in 2002, provisioning additional Cloud capacity was probably a few terse sketches on a whiteboard. The gauntlet had been thrown down and teams had to comply.

The Amazon API Manifesto is i) an example of an enterprise-wide paradigm Change regarding APIs and ii) evidence that such a Change can result in significant results if we consider the success of Amazon Web Services today.

Speedboats and Aircraft Carriers

Although the will to partner and collaborate could be strong, the legacy organization may be reluctant to achieve this. This reluctance may be due to lengthy project timelines or governance related to change and release management. Invariably, it could also be due to functionality deep within the organization which may not be easily exposed to third parties. This can be remedied in the long-term with cross-enterprise agile ways of working. However, it is possible to achieve results in the short-term by establishing a capability at the fringe of the organization.

This capability, which I refer to as the "API Marketplace" is an intersection point between the established enterprise and third-party providers. It can leverage the might of the enterprise in an agile way to satisfy aggressive demand. Martin Fowler refers to this as the "two-lever" approach. The capability is underpinned by principles of people, process, and technology. We discuss this in further detail later in this book.

The first lever represents the traditional enterprise, much like an aircraft carrier, steady and resolute in its operation. The second lever, much like a speedboat, is nimble and without the same organizational responsibility, has the ability to change direction quicker. Our Marketplace initiative had to pivot on several occasions. Although roadblocks are disruptive to delivery, our versatility allowed us to quickly change direction to keep moving. For the Minimum Viable Product (MVP), a backend platform we were planning on integrating into was suddenly eliminated due to organizational concerns regarding API access as it could impact the revenue streams of existing access channels. Under typical circumstances, this would have dealt the initiative a death blow.

With good leadership and determination, a similar but lesser-known backend was found which we integrated into with fewer challenges. This required us to shape a new API product around the new backend.

The key lesson learnt is that it may be prudent to start with a lower profile API product to establish the foundations of the platform – without raising organizational concerns (e.g., cannibalization of existing revenue streams). Lower profile could also translate into lower consumption. This provides a perfect opportunity to define and refine the operational processes and support around the Marketplace. In this fast-moving realm, it is important to get an API product published and consumed as quickly as possible.

Patterns of Integration

Integration has always been possible at different levels. Organizations connect to one another through well-defined interfaces, possibly built to achieve a specific function. The communication for this is also highly secured using dedicated network channels such as leased lines. This is typically referred to *Business to Business* (B2B) integration. Due to the highly sensitive nature of these integrations, these interfaces are available to a small subset of partners.

However, a *Business to Consumer* (B2C) integration pattern allows an organization to unlock customer data for many *third-party* providers *only* with the customer's permission. This pattern has revolutionized the integration landscape as the end customer, the true owner of the data, decides who has access to it. The security model which makes this possible is called *OAuth* and is discussed in more detail later in this book. This has also resulted in a standardization of interfaces as maintaining individual service contracts for each provider would be untenable.

Enterprise-wide Impact

In traditional Enterprise Application Integration (EAI), both consumer and provider have been well within the safe boundaries of the organization. Although internal security mechanisms are well-advised, the safety net of the "internal network" helped allay fears that the integration was only accessible to known consumers. By building an API Marketplace, integrations are built *primarily* for *external* consumption.

This is a significant game changer and although application teams may be satisfied by fronting the interfaces with an API Gateway, this has an enterprise-wide impact and will require participation from various teams – ranging from Information Security to Networks to Forensics, to name a few. Information Security signs off that customer or organization data is only released based on specific security authorization frameworks such as *OAuth*. It is important to highlight that the Information Security team is a key stakeholder of the API Marketplace and engagement should be ongoing. Information Security should approve every API product to ensure that the right level of information is provided to the right parties with the right level of security. From a technical or development perspective, it may appear to be relatively easy to expose or update an API product to provide additional data. However, Information Security has a greater view regarding the sensitivity of data and, as essentially the guardians of enterprise and customer information, must always be consulted.

The Network team will also have to determine how requests, now originating from the Internet, traverse the organization's boundary and are routed to internal services. At this junction, it may be necessary to pause and reflect on the gravity of establishing an API Marketplace from the perspective of a Network Administrator.

Suppose you were the Head of the Secret Service, responsible for the safety of the US President. If the President stayed within the grounds of the White House, your job is simple – the parameters of the White House are well-defined: entrances, exits, staff, visitors, etc. However, the instant that the President leaves the White House, your job gets inherently more complex as there are significant variables to contend with.

The same is true for the Network Security team. Since the establishment of the organization, the parameters of the network had been well defined. The firewall kept all unwanted users and traffic out and the internal network safe. External users originated from well-defined IP sources, possibly using leased lines. Now, here comes along an API Marketplace initiative that provides external developers access to company resources via the *Internet*! It is therefore important to keep Network Security engaged, preferably from the start, to ensure the necessary mindset changes are made, fears allayed, and possible technical changes can be planned for and made timeously to avoid delays.

It is also important to engage the Forensics team as they will use the audit data from each transaction to piece together the customer request, via a third party, to the enterprise. This is critical in the event of customer queries or disputes and could save the organization significant amounts of money. Trace information, analyzed in real-time, can also be used to determine and stop fraudulent requests. Forensics teams can also leverage their experience to provide insight into how attacks could originate.

There are other teams in the organization which should be consulted and informed, such as product management. The key takeaway is – although the API Marketplace may operate on the *edge* of an organization, it is supported by internal capabilities *within* the enterprise. Stakeholder management is crucial and is one of the enabling capabilities of our Platform. Education is key – take nothing for granted. At the start of all our engagements, a YouTube video was created and replayed providing a definition of an API, how it could be used, and the benefits. By doing this, our audience had knowledge and context and were more comfortable to engage.

The Gravity of a New Digital Channel

As a developer, I'm certain that there will be groans of disapproval from the development teams at this point. Information Security, Networks, and Forensics all sound like red tape – which a technical team views in the same light as Superman regards kryptonite. Fair enough – Krypton is his birthplace, but it now saps his power. The same can be said for red tape – necessary but draining.

From our experience, the heady efforts to establish an API Marketplace quickly snowballed into primarily a technical initiative. Our single objective was to expose an API which provided enterprise data with customer authentication and authorization. This was also fueled by the initial project mandate which was to demonstrate an MVP to the leadership team of the organization.

Within the oxygen-infused bubble of the newly established digital innovation lab, the technical delivery team worked against the clock to achieve the mission. It was not plain sailing – at times we bumped against the walls of the bubble as we encountered organizational platforms and systems that *had* to be used. An example is the enterprise API Gateway, which up until that point, was only used for internal consumption. However, we flashed our "MVP" and "Proof of Concept (PoC)" badges at every checkpoint and with some fast-talking and promises to adhere to enterprise standards on future iterations, albeit with fingers crossed behind our back, the team was able to navigate around those challenges.

As almost all Technical Delivery teams do in a bubble – we delivered.

Thrilled with achieving a seemingly insurmountable task in record time, which could probably be attributed to the high levels of oxygen ingested, our next question was *when* this could be launched to external developers. The *expected* timeline from the delivery team was weeks or possibly a month or two. The *actual* timeline was closer to nine to twelve months. Timelines as lengthy as these are likely to kill any developer spirit. Our move out of the digital innovation lab to make way for the new MVP kid on the block helped neutralize the oxygen content in the air, and we soon realized that technical delivery was just one dimension to be considered when operationalizing an API Marketplace. We were building a new *Channel* into the organization!

Enabling access is an evolutionary transformation. As an example, consider the evolution of access into a banking institution over the years. They began with well-secured physical buildings which were only accessible during specific office hours. By providing Automatic Teller Machines (ATMs), you could access cash around the clock – however in establishing the capability, the machine needed to be highly secured and well managed. The mechanism to get cash *into* the ATM also needed to be considered, not only from the security perspective, but also logistically given the geographical distribution of the machines. Fairly easy as a concept in a "lab" environment – completely different in a real-world context.

Another step in their evolutionary journey was providing access via web and mobile application channels. There are countless challenges – I'll highlight just one which probably never featured in the "lab" environment – phishing. Client login credentials could be easily socially engineered by simply calling an end user posing to be an employee of the financial institution. Mechanisms like two-factor authentication (2FA) are prevalent today – however, these were not readily available when the channel was first established.

With the experience gained from establishing other channels, organizations have far more insight into potential vectors of attack. Attacks on a bank's physical buildings and ATMs may also be easier to defend as threats are tangible. With a digital channel such as an API Marketplace, the attacker could be on the other side of the world. ATMs could only lose cash. An API could leak customer data, which in today's world of General Data Protection Regulation (GDPR) could cost an organization far more in reputational damage.

Establishing a digital channel is not a trivial exercise. This needs to be considered, not only from a development or technical perspective, but from a wide range of viewpoints. A single security incident can cause reputational damage but loss of trust in the platform could potentially impact the API product roadmap, possibly its very existence.

Of all the channels, an API Marketplace is probably the fastest time to market – it is unburdened by the need to have a physical location like an ATM and is not tethered to a user interface like web. However, the speed must always be tempered with responsibility.

Developer Ecosystem

An API Marketplace exists to serve third-party developers. Without third-party consumption, there would be no traffic. No traffic means no revenue. Revenue sustains the Marketplace which exists to achieve the Vision. Available API products should always be reliable and available to sustain existing consumers. A well-defined roadmap will help to attract new developers to the Platform.

The API Marketplace developer portal is essentially the shopfront for the Platform, and significant effort and focus should be made here. Although primarily meant to support technical integration, the portal should be geared to a wide audience. A startup considering the use of the Platform and API products may want a 10,000-foot view of how it works. Videos and customer case studies can easily convey the concept. It is also important to cater for varying levels of developer skill. Take nothing for granted, and concepts such as *OAuth*, which may be easily understood by the internal delivery team, need to be demystified and explained to ensure understanding and adoption.

An inherent benefit of an API Marketplace is a sandbox environment. Techniques to implement and manage this are discussed in a later chapter. From an external developer perspective, it allows development and integration testing early in the development lifecycle. Developer access and sign up to this environment must be achieved by self-service and fully automated. Some developers are resilient, most may not be – access and ease of use is a necessity. The portal should be well documented, provide sequence diagrams to show process flow, step by step guides, and code samples. This is also discussed in a later chapter.

Roles

At the start of our own project that led to the creation of this book, we began with a technical-heavy team. Some of the members included front-end developers working on the portal, integration developers assimilating backend interfaces, and DevOps engineers building on-premises container platforms. In hindsight, I now understand the exasperation of our agile coach who constantly tried to get the team to focus on the greater cause rather than just meeting the next sprint target. Our project team included personnel from several countries, across continents and time zones, and there were days we spent more time on web conferences than with our families.

As the Marketplace evolved, so did our staff complement. With the benefit of time, we were fortunate to work in a variety of combinations – from a purely startup formation to working with conventional team roles. Due to product demand, we needed to create product squads – each working on a specific domain. As the Marketplace has matured from a startup to an operational platform, the following core roles underpinned the team:

- Program Executive
- Product Owner
- Delivery Lead
- Operations Lead
- Engineering Lead

As any fan of Star Trek will relate, these roles map to those of the Starship Enterprise. Each is highly capable and performs a vital function, and the overall contribution leads to successful missions. What works impeccably well is that each member has full autonomy to execute and is always supported by the rest of the crew. Available personnel are brought in to assist with delivery objectives – for example, the Product Owner might scan through audit traces to help the operations team piece together a customer's journey when investigating a dispute. A common requirement across the team is that everyone should roll up their sleeves and get into the detail.

As the captain of the Platform, the **Program Executive** steers the ship based on objectives set out by the digital leadership of the organization. Although the API Marketplace functions as a speed boat, it is part of a greater fleet and this role must carefully balance the cautious outlook of an established enterprise with an agile, but sometimes hasty delivery team. The Executive is also a champion of the API Marketplace within the organization and has the unenviable task of securing funding for the build and early phases of the program – until it can sustain itself. Ensuring an API Marketplace is viewed as a serious digital channel for the enterprise is also a significant challenge. It is important to sell the concept and capability internally, as such a revolutionary concept could easily be classified as a research and development effort, and not taken seriously. As adoption and revenue increases, it will become easier.

The **Product Owner (PO)** is responsible for shaping the API products. The technical delivery team may underestimate the level of complexity required by a third party to consume an API product. The PO understands the needs of the third-party developers, the capability within the enterprise, and identifies how capability can be mapped to fulfill need. This is also to be tempered with business value as the Marketplace needs to be self-sustaining and revenue generating. Although many API products could be pre-defined based on regulation, there is ample opportunity to define and publish more. The PO works closely with the Program Executive to define the roadmap of API products. Organizational direction is one input; third-party demand/requirement is another. A further responsibility of this role is to internally market the potential of the API Marketplace to internal teams within the enterprise and shape offerings. This is no mean feat as it potentially requires partial funding to be provided by that team to build the product.

The **Delivery Lead** is tasked with ensuring the goals and objectives of the product roadmap are met. Areas of responsibility include scheduling incoming requirements from the Product Owner based on available development capacity. This person also works closely with backend platform teams to determine the availability of interfaces for consumption. This is sometimes a precarious balancing act as any delays from backend teams could result in lost development time. When working with an offshore delivery team, the Delivery Lead has the unenviable task of also liaising between remote and local personnel. With the insight into backend availability and delivery capacity, it may also be necessary to shift the release date and update of API products. The aim is to keep the platform constantly moving. In the development process, the rigor of bi-weekly production drops helps immensely. These can be intentionally timed to coincide with the end of a delivery sprint. The drops not only maximize the potential of the development team – but the team is aware their efforts are constantly moving to production and any resulting issues or updates can be done quickly.

The **Engineering Lead (EL)** works across the various technology areas of the platform. Being intimately aware of each layer in the stack is an advantage as it is often necessary to dive in and get involved in the detail to unblock an issue. An API Marketplace also provided us with the unique opportunity to test new approaches and technology within the Enterprise. The EL is tasked to have a detailed understanding of the technical landscape and is often called upon to share this view with supporting teams within the organization. A further responsibility, personally a privilege, is to define solutions which meet new requirements with input from other members of the team and input from backend platform teams. From a governance perspective, the EL also works with enterprise, domain, and solution architects for the approval of platform and solution designs. The EL must have a full view of the end-to-end solution, be able to decompose it into work items which can be delivered by the team. What works well is an EL who can, and often does, get into the detail – from writing code to create a quick proof-of-concept to consuming a new backend platform interface to mediating between developers during integration testing. The EL is also responsible for scoping the effort and timelines of delivery, with assistance and input from the Engineering team. Experience plays a big part as this will help to support the definition of the API product roadmap.

Finally, the **Operations Lead (OL)** is essentially the pivot point of the team. Although the primary focus is on the reliability and stability of the Marketplace execution platform, this role carries accountability for the availability of supporting organizational services and backend platforms. The Marketplace support team reports into the Operations Lead. Reporting and analytics dashboards, discussed later, are a mainstay for this role. For day-to-day operation of the Platform, resolution of outages, integration, and coordination with external teams is a key requirement. The ability to understand the complexity and dive into the detail is also mandatory as it allows the individual to know *who* to pull in *when*. From a revenue generating perspective, this is possibly *the* most important role since downtime translates to lost opportunities.

Finally, it is important to highlight the following: the roles are interconnected. The Product Owner is supported by the Engineering Lead to determine if a potential API product is viable. Similarly, the Engineering Lead relies on the Product Owner to communicate delivery delays to the Program Executive. Hierarchy is also kept to an absolute minimum, and all team members are free to engage with anyone in the above roles to fulfill an objective. Again, what binds the team together is mutual trust and respect and most importantly, we all share the same Vision. Everything we do is a firm step forward in the journey to achieve that objective.

A Guide to This Book

In Chapter 2, we consider regulations introduced which have forced organizations to build API Marketplaces. In Chapter 3, we delve into consumption and discuss how to support third-party developers. Chapter 4 reviews mechanisms to generate revenue from an API Marketplace. In Chapter 5, we review in detail the technology elements and practices used in our Platform. The focus of Chapter 6 is Security, which underpins the Marketplace.

Chapter 7 is dedicated to how APIs should be designed with Chapter 8 providing a view into our development and API delivery process. In Chapter 9, we discuss the Sandbox environment and ways it can be set up to support external developers. Chapter 10 provides insight into the operational dimension of an API Marketplace. Chapter 11 provides a brief summary and possible first, or next steps for your implementation. You may skip ahead to the chapters which interest you.

If you have any thoughts, suggestions, or general feedback, please do not hesitate to let me know. I view an API Marketplace in much the same way as a living, breathing organism. Some aspects are similar, like walking or speaking. Some incredibly different – like language and dialect. The goal of this book is to share my experience building an API Marketplace to help others craft their own.

CHAPTER 2

Regulation

The Financial Services (FS) industry has always been a trailblazer with regard to technology adoption. This is evident from the launch of Automatic Teller Machines (ATMs), to telephone banking to web-and-mobile application-based banking. Given the sensitive nature of customer data and associated transactions, the gateway to FS providers has been well guarded – and understandably so. In this chapter, we examine the factors which led to customer data and financial backend services being shared with third parties, which has revolutionized the industry. Like tectonic plates colliding in the middle of the ocean, the tsunami effect has been triggered, and the wave of change has reached many geographies across the globe.

It stands to reason that if API Marketplaces are required and can be established in such a stringent sector like Financial Services, then other sectors, such as Telecommunications and Healthcare, can and will follow suit. In this chapter, we deep dive on the impact of APIs on the Financial Services sector. We start at the epicenter of this seismic event – Payments – and then move on to Open *Banking* and finally examine the effects of further shockwaves on the industry in the form of Open *Finance*.

Background

Digital payment services have underpinned the e-commerce boom. From simply capturing credit card details to paying for the items in an electronic shopping basket, the capability has improved significantly. On the face of it, the participants in the transaction should simply be the end user, the online retailer, and the Financial Institution. Due to the myriad of banks, complex agreements, and interfacing mechanisms, innovative Financial Technology (FinTech) companies have established themselves as a new, integral participant by stepping in to abstract the complexity and providing an easy to consume service for online retailers.

© Rennay Dorasamy 2022
R. Dorasamy, *API Marketplace Engineering*, https://doi.org/10.1007/978-1-4842-7313-5_2

One such service is payment initiation. Figure 2-1 shows how an online retailer can simply integrate into a single payment provider which can leverage its network of interfaces into various banks instead of directly integrating with each bank.

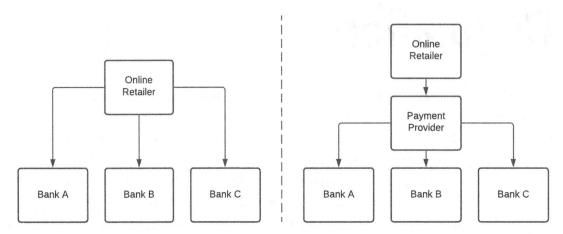

Figure 2-1. *Direct vs. brokered integration strategy*

Screen Scraping

Using the online banking channel, third-party payment providers have been able to achieve integration into banks through the practice of screen scraping. Screen scraping is the technology that reads and extracts data from a target website using computer software that impersonates a web browser to extract data or perform actions that users would usually perform manually on the website. To make the payment, the customer would provide their banking credentials (username, personal identification number (PIN), and password) with the provider, who would use this information to kick off an automated process to log in to the user's online banking portal and make the payment.

A benefit to the end user is convenience – it saves time connecting to the online banking portal, capturing the banking details of the retailer, setting up a payment, and sending confirmation of payment. The process is also streamlined to fit neatly into the checkout journey, and most customers do not know that they are logging on to their online banking directly. As traditional interbank electronic funds transfer (EFT) can take several hours, even days to reflect, a benefit to the merchant is that the payment provider can offer confirmation of payment in real time. As the payment provider connected to the user's online banking portal, verified funds and performed the transaction, the merchant can be assured that the payment was done – instead of relying on a confirmation of payment provided by the end user, which could be subject to fraud.

The inherent drawback of this practice is that accessing a customer's financial information using screen scraping has generally been found to be less secure from a data privacy and consumer protection perspective. As it poses risks to the integrity, safety, and efficiency of payment systems and to the customer, there have been a growing number of interventions from banking regulators to curb this approach.

Screen scraping allows the practice of sorting at source. This allows a payment provider with bank accounts with a number of different banks to sort the payment instruction per bank and relay them on to each respective bank – which would in turn process them as internal transactions. Although sorting a source model may sound like a more optimal way to reduce costs and increase the speed of clearing, it is prohibited under certain regulatory policies and rules as it reduces interbank clearing. Screen scraping has been a popular mechanism of payment initiation and account aggregation because of a lack of legal frameworks and policies in the banking sector that allow the sharing of customers' financial information securely with third parties.

Application Programming Interfaces (APIs)

To address this issue, banks have been exploring APIs as an alternative to share customer's financial information and to support innovative payment solutions to improve the customer experience. APIs, in a traditional banking context, have been largely internally focused, proprietary, non-standardized, and inaccessible to external consumers – known as "closed APIs." Conversely, "open APIs" are used by third parties to create innovative applications and products that extend the reach to customers and improve the user experience.

A benefit of APIs in banking is that they can be leveraged to share customer data with third parties in a secure manner *with* consent from the customer and *without* sharing login credentials. Third-party applications can connect directly into the banks' systems from the public domain to obtain account information, initiate, and track payments. If the API is owned by the bank, there is concern that this could give the bank too much power as it controls which data is shared. This could result in banks playing a gatekeeper role, which could be anti-competitive and inhibit innovation. The concept of "Open Banking" emerged as a way for third-party providers to securely gain access to customers' financial information from banks using open APIs in order to leverage innovative technologies and improve customer experience. We delve into Open Banking in more detail in the next section.

Open Banking

Due to increased demand from customers for access to and control of their data and from third-party providers eager to disrupt, the banking industry faces an imminent revolution. Open Banking presents an opportunity for a graceful, controlled transition and, more importantly, for banks to remain a vital part of the new ecosystem. Customers have greater control of their financial data, allowing them to make more informed decisions and better manage their money. Increased competition will result in broader, more diverse service offerings and innovation from third-party providers and banks alike.

Objectives

We consider some of the objectives for an Open Banking policy:

- **Financial stability and security**: Sensitive customer data shared across platforms must be secured to preserve confidence in the entire financial ecosystem.

- **Transparency and public accountability**: Customers should understand the risks involved with the use of their banking credentials, including the limited liability accepted by many third-party providers. Any open-banking implementation should outline the processes and timelines for a third party to be granted access to financial data that customers have elected to share. The sharing of data with other parties in the value chain should be prohibited to protect customer data rights.

- **Standardization and neutral technology**: Standards for APIs, data processing, storing, and cybersecurity must be clearly defined to allow easy integration to multiple banking platforms without the need for customized development.

- **Promotion of financial inclusion, competition and innovation, and cost-effectiveness**: Open Banking may help to create a level playing field for all stakeholders to offer services and solutions. It should allow banking services to a wide range of customers – from offering high-earners a personalized investment product to assisting underbanked customers to access banking services. From an implementation perspective, smaller banks and third parties should be able to participate without significant investment capital and technological infrastructure.

Terminology

When navigating Open Banking regulatory frameworks, you may encounter many new terms and classifications. We consider the most common ones and discuss how they fit into the framework.

- **Account Information Service Providers (AISP)** help customers by providing a consolidated view of their financial position by aggregating and analyzing transaction information from one or more of their payment accounts. This may help a customer to establish credit worthiness by checking earnings and expenses from multiple sources.

- **Payment Initiation Service Providers (PISP)** initiate a payment transaction on behalf of the customer via a different platform than the one belonging to the bank where the account is held.

- **Third-Party Provider (TPP)** is an entity authorized to access accounts on behalf of customers but that does not operate those accounts themselves. Types of TPPs include PISPs and AISPs. An example of a TPP is a FinTech.

- **Account Servicing Payment Service Provider (ASPSP)** provides and maintains a payment account for a payer. This is essentially the Bank or Financial Institution which holds the customer's account and money.

Figure 2-2 provides a visual representation of the terms and classifications and how it fits together.

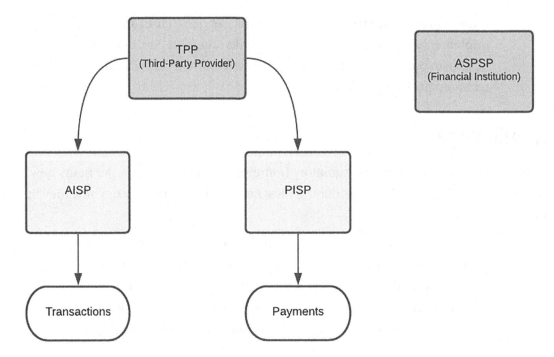

Figure 2-2. *Visual representation of Open Banking participants*

Benefits

Open Banking can provide a number of benefits to all participants in the ecosystem. Customers can enjoy a less admin-intensive, more streamlined online retail experience by leveraging payment services. This saves time previously needed to log on to banking portals and sending confirmation of payment. Account aggregation services allow easier comparison and switching. The sharing of transactional data with third-party providers is also safer as the customer has fine-grained control over which data is shared, the duration and the ability to revoke access. Access to account history can allow third parties to offer personalized products and services and allows more accurate risk ratings. Payment methods, such as mobile wallets, are also available as an alternative to card and transactional account payments. Consumers also benefit from increased competition as this will potentially lower fees for financial services and raise service levels.

Third-party providers have more business opportunities as Open Banking creates a level playing field for non-bank providers. This will allow them to offer innovative account and payment solutions that could improve the customer experience. Insight into a customer's historical account data could allow better risk rating and product matching.

Although it may appear, at first glance, that Open Banking will impact banks negatively, there could be many benefits. Customer trust can be maintained by engaging in a transparent, open relationship by providing the capability to easily and safely share data and control how money is managed. Confidence can also be instilled by demonstrating digital capability and embracing innovative solutions, with the necessary security controls, to offer customers optimal or premium products and services. Banks can create new partnerships and access new revenue streams through an API-based platform type business model. The reach of the bank also increases as the products and services of third-party providers could reach a wider audience in shorter, more aggressive timeframes.

Merchants can also grow their product offering and extend reach to markets that were previously difficult to access. An example could be the ability to make a payment from a transactional account which would allow access to customers without a credit card. Alternate payment methods could also result in lower card transaction costs. Open Banking has the potential to eliminate various fee elements of card transactions that are part of merchant service charges from the issuing banks, processors and schemes, which is also a benefit for customers.

The payment system benefits from increased competition as the levelled playing field will potentially bring innovative payment solutions. Open Banking can enhance the transparency of payment flows by removing fake and fraudulent third-party providers and building technical and data-sharing standards. It also allows a more efficient infrastructure that underpins payments that are efficient for clearing and settling transactions.

Risks

There are a number of risks associated with Open Banking implementations. Awareness and upfront mitigation are key to enable the Marketplace to deal with these challenges. As the solutions are digital, this could result in exclusion for those customers who do not have access to the Internet or smartphones. Any new channel into a financial system introduces the possibility of fraud. A customer's financial data could be used for purposes that are not mandated by the customer. Open Banking could expose a customer's data to theft and inappropriate use. Weak security measures could result in a loss of funds due to criminal activity.

Customers may not understand the risks when sharing their financial data and the limited liability accepted by many third-party providers. This may be addressed through a strong customer education campaign. In addition, the messaging and warnings must be clear and concise during the customer consent process. Customers should also be made aware of the mechanisms available to view and revoke third-party access.

Third-party providers are not subject to the same regulations as banks and could expose banks to reputational risk through the mishandling of data. Sensitive customer data could be shared through accidental or malicious employee activities. Third parties may be easier targets for cyber criminals as their security mechanisms may not be as comprehensive as banks. Initial, scheduled and spot reviews of third-party systems and/ or independent security assessments could ensure the necessary security controls are established. Depending on the nature of the API product consumed, this could be a mandatory requirement.

Implementation and operation of a product or service which consumes Open Banking APIs requires a significant investment from new entrants with regard to design, development, support, and maintenance. This should be clearly communicated to potential providers by the API Marketplace Product Owner.

Banks also face reputational risk through fraudulent or rogue third-party activity. Unauthorized use of consumer data can have a negative impact on consumer trust in the bank. This could be mitigated through thorough review and screening of third parties wishing to integrate into the Marketplace. A pre-emptive strategy is to communicate a strong market message ensuring customers and third parties are aware of security responsibilities throughout the Open Banking journey.

One of the most significant risks faced by banks is disintermediation. Third-party providers may reduce the bank's role, potentially leading to partial loss of customer relationships, which could in turn lead to loss of revenue. Open Banking, like ATM, online or app-based banking, is a channel that a customer uses to interact with the bank. A strong bank-customer relationship will help establish loyalty and trust. Banks can use customer data and activity, via any channel, to better understand behavior to provide personalized products and services. The potential of disintermediation could be viewed as motivation for banks to raise their game to retain the customer relationship.

Open Banking will result in a change of business model for banks as there are significant changes to operational infrastructure, onboarding, transactional monitoring, and security checks. This could increase costs for banks and result in competitive challenges. This is best mitigated through a forward-looking view of the financial services landscape. A clear and well-defined roadmap, which takes into consideration the experience of other countries and organizations further ahead in their journey, will help ensure the readiness of banks to enable Open Banking.

Merchants may have to contend with the exposure to reputational risk if customers lose their data or payments are intercepted, third parties not able to honor financial obligations and transactions originating from fraudulent activity. Payments systems may be subject to operational risk in the event of a system malfunction, human error, and cyberattacks. This may affect integrity and confidence in the payment system. Access to banking APIs may allow more third parties to sort-at-source which reduces interbank clearing, which will impact interbank clearing houses.

Prescriptive, Facilitated, or Market-Driven Approaches

Some countries have taken a prescriptive approach of mandating banks to share customer-permissioned data and requiring third parties that want to access such data to register with regulatory or supervisory authorities. The UK took a regulatory approach and incorporated Open Banking standards in 2018, which required the largest banks as Account Servicing Payment Service Providers (ASPSP) to develop Open APIs to provide access to Third-Party Providers (TPPs) for customer accounts. The Open Banking Implementation Entity (OBIE) was created by the Competition and Markets Authority (CMA) to deliver APIs, data structures, and security architectures. The European Union has passed the second edition of the Payment Service Directive (PSD2) which leverages APIs as a mechanism to unlock customer data and enable consumer choice. However, it took a lot of time to analyze and agree on the most optimal solution – as third parties, banks, and regulators had different objectives, ambitions, and concerns which needed to be balanced. As a result, the UK's and EU's regulations took some time to implement, and many banks missed their deadlines. Regions like Bahrain, using a PSD2-style regulation, established a set of guidelines and standards to ensure consistency in implementation and to boost adoption. Banks were also given a deadline by which they had to comply.

Other jurisdictions have taken a more facilitative and flexible approach by issuing guidance and recommended standards and releasing open API standards and technical specifications. The common pillars of Open Banking include consent, data privacy expectations, and data security requirements. Instead of mandating desired outcomes at the outset, regulators allowed third-party providers to use secure workarounds until the infrastructure can be established. As an example, some regulators allowed screen-scraping practices to access customer-consented account information before APIs were provided. Remaining regions have opted for a flexible, market-driven approach, with no explicit regulations or standards. In the following section, we review Open Banking activities from different regions.

Open Banking Across the Globe

Tables 2-1 through to 2-9 provide a point-in-time state of Open Banking in a number of countries. Key to note is the difference in strategy adopted across territories – some have chosen a prescriptive approach; others a facilitative or market-driven one. We also examine the regulatory body leading the initiative, service providers participating, access type, products, and current status. Countries starting on their journey can leverage the insights and experience of those which have started a number of years ago.

Table 2-1. *Open Banking – Australia*

Jurisdiction	Australia
Approach	Prescriptive
Lead	Treasury Department
Service providers	Phased Approach. July 2020 – four big banks. February 2021 – other banks
Access type	API
Product scope	Credit and debit cards, deposit and transaction accounts, mortgage and personal loan data
Status	<ul><li>2018: Australian government approved a framework for Open Banking</li><li>July 2020: Implemented in a phased approach, with the four big banks legally required to make consumer usage data available to consumers on credit and debit cards as well as deposit and transaction accounts</li><li>November 2020: Mortgage and personal loan data to be shared</li><li>February 2021: Other banks to start sharing data</li></ul>

Table 2-2. *Open Banking – China*

Jurisdiction	China
Approach	Market-driven
Lead	FinTechs
Service providers	AliPay, FinTechs
Access type	API
Product scope	As per the consumer (any financial data)
Status	• Open Banking is not being promoted by regulators but rather driven by FinTech companies

Table 2-3. *Open Banking – European Union*

Jurisdiction	European Union
Approach	Prescriptive
Lead	EU Commission
Service providers	All banks and payment service providers
Access type	API, Screen scraping
Product scope	Current and savings accounts
Status	PSD2 directs banks to open up their systems to allow third-party access to certain customer account information, in order to make payments on their behalf (via credit transfers) and to provide them with a view of their various payment accounts, subject to customer consent
	• The aim is to increase competition and promote innovation through data sharing

Table 2-4. *Open Banking – Hong Kong*

Jurisdiction	Hong Kong
Approach	Facilitative
Lead	Hong Kong Monetary Authority
Service providers	20 participating retail banks have made available more than 500 open APIs, offering access to information of a wide range of banking products and services
Access type	API
Product scope	As per the consumer (any financial data)
Status	July 2018: The Hong Kong Monetary Authority introduced the Open API Framework. It aims to facilitate the development and wider adoption of APIs by the banking sector January 2019: Phase I of the framework launched

Table 2-5. *Open Banking – India*

Jurisdiction	India
Approach	Hybrid Model – prescriptive and market-driven
Lead	National Payments Council of India (NPCI)
Service providers	Participating banks and payment service providers
Access type	API
Product scope	As per the consumer (any financial data)
Status	The Indian government has mandated an Open API policy In 2016, IndiaStack was introduced as a set of APIs The Aadhaar biometric digital system facilitates open API banking through government proprietary software dealing with a centralized database for authentication

Table 2-6. *Open Banking – Japan*

Jurisdiction	Japan
Approach	Prescriptive
Lead	Financial Services Agency
Service providers	All banks
Access type	API
Product scope	Bank accounts (current, savings, deposits)
Status	In 2018, Banking Act was amended to require financial institutions to develop APIs for use by third parties

Table 2-7. *Open Banking – Singapore*

Jurisdiction	Singapore
Approach	Facilitative
Lead	Monetary Authority of Singapore
Service providers	Voluntary participation
Access type	API
Product scope	Ethical use of data and artificial intelligence that will work for all players within the system
Status	Singapore is attempting to implement a different type of regulatory framework, with a less aggressive and more organic approach. It is not planning to force regulations onto financial institutions

Table 2-8. *Open Banking – South Africa*

Jurisdiction	South Africa
Approach	Market-driven
Lead	South African Reserve Bank (SARB)
Service providers	Voluntary participation
Access type	API, Screen Scraping
Product scope	Under review
Status	Currently, the SARB does not regulate, supervise or oversee Open Banking activities such as screen scraping and open APIs, including their effectiveness, soundness, integrity or robustness The SARB is of the view that Open Banking activities should be regulated and reformed, risks should be managed, and safety considerations embedded, all the while ensuring that customer experience is ensured and enhanced Consultation process currently underway

Table 2-9. *Open Banking – USA*

Jurisdiction	USA
Approach	Market-driven
Lead	Consumer Financial Protection Bureau
Service providers	Voluntary participation
Access type	API, Screen scraping
Product scope	As per the consumer (any financial data)
Status	There is no legal requirement for Open Banking, and the decision on how data sharing occurs is up to financial institutions Entities still use screen scraping rather than Open APIs. This includes web-based financial management tools that aggregate a customer's financial data

From Open Banking to Open Finance

Open Banking is just the first stage in the metamorphosis of the Financial Services industry. Open Finance is the term used to describe the extension of Open Banking data sharing and is also built on the principle of consumers owning the data they create on financial service providers' platforms. The data, with consumer consent, can be shared with approved third-party providers to develop and offer innovative products and services. While Open Banking only focuses on accessing banking transactional data or making payments on a customer's behalf, Open Finance goes wider. It includes all consumer financial services data such as savings, debt, investment, pensions, alternative lending, and insurance. For insurance, customer data sourced from the incumbent service provider can be used to identify personalized and best priced insurtech products, while in alternative lending, historical transactional data can be used for more reliable credit scoring and affordability analysis. It has the potential to transform the way consumers and businesses use financial services.

There are many lessons from the Open Banking journey which can be used to make Open Finance a success:

Standardization: Standardized access to data is key to avoid market fragmentation. In the way power supplies and electrical sockets are consistent in a country, providing a standard API definition will allow third parties to focus on providing value to the customer rather than on the different nuances of each service provider. A rule-based approach for data sharing – as with Open Banking in the UK – may be preferable to the principle-based approach applied in PSD2.

Regulation: Legislators, regulators, and public authorities should take note of the rapid development of Open Banking. Although the practice of screen scraping has an inherent security flaw of shared client credentials, it was allowed to continue for a number of years. Open APIs have quickly risen to the fore as an alternative and has revolutionized the banking industry. As this wave is likely to move through the banking sector, other industries such as insurance are likely to be impacted in the future. The regulator has a key role to play as strong direction and a suitable framework is required that will support the industry to create standards and infrastructure to balance the different public interests involved. It is also vital to continue the collaboration between incumbent financial service providers, FinTechs and regulators to help promote the ecosystem.

Commercial models: A key consideration of Open Finance is the funding model as the needs of all participants in the ecosystem have to be considered. As per specifications, like PSD2, banks may not charge for data sharing and payment data. Given the large-scale investments banks have made to enable this, this may not be an appealing initiative to pursue outside meeting the core regulatory requirement. Open Finance can make space for competition and innovation beyond the regulatory minimum. Premium APIs, which use Open API technology, can enable Open Finance by allowing data sharing across a range of different sectors.

Dispute mechanisms: As disputes could result in reputational damage to financial service providers and third parties, it is important that all stakeholders have a complaints management process in place to enable them to process complaints or issues raised. To address data privacy breaches and data misuse, a liability framework may be required to hold financial service and third-party providers accountable.

Customer focus: Customer financial data is the source ingredient of the Open Finance ecosystem. As it always belongs to the customer throughout the lifecycle, it is imperative to always have the customer in sharp focus. Customers should clearly know how their data is collected, shared, and used. Informed consent is a key mechanism to make consumers aware of the terms and conditions of what they are consenting to and how their data will be used. Customers should also have the right to revoke access and that previous data shared be "forgotten."

Customer education is a key responsibility of financial services providers and third parties and will help in establishing trust. If potential customers do not trust the ecosystem, they will not give consent to sharing their data. Credible third-party providers are also an essential element in securing and retaining customer trust.

Sample Applications

Open Banking and Finance has enabled banks and third-party providers to launch new products and services. We highlight a few of these applications – YOLT which was built by a bank, CHIP which use cutting-edge Artificial Intelligence (AI) technology, bunq which uses Open APIs to extend their existing product offering, TrueLayer which provides a platform capability to third-party providers to abstract integration complexity, and Revolut which provides an account aggregation capability across banks.

The speed, low costs, and innovation of FinTechs have helped to extend existing capability and to build digital applications and platforms.

- **YOLT**: ING has created one of the biggest third-party trusted entities called YOLT (which started in the Netherlands in 2016 and is now in the UK, France, and Italy). YOLT's app consumes open banking API's to aggregate account information across banks and give recommendations to customers. YOLT's mission is "To give everyone the power to be smart with their money." They have for now +-500,000 clients; however, one of the downsides is that their App/functionality is "read and advise" only. Any recommendations that the app makes need to be actioned in the source banking systems.

- **CHIP**: CHIP uses Artificial Intelligence (AI) to calculate how much you can save and takes funds out of linked current accounts and places them via direct debit into a separate savings account hosted by Barclays Bank. Savings percentages (up to 5%) are gamified depending on your social promotion of CHIP – an extra 1% per signed up friend.

- **bunq**: bunq, long before PSD2, opened up their API. bunq let developers build unique apps that enrich the life of all bunq users on top of a fully licensed bank. Using the bunq API, developers can connect to transactional data, push notifications, payment requests, cards, joint accounts, and limits and budgets.

- **TrueLayer**: TrueLayer's API platform makes it easy to integrate financial services, like Open Banking and payments, into any app or any website, anywhere in the world. TrueLayer enables connections to all bank APIs across Europe, regardless of the standards or protocols used.

- **Revolut**: With the new feature, German customers can now connect their accounts at Comdirect, Commerzbank, Deutsche Bank, ING-DiBa, and Sparkasse with the Revolut app and view all their finances in one place – directly from their smartphones, developed in cooperation with Europe's provider of financial APIs (programming interfaces), UK-based FinTech, TrueLayer. The use of the TrueLayer platform ensures that account information from major German banks is securely integrated and updated in real time in the Revolut app.

Summary

In this chapter, we reviewed how Open Banking and Open Finance has come to the fore in the Financial Services industry. It has essentially been driven by having the best interest of the customer in mind. Practices such as screen scraping jeopardize the security of the customer through sharing of credentials – APIs are a mechanism to remedy this. New payment methods and account aggregation will allow more convenience for customers and personalized service – specifications, such as PSD2, have enabled third parties to achieve this. More competition in the market could allow more customer choice, drive down costs, and improve service levels – Open Banking standards were introduced to do exactly this.

We extolled the benefits to all participants – from the promise of financial inclusion to billions of unbanked across the globe to levelling the playing field for third-party providers. This movement is not without risk – and we have highlighted some and provided potential mitigation. What is extremely exciting at this time is that the wave of Open Banking is spreading globally. Although different territories have adopted different approaches across various product sets, the primary objective across all is the democratization of customer-owned data.

We have also highlighted that this is just the beginning. Open Banking is the herald of a greater Open Finance initiative which will have an impact on more sectors within the Financial Services industry. This allows an unprecedented opportunity to re-design financial services for maximum scalability and efficiency. The golden thread tying everything together is regulation. A key objective regarding regulation is that data sharing and Open Banking should strike a balance between risk management and incentives for promoting innovation. Regulatory frameworks should set clear roles and responsibilities in line with market changes.

Although some organizations have been pro-active in building the capability to enable Open Banking, many were not prepared. A well-planned and executed API platform strategy can provide an organization with the pre-requisite knowledge and experience to participate in and guide the regulatory consultative process.

It is indeed interesting to note the ripple effect from a single requirement, specifically payment initiation, trigger the next change, which is access to customer account information. This brought about regulatory changes which essentially forced organizations to change their policies and allow access to third parties, with customer consent. The fracture has not stopped there – this has spurred change in other areas of financial services, such as insurance and lending.

If we apply the same set of principles to other industries, such as Telecommunications and Healthcare, it stands to reason that a user's mobile transaction history or health information belongs to the user and should be accessible to third parties, with the user's consent. Providers such as Google and Facebook have baked this capability into their product offerings. In much the same way that regulation was passed that allowed users to retain their mobile numbers when moving to a new network, I think it is simply a matter of time before mobile transaction data, possibly even call history, is democratized. The sector just needs a compelling requirement that will trigger change. There are plans in many countries to provide a national healthcare service. Access to existing patient records and data from the private sector may just be a tipping point for change in this industry.

Some organizations have adopted a wait-and-see approach and will react to regulatory changes. Many have spotted the potential of establishing a platform business and are pre-empting regulation or taking a strategic position by getting an early start to their API Marketplace implementations.

CHAPTER 3

Consumption

One of the key areas which requires a significant amount of attention is the *interface* to the API Marketplace. Although the star of the show is the actual API which provides the functionality, the star needs a stage and theatre to perform. If the stage is too small or the theatre too difficult to access, then the brilliance of the API will be lost. It is important to always keep this in mind throughout the journey. Without third-party consumption, there would be no traffic. No traffic results in no revenue. Revenue sustains the Marketplace which exists to achieve the Vision.

The Marketplace provides *Products* which can be consumed by multiple third parties. Some products or APIs essentially sell themselves due to regulation or demand for specific functionality. However, most of the products must be actively marketed to showcase their capability and to encourage adoption and usage. We discuss mechanisms to achieve this in the sections below.

Marketplace APIs vs. Internal APIs

The Delivery team should always keep in mind the *context* of the API Marketplace. From my experience as an integration developer, when exposing or consuming an interface for an internal project, we had the benefit of direct communication between consumer and provider teams through in-person meetings, phone calls, or email, to flesh out the detail beyond the interface specification document. This was possible as the nature of the integration was typically one consumer to one provider.

A successful API Marketplace will have *many* consumers, and although it is possible, having a one-on-one session with each consumer to walk through integration queries is not tenable or scalable. This also differs from internal integration projects where delivery leads do not hesitate to set up as many sessions as needed to resolve interface challenges. Third parties could have several API providers to choose from, and if the Marketplace is not appealing or easy to consume, they will typically move on. A good

© Rennay Dorasamy 2022
R. Dorasamy, *API Marketplace Engineering*, https://doi.org/10.1007/978-1-4842-7313-5_3

Marketplace is one which abstracts and simplifies the complexity of backend platforms and packages it for easy consumption.

An API Marketplace is not your typical, run of the mill, integration "plumbing" exercise, connecting one system to another. The API exposed to consumers must be thoughtfully and carefully constructed. As mentioned in the Amazon "API Manifesto":

All service interfaces, without exception, must be designed from the ground up to be externalize-able. That is to say, the team must plan and design to be able to expose the interface to developers in the outside world. No exceptions.

Personas

A pitfall many organizations fall into is to only have a technical portal with rafts of three-letter acronyms. In our race to build a Minimum Viable Product (MVP), we did exactly that. Our landing page had some vibrant icons and graphics with some terse text hurriedly put together while we focused on the technical aspects. Again, from experience, the first iteration of the portal the team puts out will probably be the longest running as the team's focus switches to making new API products available. ·

Due to its nature, it is easy to categorize an "API Marketplace" as technical and to only focus on Engineers and Integration Developers. It is also important to consider the Marketplace from a commercial perspective and how it can be leveraged to provide business value. Companies are essentially trying to build new products and services to solve old problems in more efficient and convenient ways. Consumers need to understand the intention and benefits of an API Marketplace to determine how they can use it to achieve their organization's objectives.

Although User Experience (UX) in an API construct may seem superfluous, it is an essential element of the Marketplace adoption. UX for different personas helps provide pertinent information to the right audience at the right time. This could be achieved as a separate portal or as clearly defined sections in a single portal.

In the next sections, we consider meeting goals for business and technical personas across these areas:

- **Attract**: Grab the attention of potential users of the Platform, cater for a wide spectrum of user – from established organizations to FinTechs and Startups.

- **Educate**: A more detailed understanding of your platform will result in more efficient use and possibly more widespread use of the various product offerings.

- **Build trust**: The intention of the Marketplace is to empower external organizations by using internal products and services. Potential consumers of your Platform need to be confident of its capability and reliability.

- **Transparency**: Fine print and obscure information will impact the relationship with third parties and potentially damage the reputation of your platform in the market.

- **Collaborate**: Keep your customers engaged and use feedback to optimize your platform and drive your product roadmap. The relationship is ongoing.

- **Lead**: The owner of the domain who is responsible for the content of the portal which supports other initiatives inside and outside the organization.

Business Value

The first viewers of your organization's API Marketplace Portal will most likely be from a business development perspective. This individual or team will review the API products to determine fit as a foundational element for a product or service still being conceptualized or built. Figures 3-1-1, 3-1-2, and 3-1-3 are a great example that illustrate how Twilio has achieved this for its Messaging API.

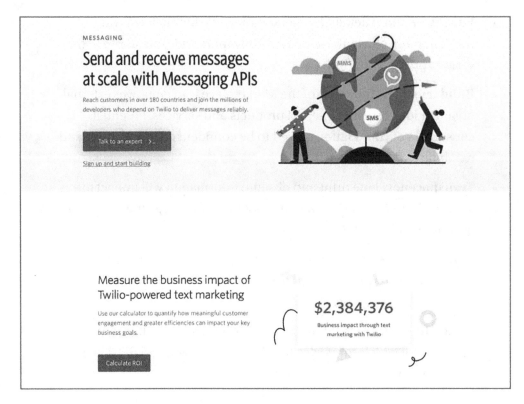

Figure 3-1-1. *Non-technical overview of Twilio's Message API*

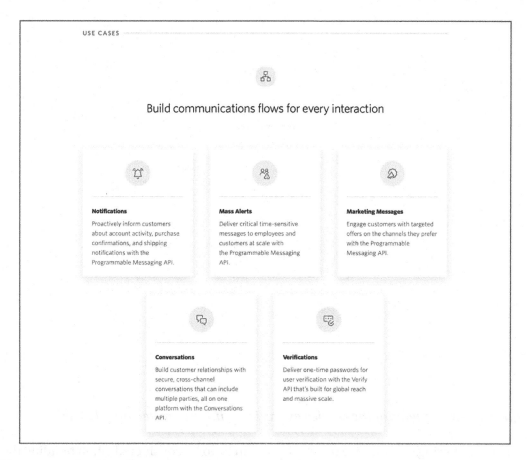

Figure 3-1-2. *Simple, easy to relate to use-cases*

Figure 3-1-3. *Benefits of the service expressed without any technical jargon*

In the following sections, we review the key areas to be considered when building the "Business Portal" of your API Marketplace.

Attract

Although you can use a "Field of Dreams" strategy of "*If you build it, they will come*" – it may be more effective to actively market the Platform. Posts on social media, launch events, articles, and interviews on Technology, Entrepreneurship, and Startup websites will help draw potential users in. The key message on your main page, possibly the first thing a user sees, is your "elevator pitch" – how can *our* API Marketplace help *your* organization? This could include a 2- to 3-minute video, showing at a high-level, preferably in a non-technical context, how the Marketplace provides services and capabilities upon which new products can be built.

Be sure to extol the benefits of adoption. This can be done through motivation, "by using our platform today, you have a first-mover advantage to power your business and leapfrog the competition," or through fear – "in Europe, governments have issued regulations that require all banks to abide by the Payment Services Directive by the end of 2018. Our government is investigating similar regulation."

Educate

An empowered third party will understand the purpose of the platform and can leverage the business capability for commercial use. Your audience, at this time, may not have any technical background. Metaphors and analogies are important to convey the key messages. **Explainer videos** detailing core concepts such as *"What is an API?"* and *"What can you do with it?"* will help considerably. Test the use of this material when communicating with internal backend teams. As the delivery team is constantly immersed in the detail, it may be easy to take for granted certain concepts and functions around APIs. Be sure to keep in mind that there is a relatively steep learning curve for those new to APIs.

Case studies detailing the journey of users of the platform successfully leveraging APIs to launch new products and services will also help potential customers understand how the Marketplace can be used to achieve a business purpose. It may also help to provide details around the time and effort required to use the platform. Be sure to provide accurate information as being too optimistic may result in the third-party setting unrealistic launch timelines leading to integration fatigue. Being too pessimistic may result in the platform not being used. Encourage iterative adoption of Products. It would be more beneficial for both consumer and provider, to start and finish with one or a few products than starting with many products and later abandoning the effort.

Focus on **business value** instead of API products. For example, a *Customer* API which returns the name and address information of a customer can be used for *identity verification*. It could also be used to streamline the registration or sign-up process for third-party applications. Highlight that onerous registration forms result in high drop-offs for potential users and the *Customer* API could help alleviate that. Similarly, an *Accounts* API can be used to determine a user's financial behavior, which can result in better or personalized service offerings. In developing countries, where the concept of API Marketplaces is only beginning to emerge, highlight the value that has been created in other markets which have an active API ecosystem.

Mailing lists and regular **blog** posts will also help keep current and prospective customers engaged. This will also help to define the product roadmap. The Product Owner can use these communication streams to determine interest or potential uptake of a new API. Third parties can also be made aware of new versions of products, releases, and patches.

As an API Marketplace is constantly evolving, customer education is an ongoing activity. This is one of the greatest rewards of working on the Platform – the cycle of innovation and optimization never stops. You need to ensure that the users of the platform can leverage its full potential.

Build Trust

Consider the API Marketplace from the perspective of a potential third party. This entity is potentially using the Marketplace as a foundational element of its business operation. The consequences for the organization could be catastrophic if there are any stability or reliability issues with the platform. What has helped our implementation adoption considerably is that we have a nationally trusted brand with millions of customers behind our Marketplace. The members of our team are always aware that this relationship is reciprocal. Any issues or fallibility of our platform could impact the trust and brand of the organization we represent. I like to consider the trust earned through this mechanism as "inherited." Essentially, you trust me because you know my parent. I believe trust should also be "earned."

This can be achieved by having a close relationship with the users of your platform. During early or pilot phases of the platform release, work closely with third-party providers. When launching a recent product, we had weekly, sometimes daily, calls with an enthusiastic Developer. This interaction not only helped us flesh out issues with the API Product we were releasing but provided insight into the use of the product. The confidence of the external development team in the product also improved significantly as they could see the commitment from the provider. Word also tends to spread quickly in FinTech and Startup communities.

Adoption of your Platform will be impacted by positive *and* negative feedback. Endorsements from established third parties, preferably in their own words, in the form of a **customer testimonial,** may help convince potential users to use your Marketplace. Again, these are not easy to attain, and there may be a significant amount of work from the full team to achieve this. **Reference customers** will also help establish trust. Implicit trust can be secured if potential users of the platform see a known brand or product which uses the platform. It is important to identify and target one or more established brands who must be actively engaged to use your Marketplace. A key lesson we learnt out of practical experience regarding timeframes is if you are aiming for your Platform to be used by Black Friday (fourth Friday of November), you need to start integration activities by June.

A key construct of an API Marketplace is a **partnership** between Marketplace and third-party provider. As indicated previously, the Marketplace requires consumers of the Platform to survive. It is important to highlight that another key partnership is between the Marketplace and the end user of the organization. The end user places their trust in the Marketplace to only allow access to information or data to third parties that they have granted permission to. To the API project teams reading this – be aware this is not only a massive responsibility to uphold, but also an incredible honor as your efforts enables this three-way relationship.

Transparency

Strong, enduring relationships require transparency. Although third parties are consumers of the Marketplace, be sure to remember that they are intrinsically linked to the success or failure of the platform as much as the internal team. The simple reasoning behind this statement is – if the Marketplace fails, it will impact their organization, possibly their ability to continue operating.

Be honest about **timelines**. Marketplace launch, API product capability, availability, and roadmap. This may not always be possible due to competitive pressure. But always aim to under-promise and over-deliver. A key lesson learnt early in our journey is that we should always be one step ahead of our developer community. With the launch of our Marketplace, many third parties signed up to use the Platform – far more than anticipated. Unfortunately, some of the API products in our Marketplace were not ready for commercialization due to internal approvals required. In hindsight, it would have been prudent to remove those API products from our catalogue or clearly indicate in our portal that timelines for commercial availability were still to be established.

Pricing – in the form of costs or incentives – should be clear, unambiguous, and free of fine print. The third party will most likely have to invest time and money to consume the products of the API Marketplace. In addition, the third party will also need visibility into the costs of using the platform. That is, if the costs are per transaction, tiered or flat. There could also be an incentive to use the Marketplace in the form of a lead or referral commission. Essentially, the third party requires as much financial information as possible to determine the commercial viability of engaging with your Marketplace. During the early phases of the Marketplace, it may be necessary to allow free access to APIs to stimulate adoption. Be sure to communicate to consumers that this is subject to change and will be reviewed later. If pricing is simply not available, due to external factors, be sure to clearly indicate this.

Service-Level Agreements (SLAs) and resolution timeframes must be clearly defined. The inherent benefit is that the SLAs can be used across several providers. These can be tiered – higher tiers would receive more support and faster resolution – albeit at a higher cost. Upfront agreement also sets the correct expectations regarding resolution and will significantly assist the Marketplace Support team when fielding operational queries. Again, be sure to be honest regarding resolution times – as too optimistic timeframes will result in a loss of confidence with prolonged outages and too pessimistic an outlook may impact adoption and confidence. Where unclear or still to be defined, clearly indicate as such and ensure clear communication in the event of an operational issue.

Collaborate

Consider offering one or a few obligation-free **consultation** sessions. This is especially the case in developing markets where prospective customers want that extra reassurance by discussing questions or scenarios in person. From experience, technical support teams may not be the best suited to assist prospective users at this point in the customer journey. The Product Owner, with support from the technical team, should facilitate these sessions. Technical teams will be able to assist with development or integration queries. However, the Product Owner will be able to position the Marketplace for commercial success.

A **register your interest** lead-generation form is a necessity. A follow-up email or phone call within 24 hours is mandatory. FinTechs and startups operate at incredible pace, and the potential opportunity is at risk of being lost if not followed up on timeously. During the follow-up, the Product Owner will be able to determine the maturity of the prospect, where the organization is in their journey and the level and area of support required (including whether the questions are commercial or technical in nature).

As the Marketplace evolves and adoption increases, it may be necessary to provide **tiers** of support. As the number of staff in the delivery team may be fixed, it might not be possible to provide all third parties with the same level of time and attention. Higher, paid-for offerings will result in closer engagement as it could also fund dedicated Service Managers. While the Marketplace is in its early phases, be sure to capture every customer query (be it potential or current) in a Service Desk and follow up.

Lead

This effort is best led by the Product Owner (PO) as this will form the foundation of the sales pitch for external consumers. The PO will also extol the benefits of having representation in the Marketplace to internal platform teams. Always keep in mind that an API Marketplace has many consumers – a Business *and* Technical audience from external organizations. Knowledge gained from these relationships can also be used to demonstrate capability to internal teams and to stakeholders. Be sure to give this the right level of attention and focus.

Technical Developer Portal

With more than 20 years of experience in the technology industry and as a proud developer myself, when it comes to technical sources of information, I have extremely high standards *but* low levels of tolerance. I expect quality and precise information to assimilate a product or service. Although all developers eventually end up at StackOverflow, my confidence in the capability and maturity of a product drops if I must resort to this measure frequently. If there is suitable information or resources available, I don't mind spending the time and effort learning or understanding concepts to use the technology. The Developer Portal is the foundation upon which the relationship an API Marketplace establishes with a technical audience.

Figures 3-2-1 and 3-2-2 provide a view of Twilio's technical documentation for its Messaging API. Figure 3-2-1 shows the next level of detail by identifying the various channels for sending a message. In Figure 3-2-2, the documentation provides the low-level technical details for API use.

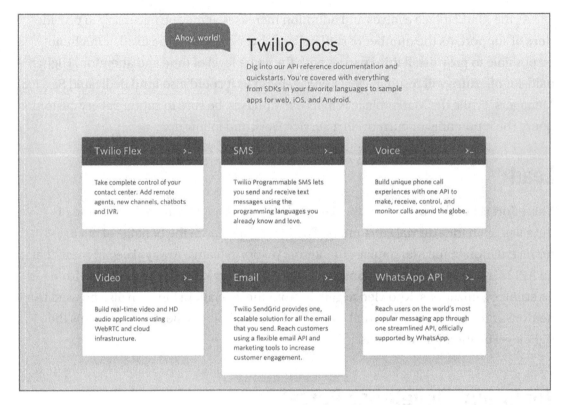

Figure 3-2-1. *Gradual introduction to the different messaging channels*

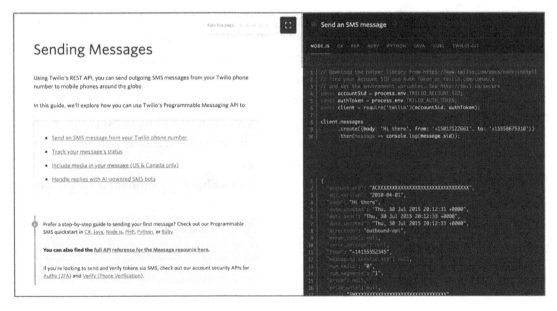

Figure 3-2-2. *Technical instructions and code samples for API consumption*

We consider the following areas to build a Marketplace that your developers will believe in and be loyal to.

Attract

Technical consumption of the API Marketplace may be the result of a second wave of review, the first being a business development assessment. The technical team will be tasked with providing an **impact assessment** to integrate into the Marketplace. Criteria such as the standard of documentation, self-service, sample code, availability of test data, and developer support will be examined. The feedback from this assessment will help determine timelines and cost to integrate.

Although the goal of an API Marketplace is to attract third-party providers to the platform, this needs to be tempered with a required **minimum level** of skill and experience. Be sure to keep this in mind when defining your target audience. The risk of bringing in novice or junior developers is that the team will have to provide more handholding and support.

User groups and community sessions can also be used to demystify the concept of an API Marketplace and to introduce interested developers to the platform. As the goal of an API Marketplace is to democratize access to data, consider entrepreneurs who could consume the products to launch a diverse set of applications. **Hackathons** are an excellent mechanism to encourage participation and to stimulate interest. A positive side effect is that they could help you find talented developers to join your delivery team.

A novel approach we observed from an implementation was the engagement of an external organization who invited a diverse set of developers to a 3–5-day bootcamp. During this time, the developers were paired with an expert for support and built an application which used the API Marketplace.

FinTechs and startups are also eager to consume APIs to bootstrap application delivery. Be sure to post articles in sites frequented by such organizations and encourage participation. Marketplaces are **viral** and if the developer experience is positive, word will spread. It is important to build and foster a developer community, and this needs to be a key goal for the API Marketplace.

Educate

Technical consumption of an API Marketplace requires at a minimum intermediate developer experience, preferably 2–3 years of hands-on coding or integration experience. Although you can educate novice developers, I do not think that the objective and material of the portal should include tutorials on how to make REST API calls. There are great online tutorials which will help developers come up to speed with APIs.

However, be sure to cover API Marketplace *specific* concepts, such as OAuth, in **blueprints**. Delegated authorization, which is one of the basic tenets of a Marketplace, *must* be clearly and concisely detailed and explained. We have had many new API consumers who did not clearly understand the process flow until they could trace the calls against a sequence diagram. Many integration developers are only familiar with a client ID/secret pattern.

For each of the API products, try to provide **code samples** in many programming languages. Some of the benchmark developer portals provide samples in: Node.js, C#, PHP, Ruby, Python, Java, and cURL. One of the greatest benefits of an API Marketplace is the neutrality of access – HTTP. Be sure to leverage this to accommodate a wide range of developers. From personal development experience of consuming a product from one of the major cloud providers, **code labs** can make a massive difference. Code labs are different from code samples as they step a developer through the process of consuming an API. Think of a code sample as a ready-made cake and a code lab as a recipe.

As the marketplace matures, consider providing **patterns** or recommended practices for integration. A typical example is consuming APIs from a mobile application. Given that a wide range of providers may have similar challenges with integration, providing a pattern will help ease the integration friction and allow easier consumption of your API. The answer, in case you're wondering about consuming APIs directly from a mobile application, is never to store credentials in the app but rather to use user-authenticated tokens to make the API calls.

Blog posts and **podcasts** are also an excellent way to stay connected to your developer community. These tools can be used to share details of your Marketplace journey and to give users a view into your roadmap. Raise and address hard-hitting issues in the podcasts – such as timelines for regulation and how to plan accordingly. These give greater insight into the internal working and operation of the platform.

As the platform matures and scales, consider **developer certification**. It does not have to be an extensive program – but just a basic theoretical assessment and practical exercise to ensure that a developer grasps the concepts of the Marketplace. This may become a mandatory requirement for more sensitive API products.

Finally, a downloadable Postman collection will help potential developers immensely. Postman is regarded as the de facto tool for API development and is discussed later in this chapter. Be sure to include documentation detailing each value of the collection with a step-by-step guide. The Postman collection is approximately 40% of the effort. The remaining 60% is the accompanying documentation. If possible, consider enlisting the services of a technical writer to help compile this material. Unfortunately, some of the best developers are not necessarily the best at providing documentation.

Build Trust

Trust, in a Developer Community, must be earned. This can be achieved by paying attention to the detail and insisting on a high standard of delivery. By assisting developers with challenges they cannot solve on their own using the available technical literature, developers will feel supported. Timely response to support requests is also mandatory. Prompt feedback – even as simple as *"we are investigating and will get back to you"* is essential. With that in mind, it is imperative that there are processes within the support team that allow development issues to be escalated and attended to.

I would like to highlight that developer support is a balancing act. As much as we want to support developers in consuming our Marketplaces, we would like our customer base to be self-reliant as much as possible. That is – the first port of call should be the documentation of the Portal, and then if there is still a significant gap in understanding, a question should be raised on the developer forum to solicit community feedback. If all else fails and the consumer is convinced there is a problem with the internal functioning or something that they cannot solve without intervention from the Marketplace team, a query should be logged. In addition, the query should include details of their troubleshooting and investigative efforts as well as *their* reasoning to believe it is an issue outside their sphere of control. This may seem like a tall order – however, having a strong developer community not only alleviates pressure on your Support team but also raises the bar for the overall standard of the Marketplace. That is, the quality of API products will improve as it will be subject to more challenging review from consumers.

It is also essential to **walk the talk**. If an API Marketplace is a new digital channel to access data, your processes should also be *digital*. There is nothing more frustrating for a developer whose curiosity has been piqued to not have immediate access to get their hands dirty. An example is having a fantastic developer portal which outlines amazing functionality and capability with a *Schedule a chat* or *Contact us* form. Self-service is an absolute necessity. I would like to highly emphasize this as it allows a seamless transition from conceptual to tangible.

By providing immediate access to functionality, your API Marketplace moves from a categorization of "marketing/vaporware" to tangible code. Speaking from experience, developers detest vaporware. Skepticism immediately increases and scrutiny to find chinks in the Marketplace armor intensifies. Be sure to allow immediate self-service access, at least to a Sandbox/Simulated environment, when an API product is released.

Transparency

Open, unambiguous access to information is also a way to *keep* the trust of your developer community. Provide insight into the API Product roadmap as much as competitive pressure will allow. Third parties can use this information to plan and schedule their releases accordingly. If possible, consider a consultative process with third parties regarding potential API products to determine potential demand/uptake early in the product lifecycle. This will help direct efforts/focus on APIs which will be readily consumed. Although a catalogue with hundreds of API products is impressive, if there is minimal use or uptake across most of the APIs, it only serves to increase the areas to support and maintain and diverts attention from APIs which are used more.

Consider a **beta** program which allows early-stage API product access to a subset of trusted third parties. This process will allow the team to optimize and refine the product – from shaping an interface to performance engineering to updates in documentation in a safely demarcated "staging" environment. The beta tag provides a clear indication that the products are still under construction. When our Marketplace was launched to the public, our Product Owner skillfully included the "beta" reference to allow us room to maneuver during the early phases of our launch. With permission from Information and Network Security, it may also be possible to connect beta release APIs to internal Quality Assurance (QA) backends to allow for more in-depth integration testing. This should be done after serious consideration as providing third parties access to an internal environment could open a Pandora's box.

A novel feature observed on several established Developer Portals is an API **status** page, which is also available as an API. This allows consumers to tap into your operational platform and the ability to take pre-emptive steps in the event of a service or API outage.

Status also includes historical data so that consumers and the Operations team can quickly identify poorly operating products and to seek remediation efforts on the internal or backend platform. By providing this level of visibility, it is a signal to a third party that you are serious about the stability and reliability of your platform, and you are taking measures to provide immediate alerting/notification in the event of an issue.

Once an API is in production, any updates for new functionality, or to patch or fix issues, must be clearly documented in **release notes**. This should become part of the deployment cycle as third parties must be kept informed of any changes to an API.

Collaborate

Be sure to encourage feedback from your consumers regarding API products and, where possible, attempt to address the feedback in subsequent releases. Some feedback, such as prescribed regulatory interfaces are too complex to consume, may not be possible to accommodate changes. Feedback is a gift, and if a consumer took the time to send through feedback, it is probably significant from their perspective – always be sure to close the loop with the user. Continuing the scenario above – the feedback regarding complex, regulated interfaces would be to emphasize, then indicate that regulation mandates the interface and finally provide suggestions to assist, such as sample code or labs.

Set up an area on the technical developer portal, possibly a dedicated section in your message forum for **feature** requests. As third parties are consuming your APIs, they are in the best position to determine product gaps and potential areas of improvement. This is a fantastic input into the product lifecycle and can make a good API great. Again, based on the scale and reach of the API, the priority or scheduling of the request is linked to the number of votes for the request. This is one of the biggest benefits of an active developer community – the users can help to drive the product roadmap forward.

For integration solutions within an enterprise, all service consumers are notified of a change well in advance, and some governance processes require approval from all consumers before the change can be made. As an API Marketplace sits on the fringe of an organization, the delivery team may not consider the wider impact when updating an API. That is, from a responsibility assignment RACI (Responsible, Accountable, Consulted, Informed) matrix perspective, a third party may not be Consulted or even Informed. A lightweight change management process should be followed to ensure that all service consumers are at a minimum aware of any maintenance or releases to any APIs consumed.

Lead

This effort should also be coordinated by the Product Owner (PO) with significant input and direction from the Engineering team. Although the content is highly technical in nature, it could be argued that this would be best understood and delivered by a technical team. My counterargument is that a technical team is *not* suited to lead this effort as they may be too close to the detail. The Product Owner will provide a view from a third-party perspective. As the Product Owner is ultimately accountable for the success and uptake of APIs, they should lead the effort for both portals, Business and Technical, as it is customer facing. By now, it should be apparent that a Product Owner *must* be semi-technical.

Developer Advocacy

Even a good product, with good documentation, needs to be evangelized. I observed and appreciated this approach from a major cloud provider while learning how to use a new mobile application development platform. At first, I could not understand why it was necessary at all – the documentation, code samples, and labs were amazing and even novice developers could get up and running in a short space of time. However, as I progressed deeper into the platform, I ran into scenarios which were not covered by any documentation. It was at that point I understood the value of a Developer Advocate.

Although they might not know it, I got to know them by first name by watching, re-watching, pausing, and writing code in-step with their video tutorials. I marveled at how their solutions were far simpler and more elegant than the complex ones I anticipated. In addition to learning more about the platform, I also learnt how to use *Node.js* more efficiently. The difference between the documentation and the Advocate was that the latter used the product to solve a real-world scenario.

Imagine pieces of Lego blocks lying on a table. Although you might be able to assemble a basic structure on your own, you probably would stick with familiar pieces. Watching someone else use an unfamiliar piece to achieve a specific function would help put that piece into perspective and give you the confidence to use it in the future.

Simply put – API Marketplaces, especially in developing markets, need strong Developer Advocacy. Video tutorials covering concepts such as delegated authorization in a fun, easy to understand context will certainly help alleviate developer anxiety. The access mechanism allows viewing of the material *anytime* and as *many times* as needed to understand complex concepts. With the recent boom in online meetups, it is now easier than ever to join a user group. This should be leveraged as much as possible to get potential developers, albeit with the pre-requisite experience and willing-to-learn mindset, up and running on the platform. The inherent benefit of user groups, meetings – in person or online – is that it allows two-way communication between Marketplace and developer. I consider this interaction as mutually beneficial.

Developers can get hands-on support from the Marketplace technical delivery team. The delivery team can also view first-hand the viewpoint from a developer. Sometimes developing in an ivory tower may result in theoretically sound, but impractical products. Such products typically get shelved. A key mantra of API Marketplace product development should be simple, practical, and reliable. Any member of the team should have the confidence to easily explain how to consume the product to an external user.

For our launch event, the Product team secured funding for T-shirts and mugs. I chuckled at the effort and initially chalked it down to a marketing maneuver. I was extremely surprised to see how proud the delivery team was to wear the T-shirts, and it was at that point that I realized the importance of these tokens. "Swag," also known as "merch," provides a physical connection to an intangible entity. To this day, I still have the (unused) mug on my desk as I am proud of what we have achieved. It is one of our key objectives to have our developer community feel connected to the Marketplace and the same sense of belonging and support.

Developer Support

An API Marketplace is unique when compared to other integration environments since support is required during development and for operational execution. This may seem to double the support capacity required – however, supporting developers will ultimately result in more operational use of the platform. Developer support also differs from operational support as the nature of queries are different.

Our most common query was around the seemingly complex delegated authority model. To remedy this, the team worked on material that could clearly illustrate the concept. It may surprise you that the content was a simple set of images assembled into a slideshow. We successfully used this on several occasions – for both internal and external developers. It helped frame the end user, the third-party provider, and our organization. As we stepped through the flow on calls with API consumers, testers, or solution architects, I could almost sense the "penny-drop" moment when it clicked, and they understood exactly how it worked.

As our Marketplace grows and evolves, we are refining and optimizing the developer support process. In the early phases of our release, most developer queries were dealt with by our first-line support team. However, if first-line support was not able to assist, the query moved to the internal team for deeper technical or product support. For some requests, we attempted to resolve them via email. However, nine times out of ten, our highest success rate was an online discussion with the third-party developer.

To be completely honest, this is a work-in-progress for our implementation. What has helped incredibly is that our Product Owner has an exceptional relationship building ability. The PO also engages the third party when the request transitions between first-line support and backend support to be able to frame the requirement and to ease any friction before the online discussion. Be sure to keep in mind that by the time of the discussion, the third party is likely to be upset that the issue was not resolved, and first-line support is exasperated as their attempts to solve the issue have not been successful.

For the online discussion, we had representation from the first-line support engineer who had been interacting with the user – for continuity. Senior engineers and the Product Owner also attended the session. Our intention was not to scare the external developer. Exactly the opposite. We wanted to show that the third party was important to us and our entire team valued the relationship.

The number one rule around these interactions is to *listen*. Firstly, you must listen clearly and attentively to the triage from the first-line engineer around the issue – in preparation for the discussion. Based on the feedback, the team should be ready with the relevant material or information. Secondly, you must listen clearly and attentively to the external developer. The feedback or queries during the initial part of the session will help you to build a better platform. Once you are sure that you have a firm grasp of the problem or situation, then offer a solution. If you need to investigate further, clearly indicate so. Attempt to follow up a day or so after the call. This will demonstrate that the API Marketplace is sincere about the developer's success.

A positive side effect is a better, personal relationship with our developer community. We have put voices and faces to client IDs and email addresses. We know the types of applications our developers are building and how our APIs are consumed. In almost all our interactions, developers proudly showed off their applications. For new product releases, we have also invited third-party developers for full-day sessions to run end-to-end integration tests. This has helped us to identify and flesh out potential issues before extending the offering to more third-party providers. The feedback received was used to update and change how the product worked.

Although these interactions are not subject to intense time pressure, like those in an operational context, we still attempt to handle developer support requests with the same attention and rigor as operational issues. From a priority perspective, the operational environment comes first. Our Marketplace fields support requests via email and Slack. The first-line support engineer will attempt to resolve configuration or simple issues. For more complex issues, a service desk request is logged for tracking and to assign to the relevant member of the team for investigation and resolution. If required, the issue is escalated to the Product Owner who will schedule an online discussion with the external team.

Finally, and as discussed earlier in this chapter, we encourage external development teams to be as self-sufficient as possible. If there are technical issues with API integration, HTTP trace information regarding the requests and responses and possibly code extracts are requested. Essentially, this is a *"help me help you"* engagement. An altruistic aim of the API Marketplace is that the platform empowers, fosters, and builds our local developer community. We discuss this in more detail in the following section.

Ecosystem

I've been extremely fortunate to have been on an API Marketplace implementation for several years now and have marveled how the ecosystem has evolved over time and as the initiative has matured. We started in a little fishbowl, just a few members of a delivery team, with the goal of delivering a Minimum Viable Product (MVP). Initially, there was no real connection to the outside world and a few tenuous links to backend platforms.

As the platform was readied for production workloads, we moved into a larger tank, working closely with different enterprise teams to achieve more stability and reliability. Our respect and appreciation of the enterprise capability grew as we understood the value it added to our implementation. It may be easy to glance over internal enterprise teams in the context of an API Marketplace ecosystem. I now consider this one of the key supporting elements of the platform and an essential part of our ecosystem. Without a doubt, the tether to an established enterprise, in the form of process and governance, may be viewed at times as a millstone slowing the pace of change. In hindsight, almost all of these requirements have resulted in a more stable, reliable, and enterprise-class platform.

We were incredibly lucky to have, as our first mainstream consumer, an internally sponsored super-app. We had moved from tank to dam. Bigger body of water, far more serious, but essentially a "safe-space" to verify the platform from an operational context. As more role-players entered our ecosystem, we had to balance super-aggressive delivery requirements and operational issues deeply rooted in backend platforms. This resulted in possibly the greatest expansion of the Marketplace. The number of integrations to backend platforms grew exponentially in the space of a few short months. What helped incredibly was the impetus of the super-app since our links into more backend platforms were able to grow as the juggernaut smashed down barriers and tore through red tape. With each new integration, we had to build a new relationship with a backend – not only for development, but also for operational support.

We have since moved on to open-water. Spurred on by the success of supporting the load of a high-performing internal consumer and earning our stripes in the process, we are now working more with external third parties. The size and scale of the third parties range from single-developer entities to well-known FinTechs to established online retailers. However, we treat all with the same level of respect and commitment.

What continually amazes me is the symbiotic nature of the ecosystem. The API Marketplace will not exist without consumers and the support from enterprise services. Yet, it is a pivotal component for external consumers to leverage the capability of the enterprise services. A ripple effect, which we hope will one day turn into a butterfly effect, is that the Marketplace has stimulated the local developer community. As a leading Financial Services provider, the capability provided by our Marketplace has enabled the building of many innovative products and services. These new shoots of growth need to be nurtured and supported and will result in successful third parties who will further fuel the Marketplace. The success of the Marketplace hinges on an active, thriving ecosystem where all entities work and grow together.

Developer Engagement

An API Marketplace may use different strategies for interaction with developers. Some platforms use a community-based approach, where access is open, and members support each other to effectively leverage the platform. The interaction between developers could also result in innovative products and solutions which could include APIs from different platforms. In these engagements, the developer portal is essentially a meeting point for like-minded developers to share ideas and collaborate. Some portals also provide the experience and expertise of individual developers. As solutions are verified and endorsed, developer rank and credibility increases. Experienced members could act as ambassadors as they assist new developers.

Another approach is to choose partners based on key selection criteria. The intention is to allow a smaller subset of more experienced, established, and like-minded partners into the ecosystem. Closed-ecosystem partnerships are used for creating, extending, and improving API offerings. Developers could benefit from financial compensation, premium support, and coaching through a partner network, early access to new products, and formal accreditation. Although the developer pool is smaller, this could potentially require more management and support from the platform provider.

As developers from different organizations might not communicate directly, a partner manager may be required for support and to forward queries to the backend technical team for resolution. Sharing information or assisting fellow developers may also not be possible since they could see this as a loss of competitive advantage. It should also be noted that expected service levels in such an environment are significantly higher. If a developer posts a query, feedback and/or resolution must be provided in a significantly shorter timeframe than a community forum.

The nature of Developer engagement will be determined by the nature of the API Marketplace you will build. If, for example, your APIs help to find lost pets in a local neighborhood, a community-approach should be used. If your APIs help to find sources of plutonium for building nuclear weapons, you might want to restrict the partners who can access your platform.

Tooling

Developers work with a wide variety of tools to get a job done. Developer tools could range from email clients to code editors to Integrated Developer Environments (IDEs) to wikis. In this section, I highlight a few tools and practices which I have personally found to be useful as part of my daily delivery. There are many amazing tools and products available for API consumption and development. This is not intended to be a product comparison or benchmark. If you have experience or are comfortable with another tool, please continue to use it.

cURL

cURL, which stands for client URL, is a command-line tool for getting and sending files using URL syntax. It supports several protocols including HTTP and HTTPS – which make it ideal for working with APIs. It runs on almost any platform on any hardware and is included in many popular operating systems.

The reasons that I use cURL are as follows:

- **Universal**: As I hop between containers, virtual machines and servers, I often lose access to the powerful Graphical User Interface (GUI) driven tools on my local machine. The ability to *curl* to an endpoint to check connectivity or to simulate/replay a client request from a remote node, cut off from the luxury of a UI due to network restrictions, is priceless.

- **Simple**: I also enjoy working with cURL due to its no frills and low maintenance disposition. It focuses on its role as emissary in transporting a message between the key participants – client and server. The syntax to make various API calls are concise and online tutorials or samples are readily available.

- **Neutrality**: If a request works with cURL, or conversely does not work, it is unquestionable. Although developers may use different tools, a cURL command can be easily shared and replayed in seconds. As the command line is the lowest common denominator across all operating systems, cURL achieves universal citizenship across developer boundaries.

Postman API Client

Postman is a popular API client that makes it easy for developers to create, share, test, and document APIs. This is done by allowing users to create and save simple or complex HTTP/s requests, as well as read their responses. Postman has a number of features. The following is not an exhaustive list but highlights the elements my team and I use on a regular basis:

- **Up and running quickly**: We can consume an API quickly once we have an endpoint and request details. The Postman UI is intuitive and allows requests to be initiated in different ways. For example, the body for a request can be specified in various formats – which are selectable from a simple radio button interface. The free version has all the capabilities needed to get up and running.

- **Capability**: The tool is as simple or complex as you need it to be. Postman caters for a wide range of developer expertise – from the novice developer who simply wants to fire a request to an endpoint, to a seasoned testing engineer who wants to set up complex automated test execution.

- **Sharing**: As I typically work across machines, the synchronization capability allows great portability, and I can easily start a collection on one machine and continue working on it from another. One of the features we use the most is the sharing of collections between team members. We have often had the case where the call works for one developer but not another. API requests are extremely intricate, and for complex calls, the difference between success and failure could be due to one parameter. Sharing is easily achieved by exporting a collection via a public link. Note that this should not be used for sensitive APIs. This increases collaboration significantly and allows instant alignment between members of the development team.

- **Code snippets**: In developing integration solutions, consuming an API or endpoint from a tool is winning one battle in an ongoing campaign. The next battleground is achieving that same result from code. The code snippets feature is extremely useful as it converts the requests in Postman to a number of different languages – even a cURL command. This is extremely useful as it helps the transition from tool to code.

- **Variables and environments**: As part of the software development lifecycle, the solution must transition through many environments – from Development to Test, to Staging, to Production. It is also extremely common for a conversational API interaction, that is, the output of one request is used for the next. Variables can be used as placeholders – which are manually set or updated using a script which can significantly speed up testing. Variables, such as endpoints, can also be configured for specific environments.

Fiddler

Fiddler is a debugging proxy server tool used to log, inspect, and alter HTTP and HTTPS traffic between a computer and a web server or servers.

Our support team recently received a support request from a third-party developer who had trouble consuming an API. What set this query apart from others we received was that it included detailed HTTP trace information regarding each request and response. This not only allowed us to follow the flow of calls to ensure the sequence was correct, but it also helped the Support team identify exactly which parameter of which request was incorrect. The developer was able to provide this trace information by using Fiddler which intercepted the call and recorded the HTTP request and response.

Developer Education

As the Marketplace team uses these tools and techniques on a daily basis, it can be easy to forget the learning curve other developers may encounter. The technical developer portal should have one or more of the following as mandatory elements to support third parties:

1. Sample Postman collections for each API product. The collection must have pre-populated requests with developers having to provide minimal information, such as credentials, to make their first API call.

2. A quick walkthrough of how a tool should be configured, with special attention to areas which could cause an issue. For example, the difference between "Headers" and "Parameters" in Postman.

3. When logging support requests, the detail required for the request and *how* to get it. Using an interceptor, like Fiddler, to capture the request and response – instead of sending code extracts.

Empowered developers will result in an experienced developer community, fewer support requests, and more detailed, concise requests when they do come through. Spending the time and effort upfront will result in significant gains later in the Marketplace lifecycle such as requiring fewer operations staff and faster resolution or response to support queries.

Summary

In this chapter, we discussed strategies around the business and technical Portals of your API Marketplace. Although the spotlight is on the dazzling API product on an amazing stage, it is important to ensure that the requirements of the developer audience are kept in focus.

Each Marketplace implementation will have a different combination of API products, portals, developer focus, and engagement strategy that will make it unique. Defining this identity upfront can help the team carve out a clear path to the end state. It may also be necessary to allow the identity of the platform to evolve or pivot over time – in response to customer demand. The dynamic nature of an API Marketplace is indeed one of its biggest advantages as its flexibility allows it to respond far faster than existing enterprise systems.

In the next chapter, we consider monetization for API Marketplaces. The Consumption model has a significant impact on how the platform is monetized as the two are intrinsically linked. If the monetization model is high volume with low transaction costs, more developers are needed in the pipeline. If the strategy is lower volume, subscription-based revenue, then a smaller subset of established, loyal organizations willing and able to pay a subscription is the objective.

CHAPTER 4

Monetization

I believe that Engineering is possibly *the* biggest enabler of the monetization or commercial proposition of an API Marketplace. To many technically inclined individuals, this may seem oxymoronic as the realms are at the opposite ends of the spectrum.

Allow me to present this argument in the context of building a new passenger airplane. If the Engineering team focuses purely on speed, performance, and technology, it will undoubtedly be fast and technically sound. There are a number of other factors to consider such as the number of passengers it can carry, the fuel consumed, the range or distance the aircraft can cover, and the maintenance and lifespan. These factors determine the financial viability of the aircraft. A real-world example of this scenario is the retirement of the supersonic airliner, the Concorde, which is an engineering marvel but unfortunately, not the most economical.

In much the same way, the technical delivery team has a responsibility for the commercial trajectory and financial viability that influences the lifespan of an API Marketplace. In all honesty, I would classify this very much as a privilege and challenges the Engineering team to maintain a view on commercial objectives when designing and building solutions. Based on observation of a number of IT projects, leaving this objective to the project executive to shoulder alone will ultimately result in a technically sound but imbalanced solution. Such projects are generally shelved closer to release or mothballed due to unsustainability.

An approach which has worked remarkably well for our implementation is one which affords any member of the team the opportunity to question or make a suggestion regarding commercial aspects of an API product. This has been enabled by a project executive who not only welcomes feedback but often demands it from the team as a signal of their ownership in the platform. Whimsical pitches regarding potentially amazing revenue-generating products from the technical dugout are often fielded with incredible finesse to avoid bruised egos as these may lie outside the rules of the organizational game.

© Rennay Dorasamy 2022
R. Dorasamy, *API Marketplace Engineering*, https://doi.org/10.1007/978-1-4842-7313-5_4

In this chapter, I consider the objective of Monetization from a technical perspective, using a logical-focused lens leveraging the experience of products that didn't survive conceptualization and many that have reached implementation, some of which are now generating revenue. We unpack the strategies which are currently in use for our platform and which are constantly adapted to maximize financial potential. The key underlying theme of this chapter is the interdependence between technical and commercial – one cannot survive without the other.

The API Marketplace Flywheel

Taking inspiration from the Amazon flywheel which places Customer Experience at the core of its Growth strategy, the process which powers our platform, as detailed in Figure 4-1, is underpinned by the Developer Experience. Full credit for this process is due to our project executive, and I had to persuade him to share the blueprints for the process which essentially drives our Platform's operating model.

In a new market, this was certainly a bold decision and is enabled by a long-term outlook from the leadership team supported by a well-defined Digital strategy. Unlike many organizations, we have adopted an approach which favors quality over quantity. In support of this statement, all API products have been built in accordance and alignment with industry standards. Custom definitions would have afforded faster delivery but harder to adopt definitions.

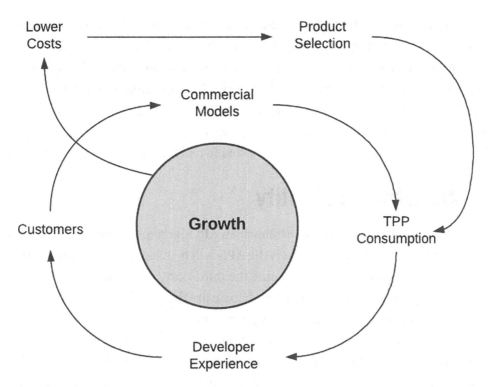

Figure 4-1. *The API Marketplace flywheel*

Our strategy is to start the wheel by earning trust and establishing developer affinity to the platform. From observation of third-party consumers, our APIs provide significant support and acceleration to the development of the product or service which will be delivered to the end user. In many cases, these users come from a market segment that the greater organization may have not been targeting. Although the primary consumers of the Marketplace are essentially the third-party providers, increased activity from the end user brings more API usage which enables the development of improved, competitive commercial models which in turn results in additional consumption of the APIs and attracted new consumers to the platform.

By leveraging economies of scale to service and support new customers with existing infrastructure and operational capability, the platform generates more revenue without incurring additional costs yielding higher margins. We have adopted a similar strategy to Amazon and have made a conscious decision to pass this benefit on to our customers by lowering costs. As Jeff Bezos wisely predicted, lowering costs results in increased traffic which invariably speeds up the momentum of the flywheel. An observation is that lower costs also reduce the barrier to entry and the platform has caught the attention of smaller consultancies who are building innovative solutions with our products.

In much the same way that a quick dash into a supermarket for one or two items invariably results in a trolley full of additional purchases, third parties who start with one API product typically leverage the onboarding process and technical integration knowledge to assimilate and consume others. Our Marketplace started with a few API products but, over time, the selection has steadily grown through existing consumer demand and new product definitions. Although we cannot claim to have the largest number of API products, those in our stable provide real business and customer value.

Your Marketplace Identity

Before you set out on your journey to establish an API Marketplace for your organization, it is important to have a clear view of how the APIs will be used. This will guide your sales and marketing strategy, will also define the third-party segment to target, and more importantly, establish the factors which measure the success of your platform. In Table 4-1, I describe some of the ways organizations are using APIs by using a comparison to brick-and-mortar stores. Note that this is not an exhaustive or conclusive list – the direction and focus of your platform will be tailored according to the needs and aspirational goals of your organization and may start in one segment and evolve to another or possibly straddle different segments.

Table 4-1. *Marketplace positioning*

Goal	Description
Minimal	This is the type of store that only provides bare necessities. No fancy items – only what is absolutely necessary to keep stock moving and to keep the lights on
	This is the type of API Marketplace that is built simply to be compliant to regulations. The regulator has issued legislation to be adhered to by a specific deadline, and this is the bare minimum that needs to be done to avoid penalties. No strategic objective for the moment – possibly a wait and see approach
Niche player	One of the stores I would have loved to visit is RadioShack. This was a dream destination if you needed anything electronics related. It pitches only to a specific market, but is a one-stop shop for anything in that category
	A comparable API Marketplace is one which only deals with a specific category of APIs. For example, a Bank might only provide APIs which deal with money – from Payments to Loans to Transaction data

(*continued*)

Table 4-1. (*continued*)

Goal	Description
Supermarket	Supermarkets are the lifeblood of communities across the world. You can dash in for bare necessities like milk or to find less commonly used items like light bulbs. They cater to a wide range of customer requirements, but product selection is based on popular product demand. So, you might be able to find the most common type of light bulb but not the one which fits an antique chandelier from the early 1900s
	This type of Marketplace is an Aggregator. It brings together commonly used APIs and allows easy consumption under a single umbrella. A single point of contact mitigates the need to maintain accounts or relationships with several providers. The inherent benefit is that with economies of scale, it will require fewer staff to support. In addition, the combined might of a larger entity representing several consumers can result in more competitive pricing and service from backend providers. The supermarket, possibly part of a chain, is likely to get far better pricing and service from a supplier than an individual would
Champs-Élysées	A famous shopping avenue in Paris is the Champs-Élysées. It features well-established stores and is a popular destination for both locals and tourists. Square footage is at a premium, and only specific brands are invited to participate to maintain the exclusivity of the space. Although each store is independent, it is intrinsically connected by the aura and atmosphere of the location
	This type of Marketplace is an ecosystem – there is no single owner, but is built around a central theme or construct. There is a one-to-one relationship between consumer and provider. Trust and confidence in the provider's ability to execute is gauged implicitly by its presence in that forum. That is, if a service provider has been admitted to that exclusive group, it had to meet specific quality criteria. Conversely, providers need to maintain a high standard of quality to retain membership to this group. This mutual trust is gained over time

(*continued*)

Table 4-1. (*continued*)

Goal	Description
Shopping mall	Shopping malls are popular attractions for many customers. There is a wide assortment of stores, and the minimum requirements for potential tenants are far less stringent. More importantly, there are utilities such as security, parking, and bathrooms which are provided as a convenience to the customer and are provided on behalf of all tenants. Many of these centers have anchor tenants which are the main attraction for customers
	This Marketplace represents a closed ecosystem. Consumers are in direct contact with providers but leverage shared capabilities – typically security and support. Common infrastructure may also host multi-tenant solutions to reduce costs and achieve economies of scale. Anchor tenants in this instance may be a well-established and trusted brand, such as a regarded Financial Institution, who also participates in this environment. This could represent a natural evolution for organizations who start their individual Marketplaces and want to stimulate growth by attracting more third-party developers and supporting smaller providers to reach a larger audience

Value and Revenue Strategies

In our fast-moving world, amplified by technology, there are new and novel ways to generate revenue today that we would not have dreamed possible years ago. As examples – social media personalities with a large number of fans and followers become influencers and are paid with more views of their content and to market and promote products. Professional gamers could make more than professional sports players. In short, it is important to understand and appreciate that *value* could be created explicitly – in the form of hard revenue – or implicitly, for example, in the form of brand positioning and customer loyalty. In this section, we consider different approaches how an API Marketplace can generate value – both implicit and explicit.

Developer Pays

Let us start with the option that will keep the Capitalists happy. After all, the financial viability of an API Marketplace will be a hot topic when the concept is pitched for funding. For this approach, the third-party provider would pay for use of the API products. From examination of successful platforms such as Twilio, there are a number of different ways in which this may be achieved:

- **Pay as you go**: This is essentially a "prepaid" concept. It was popularized years ago when mobile operators provided voice and SMS services to customers who essentially loaded "airtime" into their accounts. I am not an economist by any measure, but I've always found it strange that the unit cost of voice (per second or minute) has been magnitudes higher on these types of accounts – although the risk to the mobile operator is far lower. Even more strange is that this position is largely accepted by the subscriber base particularly over long periods of time. From a consumption perspective, the third party would pay for credits ahead of time which would deplete with API usage. Once all credits are exhausted, no further requests will be processed. The benefit for the API provider is upfront payment, minimized risk, and if tariffs are similar to mobile packages – higher unit costs. The benefit for the API consumer is reduced risk – with this approach, a specific budget can be set to prevent runaway costs and the flexibility to terminate the relationship at any time.

- **Freemium**: A number of Cloud providers offer free computing and credits to attract developers to their platforms. I have personally used many products and services because of these offers. As I became more familiar with products like Firebase, I moved on to the paid options which provided more features. Had it not been for the promotional credit, I would have been reluctant to part with my credit card details to investigate. This model can be used to earn developer trust. If used correctly, it can build loyalty to your API product. There is some risk to the API provider as a service is essentially being provided at zero cost. In many cases, given the nature of the API, this risk may be marginal as this may essentially be an internal cost to service the request. Wearing my developer hat, this is certainly an appealing option for me.

71

- **Tiered**: In the Financial services industry, we have observed a boom of Financial technology (FinTech) solutions that seeks to improve the delivery and use of financial services. These are essentially startups with a great idea but often with little capital investment. Tiered offerings allow consumers, at various stages in their organizational lifecycle, access to your products – at a price point that meets their requirements. Reciprocally, packages may be structured in a way to keep costs low – as an example, base packages may provide limited support. Tiers also provide visibility regarding the differences between levels and may be used for financial projections which is incredibly important for a startup's business plan. Each tier may provide a specified number of free transactions for a defined period, thereafter a unit cost per transaction, varying levels of support, and service availability or access to specific API products. The Product Owner will need to undertake significant research in structuring the packages as markets may differ significantly based on region, demographic, and consumer behavior. Over my career, I have observed many business models work fantastically in one market but perform abysmally in another. The products must be tailored to the consumer market.

- **Points based**: One of the most successful medical aid schemes in our country is based around the concept of "points." The idea is incredibly simple, but profound in its operation and reach. A member receives points for a healthy lifestyle – more exercise and fitness results in more points. As points increase, the users' status rises. The member can then purchase items such as airline and movie tickets at discounted prices. The benefit to the scheme provider is that healthy members are less likely to get sick and claim. This particular program has many members, now fanatical about fitness, and has become so successful that the organization has now moved into banking – the incentive is that points can be earned through spend. This is an example of an all-round win. Both consumer and provider win, and a host of external service providers participating in this program also benefit. A simple implementation of this pattern in an API Marketplace is that consumers earn credit for a specific number of transactions. The credit can be used to offset costs or possibly to purchase other products in your organization. As an example, a third-party consumer may redeem points earned through API transactions to offset their monthly account fee. This allows cross-pollination of products which will help with customer retention. In the above scenario, the consumer may be reluctant to move to another provider as this would impact the monthly account fee.

- **Transaction fee**: This may potentially be the simplest mechanism to implement. Each API request generates an event which is routed to an engine where it is mediated, rated, and billed. At the end of a billing period, a statement is generated, and the consumer pays. There is a significant amount of complexity that belies the implementation. Invoicing, collection, and billing disputes are areas which must be considered. As billing occurs after usage, there is a significant risk of running up a large bill, in much the same way as Cloud services or products accidentally left running will result in astronomical bills. Providers are equally at risk as customers may default on amounts owed and dedicate a significant amount of time on customer education to avoid such situations and to retain customers over a longer period. Although the most transparent of approaches, I consider this also be the most basic and rigid as it does not encourage or reward third-party behavior.

Before we move on, there are two critical factors which must be taken into consideration. The first is that the billing capability of the platform, for any of the above approaches, must be bulletproof, transparent, and without a single element of doubt or uncertainty. Drawing on the similarities of mobile billing, customer queries are immediately resolved using an itemized bill. Your billing platform must be capable of generating an itemized bill which clearly shows when the transaction took place, which API was called with the ability to drill deeper and provide additional information such as transaction origination, request, and response payload.

The second and possibly the *most* important factor to keep in mind is that the API product must generate value and revenue for the third party *first* which will drive revenue for your organization. It is quite possible to build and launch an API product and attach a high price tag to it providing bragging rights of high potential-value products. However, without a compelling value proposition, there will be little third-party adoption and usage, and it will stay on the shelf yielding little revenue.

Developer Gets Paid

The principle of this approach is that the third party is incentivized to use the organization's APIs. All approaches, at their core, must be viewed as a partnership as the success of one implies the success of the other. Here, the consumer is an extension of the organization and shares the spoils of the revenue. This reminds me of a conversation I had with the owner of a startup who had sold his business for a hefty sum. Although this is a formula many wish they had, he was remorseful that he had retained full ownership, the business could have been far bigger with more stakeholders.

From a financial perspective, it could be more lucrative to share a piece of a larger pie than have full ownership of a smaller one. This is a key theme of an API Marketplace – it allows your organization to reach more customers through third parties. If we consider this logically, if the third party stands to benefit from a transaction that it facilitates, it is part of the value chain and will do its best to close the deal. Let us consider ways this can be achieved:

- **Revenue share**: This is probably one of my favorite mechanisms for third-party engagement. It reflects a win-win approach and clearly demonstrates the organization's commitment that the third party is a valued partner. A key factor for the explosive growth of mobile networks in Africa is that airtime could be purchased from small vendors on almost any street corner. The incentive for the vendor is the commission made on any sale. The mobile operator simply used a well-established, widespread network for airtime distribution. A third-party provider is also far more likely to promote or feature a product or service which results in a higher revenue share. The potential revenue split could also be the tipping point in a third party's business plan to build a new product or service.

- **Affiliate**: Third parties with an established customer base can also be engaged as brand advocates to encourage adoption of your API products. In much the same way that training partners assist candidates seeking certification, there are service providers who can build custom bootcamp programs to get potential developers up and running with your API products. In addition to getting more exposure to the APIs, a benefit is direct feedback from the affiliate service provider and developers in training regarding API adoption. As much as this function could be undertaken by the internal delivery team, a specialist organization may already have an established subscriber base, the skills to build repertoire with developers, and most importantly, neutrality that new consumers may be less wary of. Partnerships with startup incubators, programs designed to support developing businesses, are also a great way to support these initiatives and an excellent opportunity to engage new organizations and showcase Marketplace value, early in their lifecycle.

– **Referral**: The success of this pattern can be seen by simply clicking through the thousands of sponsored YouTube channels. By implementing a simple referral program, developers can be rewarded if their friends and colleagues sign up with their code. This can certainly help with attracting and building an audience for your Marketplace. For some API products, the potential of a customer Lead may be sufficient benefit to compensate a third-party provider. For example, a third party could be compensated if a potential customer uses a financial loan calculator API when considering a home or vehicle purchase. As the customer's details could be relayed in the call, it provides a potential sales opportunity for the organization.

Free

The key difference between Free and Freemium is that Free API products will always be provided at no charge. Value creation in this instance is implicit – it drives API adoption and increases the number of third-party providers using your platform – whom could be potentially converted over time. A goal is that the zero cost will result in mass proliferation which will help get your brand to more potential customers.

This represents an appealing option for third parties, and as much as it may be provided grudgingly by the host organization, the potential impact and value to the third party could be significant. For example, a simple data API to provide lists of income and occupation types may be taken for granted in an enterprise but may be of great value for a startup that needs the data for their registration process. It also affords your organization the opportunity to be accessible via new channels – which are essentially apps and services built by third parties.

Indirect

In the spirit of partnership and to cement the foundational principle of a win-win model, this strategy is centered on the benefit to the end customer. A successful sales strategy is one where all participants gain value from the transaction. Value, using an Indirect strategy, can be created in the following ways:

- **Customers**: Meeting regulatory requirements, such as Open Banking, is a clear signal that the ownership and sharing of customer data is in the control of the end user. It affords users the ability and flexibility to securely access new products and services in a way which is facilitated by your platform. Essentially, *their* data but on *your* terms. It's a win-win for both user and organization.

- **Business-to-business (B2B)**: Allowing API access to external partners broadens the range of solutions available to your customers. For example, API access to your Loyalty and Rewards program could allow the end customer to participate in a reward points exchange system which not only extends the reach of your program, resulting in more points redemption, but also provides a good value proposition for the user.

- **Informational**: Customer awareness regarding changing market conditions can be achieved through sharing of information using APIs. Examples of information which may be shared are foreign exchange rates, marketing campaigns such as promotional, time-sensitive offers, and organizational updates.

- **Reputational**: Establishing a new digital channel positions your organization as a technology leader and a game changer. This could be a factor that differentiates your organization from competitors and provides significant value for your brand.

Billing Engineering

Having defined a number of strategies for billing in an API Marketplace, let us now discuss the technical engineering for practical implementation. The API product will typically define the monetization approach – some may be paid for by the third party;

others may have a revenue share or referral or free. This is typically defined by the Product Owner in close consultation with the backend supporting systems.

It is also important to identify how consumers will be billed – will the third party need to fund an account which is charged on each transaction, or will transactions be billed and invoiced later? Regardless of which mechanism is selected, it is important to build a "billing backbone" which will service all APIs in the platform. All events, even for free APIs, should be sent into the billing pipeline for Analytics and Reporting purposes, and this billing function should not be taken lightly. Whenever possible, leverage an enterprise capability. If this is not possible, consider using a hosted or managed service as this has a high operational impact.

A technical flow of an Event Billing Model is illustrated in Figure 4-2.

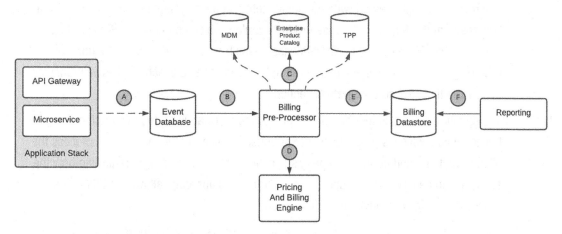

Figure 4-2. *Event Billing Model*

The steps in an Event Billing Model are described in Table 4-2.

Table 4-2. *Event billing sequence*

Step	Description
A	An event is generated from an element in the Application Stack, typically upon completion of an API request and, at this time, primarily from the Microservice component. The event contains details of the call including the product, third-party identifier, completion status, request and response payloads, and date and time. The event is inserted into a database – to minimize call latency and to allow offline processing
B	The event record is read by a Billing Pre-Processor on a batch schedule or trigger. The batch schedule allows more efficient processing as many records are processed for a specific period. Trigger execution allows near real-time processing of events
C	The record is supplemented with additional metadata from systems such as Master Data Management (MDM), the Enterprise Product Catalog, which contains an API to product mapping, and Third-Party Provider database – which contains additional configuration regarding the third party such as account to be billed. As this is achieved asynchronously, there is no time pressure for data collection
D	The enriched and mediated record, in a pre-defined format, is routed to a Pricing and Billing Engine, which is provided as an Enterprise Service. This capability will process the billing event and update the third party's account data. Note that rules regarding how the event should be billed are included in the record. This approach allows the Billing Pre-Processor to influence how the event is billed
E	The mediated record is also stored in a datastore accessible to business support applications in the Marketplace
F	Custom reports, using enriched, mediated records, are run periodically to provide a near real-time billing view of the platform. Note that these views may not be accurate revenue data – but supports the "notional view" discussed later in this chapter

A technical flow of a real-time Billing Model is illustrated in Figure 4-3.

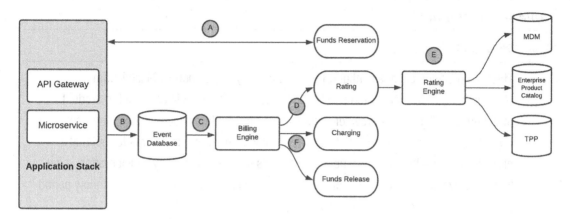

Figure 4-3. *Real-time billing*

The steps in a *near* real-time Billing Model are described in Table 4-3.

Table 4-3. *Real-time billing sequence*

Step	Description
A	A call to reserve funds is made before the API request is processed. This ensures that the third party has sufficient credit available to service the request. At the time of the call, the exact amount to be billed may not be known – a pre-defined budgetary amount based on the nature of the API product is reserved. If the minimum amount to meet the funds reservation request cannot be met, an error is returned to the consumer
B	An event is generated from an element in the Application Stack, typically upon completion of an API request and, at this time, primarily from the Microservice component. The event contains details of the call including the product, third-party identifier, completion status, request and response payloads, and date and time. The event is inserted into a database – to minimize call latency and to allow offline processing
C	The insertion of the event record triggers a call to the Billing Engine. The Billing Engine orchestrates calls across the components detailed below
D	It is first necessary to rate the event. The event record is routed to the Rating Engine

(continued)

Table 4-3. (*continued*)

Step	Description
E	The Rating Engine caches configuration data from systems such as Master Data Management (MDM), the Enterprise Product Catalog, which contains an API to product mapping, and Third-Party Provider database – which contains additional configuration regarding the third party such as billing account in in-memory datastores for optimal processing. Note that for this type of bill processing, latency is a key consideration. Low latency allows faster processing of the event which results in a smaller risk window period between balance update and additional requests
F	The rated event is then used by the Charging element to deduct a specific amount from the third parties' remaining credit. The rated event could also indicate that the third party should not be charged – for example, if the API request was not successfully processed or if the product was part of a promotional campaign. In this instance, the reserved amount is released

Analytics and Insight

Piloting an API Marketplace implementation is made significantly easier with the assistance of navigational data, preferably as real-time and detailed as possible. In a typical engineering mindset, this section was initially planned to be included in the chapter detailing Operations. After some consideration, I found that this would be suggesting that the ship is guided from the engine room rather than the bridge. As vital as operational metrics may be, it is the *interpreted* information that drives the direction and objective of the platform. As an example, consider the operational metric of number of transactions per second as an indication of speed. Without supplementary data such as the third-party provider and API product generating the traffic, as an indication of direction, this could turn out to be equivalent to stepping on the gas pedal with the gear in a neutral position – high revs but no forward momentum.

The intention of this section is to highlight the importance of knowing the historical path and progress of the platform and establishing a set of current navigational data such as position and current bearing that will be used to plot the way forward. It is important to note that not all gauges and dials on the command center control panel of the bridge will be active on Day One. These spring to life as the Engineering team instruments the platform or harvests data from disparate sources to allow data to flow in. If the Product Owner has a well-defined view of what is needed, this top-down approach will guide the Engineering team. The alternative is a bottom-up, technically driven view of some random system metrics that makes for a pretty widget on the control panel but provides a useless business indicator.

Data Collection

At full flight, there is an almost continuous stream of events within the ecosystem of an API Marketplace. Apart from the obvious API calls, potential consumers may be raising support tickets from prototyping efforts, requests to backend systems may be slowing down, end users could be in the final stages of completing a high-value transaction, or unanticipated loads could be originating from a last-minute campaign. A key objective is to capture as much of this data as possible – efficiently, consistently, and reliably.

From years of experience in various integration domains, and taking inspiration from a medical triage process, we have implemented a Sensor and Probe strategy, illustrated in Figure 4-4. For elements we have direct control over, such as the Application Stack, explicit sensors have been attached to key process flows. These publish well-defined events providing granular information regarding the request – such as the third-party identifier and transaction value. When the event is received, it still needs to be supplemented with additional metadata – such as resolution of the name of the third party, given the identifier.

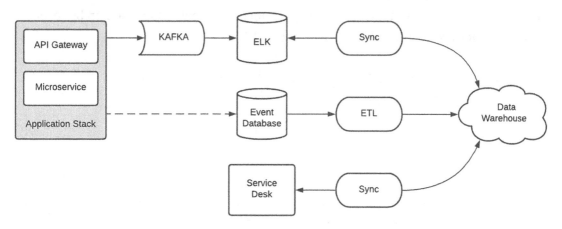

Figure 4-4. Data collection strategy

There are many instances where the data is captured in external systems. For these, we use a probing strategy. The Service Desk, which is used to capture customer interactions, contains a wealth of information and is an example of such an entity. Requests from potential third parties for access to API products or additional information is valuable Lead data. Support requests regarding service outages or transaction tracing are equivalently vital as they represent interactions which may provide Retention value. As the data is stored in an enterprise hosted application, a probing mechanism, in the form of a custom application, has been built by the technical team to query and extract the interactions. This approach has also been used to parse and extract application and audit data to expedite access in some instances where additional information was urgently required.

It is important to survey the landscape to identify the various participants and sources of information and define a strategy regarding how the data may be harvested.

Data Analysis

Early in my career, when tasked with providing Analytics for an integration platform my team supported, I pursued this task with a technical orientation. I was obsessed with gauging low-level metrics, such as requests per flow, and instrumented the platform and application to leave a trail of data that was ingested into a database. Unfortunately, my elation and pride in watching the data stream in was soon replaced by despair as I attempted to structure queries to interpret the data to determine any meaningful pattern. From this experience, my basic understanding is that context is key to analytical information, and a single analytical data point is generally made up by several underlying metrics, as shown in Figures 4-5-1 and 4-5-2.

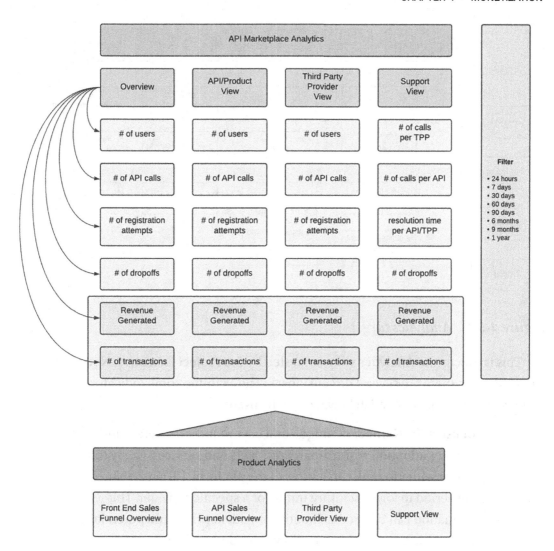

Figure 4-5-1. *Analytics source*

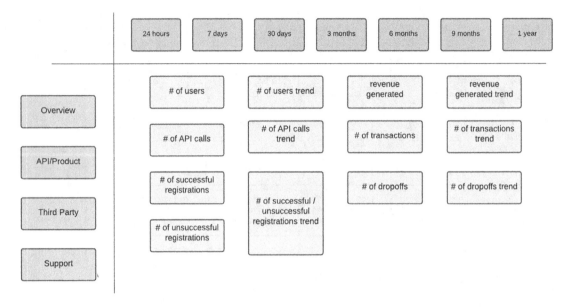

Figure 4-5-2. *Analytics target*

This is exactly the Analytics view requested by the Project Executive. Note that for each indicator, there are several dimensions. Let us examine some indicators across various dimensions to establish how it could be used:

- **# of users**: (i) Number of unique end user requests to determine customer adoption of third-party products and services, (ii) by third-party provider to rank consumers of the platform, (iii) in a defined time period to forecast future traffic for a specific provider. This information can be used to identify providers who could potentially generate higher traffic and possibly revenue.

- **# of completed transactions**: (i) For a specific API product to determine revenue generated, (ii) by third-party provider, again to rank consumers of the platform, (iii) in a defined time period to understand if the traffic was a burst or sustained.

This information is crucial to understanding the platform, from different perspectives. Not only can high-traffic APIs be easily spotted, but it is also possible to drill into the exact operations to understand how the product is used. It can also guide your third-party acquisition strategy. As an example, most of the traffic from a single consumer could be a risk indicator that more anchors are required for platform longevity. Conversely, little traffic from many consumers may be an indicator that the platform has not established deep roots within any third party. These hypotheses and conjectures are made possible by having key data available across various dimensions over different periods of time.

Reporting

With maturity of the platform, more high-value API products and the requirement of providing mission-critical support to key third parties, our team has implemented the following mechanisms to provide visibility into platform activity:

- **Dashboards**: As shown in Figure 4-6 and described in Table 4-4. In much the same way that your car's instrumentation panel provides a wide range of information, your focus is typically on the speedometer but is drawn to other indicators, such as the fuel level, which has an influence on the speed of the vehicle. The dashboard below, at first glance, may appear to have an explosion of metrics. Typically, the Product or Business Owner will focus on a specific metric and if this is not within defined parameters, will then examine other values to determine how it could have impacted the primary metric. The value of dashboards is in providing key metrics for the platform, but also details regarding factors or conditions which could impact the platform.

- **Email**: Snapshots of the dashboard are sent to key product stakeholders hourly via email. In addition, notification of the successful completion of high-value transactions is also distributed to the product team. I have been quite surprised to see queries from senior commercial staff asking if there are technical outages if the number of completed transactions are low or excited, congratulatory messages for high-value transactions. This is an indication that the regularly distributed messages are indeed being reviewed and used by the commercial team and the API is recognized as a key revenue channel.

Bi-hourly **instant messages** from the Operational Support team detailing system stability and successfully completed transactions for key API products. Again, if the numbers are uncharacteristically low, questions are raised regarding the availability of supporting systems and downstream providers.

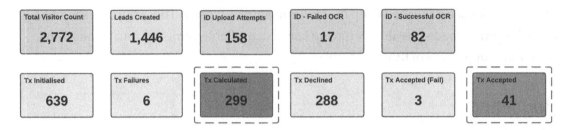

Figure 4-6. *Sample dashboard*

Table 4-4. *Reporting dashboard metrics*

Metric	Description
Total visitor count	Number of unique users accessing the application (portal or API)
Leads created	Users who completed the basic information step/form requesting further information. Those that did not proceed further may be contacted telephonically by sales agents
ID statistics	Number of identity document uploaded, successfully processed, and failures due to OCR. Failed requests are interrogated to determine if there was a problem with the uploaded image or a system failure
Transaction statistics	Number of detailed transactions and associated states calculated, declined, failed, and accepted – based on process execution logic

The key to a successful reporting strategy is to provide specific, pertinent data, which can be pulled (via web) or pushed (via email or instant message) in a format which can be quickly understood and interrogated by the target audience.

The Notional Income Statement

The Notional Income Statement is a key construct of our Marketplace which fulfills several functions. In a term coined by the project executive, it is a measure of the overall profitability at a channel capability level. As a Marketplace may have a range of products, some which may generate revenue, others which are regulated to be free, it helps to understand value across all products.

As a market maker, essentially brokering an interaction between consumer and provider, there are occasions when it may be a challenge to demonstrate value. After all, there are expenses to keep the platform running – infrastructure, software, developers, support engineers, Product Owners, and Delivery Leads to pay. As the revenue for a transaction will most likely be recognized by the backend service provider, it may result in the Marketplace categorized as an internal "Cost Center," Unfortunately, implicit value such as establishing a digital brand or empowering third parties means little to Financial Officers who simply look at the bottom line.

This phenomenon may be hugely frustrating for the team as business units which bring in more revenue generally receive higher budget allocations and recognition. Not content with simply being viewed as a "Cost Center" and wanting the organization to understand the contribution and importance of the Marketplace initiative, the project executive has wisely established a measure of "notional value."

The magnification of the Income Statement lens is increased to constantly scrutinize the performance of each API product. At inception, Product and Business owners may make assumptions which influence the decision to build the specific API. Once built, regular measurement is required to determine the product health. Assumptions, such as projected traffic volumes or third-party adoption, are constantly validated. Platform scale and infrastructure is also thrust under the spotlight to identify if this could be an impediment to the product's success. The ongoing measurement helps to gauge if a product is approaching a stage of limited returns which may require remediation or a decision to retire.

Understanding of specific products at this granular level provides deeper insight into Total Cost of Ownership (TCO). Some products, which may be more successful, may require higher levels of support and monitoring and should carry a higher proportion of the operational cost to run the platform. The detail of the line of the Income Statement allows a quantitative measure for each product.

Finally, adopting an Income Statement as our standard mechanism of measurement provides a significant advantage for reviews and assessments by executive committees who typically have a financially focused mindset. This process removes qualitative or "gut-feel" sentiment regarding the Marketplace and uses a quantitative approach to clearly understand the financial position. In some circumstances, this may signal a need to pivot to ensure longevity of the initiative. This is discussed next.

Pivot to New Business Models

The roots of the API Marketplace we hoped to establish initially hit hard ground in the form of technical readiness of third-party providers. Although the APIs followed open standards and the team was more than happy to assist with resolving integration challenges, we were disappointed to observe low adoption of APIs by third-party providers. The situation reached a tipping point when an established third party, with an experienced development team, fell behind on an aggressive integration project schedule and indicated a key delivery date would be missed.

Springing into action, the Product Owner of the Marketplace proposed a radical solution that our team would host the application on behalf of the third party to meet the timeline. Although this decision demonstrated far more faith and belief in our delivery capability than the consumer, the Engineering team initially chalked this down as an impulsive decision. After all, this was an *API* Marketplace – not an *Application Hosting* Marketplace. From first-hand experience, I can also assure you that asking an integration developer to build a User Interface (UI) is much like asking Superman to mine kryptonite.

The objective of the hosted application was relatively simple. It did require some API integration – but the absolute minimum. The third party would implement a standard redirect to launch the application that would consume the APIs in the platform. What eased the sting of the front-end development was that we were staying true to our purpose and were using APIs to leverage internal organizational capability. In all honesty, this integration pattern has become one of the biggest revenue generators for the platform!

What initially started as a grudge-purchase, as the technical team had to scramble to update deployment strategies and request design and security approval, gradually evolved as the team discovered they now possessed the ability to use the APIs directly – in ways we had been trying to persuade third parties to for some time. This approach has also enabled other providers to accelerate their integration efforts by adopting the same pattern.

In this instance, the Product Owner was well within their rights to stay firm and insist on API adoption, even at the risk of missing the deadline. However, this pivot demonstrates the versatility and flexibility of the technical platform to create new business models by adapting to varying market conditions.

Summary

At the start of this chapter, I put forward the argument that the engineering capability underpins the commercial success of the API Marketplace. We also discussed the flywheel process which, once initiated, creates a ripple effect throughout various areas of the platform. By focusing on the Developer Experience, it attracts more Customers which brings down Costs and allows aggressive and new Commercial Models which fund new Product Development which more Third Parties consume which comes full circle to a better Developer Experience. This wave of perpetual motion powers the Growth strategy of the API Marketplace.

We touched on the need of establishing an identity for your API Marketplace and contrasted this to setting up a brick-and-mortar store. By providing the comparison, I hope that you have started to formulate the type of store you would like to build and the new platforms which will soon set up shop. We then discussed the ways value can be created from an API Marketplace, and we observed how it could be achieved implicitly, explicitly, and even indirectly. Dropping down to the nuts and bolts, we reviewed engineering approaches to support various billing strategies. It is important to note that the billing strategy comes first, and the platform is engineered to support it. We then moved to a key area of Monetization – which is visibility and measurement. Analytics and Insights provides much needed visibility which powers the control panel that is used to pilot the Marketplace. We reviewed data collection, analysis, and reporting strategies. The Notional Income Statement is the mechanism we used for measurement and to determine profitability of the Marketplace. Finally, we demonstrated a way to pivot to create new business models.

Running an API Marketplace is an extremely challenging but rewarding activity. The team has adopted a startup mindset, which makes us more efficient, thrifty, leaner, and constantly on the lookout for new opportunities. This is yet another flywheel process which drives a perpetual engineering optimization process. This has resulted in a constantly evolving Platform Architecture which we discuss in more detail in the next chapter.

CHAPTER 5

Platform Architecture

Our Marketplace was born into a post Netflix-era world, one of the first projects in a newly established Digital practice. The team was not only tasked with the delivery of an Open Banking prototype but presented with the opportunity and mandate to use bleeding-edge technology. In hindsight, this has been both a blessing and a curse. The ability to use new approaches such as containerization afforded our platform a high degree of flexibility. The unfortunate drawback was that we were 2 to 3 years ahead of the rest of the organization and the new approaches we wanted to use were not yet trusted, let alone understood.

The inherent benefit of time is that it allowed our team to evolve and optimize the platform and establish trust with the rest of the organization through knowledge sharing and iterative delivery. The waves of Change soon reached our organizations' shores, and concepts and approaches that we were trialing were becoming more widespread and trusted by similar institutions. It has also allowed us to position the Marketplace as an enterprise-grade platform, pivotal to the function of the organization as opposed to a satellite installation fulfilling a niche role.

Through this process, we have a greater appreciation of supporting systems within the enterprise. We have also been humbled by the effort of operationalizing bleeding-edge technology and are now acutely aware of how people and process are essential ingredients of the final solution.

In the following sections, I provide a time-lapsed view of the elements of our platform, how it has changed, and my thoughts and plans regarding its evolution. This is done with the hope to bootstrap your implementation and to share some of the ideals and principles we have since established in ours.

© Rennay Dorasamy 2022
R. Dorasamy, *API Marketplace Engineering*, https://doi.org/10.1007/978-1-4842-7313-5_5

Elements

Like the elements in the periodic table, Figure 5-1 details the components of our Platform Architecture. Some, like the Reverse Proxy, are provided as an atomic shared enterprise service. Others, like our Microservices, have been genetically engineered, which gives our Platform its unique identity. These blocks represent the core of our Marketplace, and we are continually trying to optimize their function in order to make the platform more efficient. Each of the elements is discussed in further detail in the following sections.

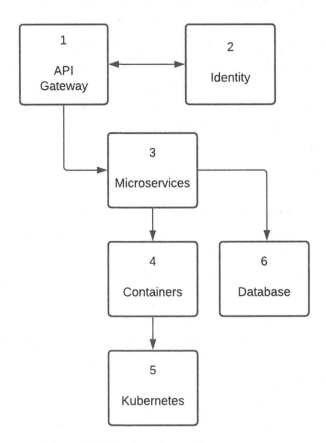

Figure 5-1. *Elements of an API Marketplace platform*

API Gateway (External/Internal)

An API Gateway is essentially the entry point to the enterprise. In our deployment, it was stationed on the edge of the Demilitarized Zone (DMZ), and a second, separate instance is positioned as the entry to internal services. The core functions are Security,

API Management, and Monitoring. A key standard for our organization is that all APIs, internal and external facing, should be accessed via an API Gateway. A great feature of API Gateways is the ability to throttle user requests. Although this can be custom developed, the benefit of using an off-the-shelf product is that it alleviates the operational workload from the team. Tasks such as security configuration, certificate management, API product updates, and versioning are provided out of the box.

Several Cloud providers offer a Platform-as-a-Service (PaaS) API Gateway, which can be easily provisioned. The benefit of a PaaS offering is that the scaling and management of underlying infrastructure is handled by the Cloud Provider. As an established Financial Institution, we have a commercial off-the-shelf product, which is managed by an internal team and supported by the software vendor. To allow the Delivery team some autonomy, a separate Developer Organization within the Gateway was created for our API Products. This is essentially a logical separation of the API Gateway infrastructure. We are allowed administrative access in the Development environment but must adhere to strict governance as we progress to Production.

Identity

This block hosts many capabilities which is critical to the function of the API Marketplace. One of the most important is the Access Control Authentication Policy, which, in layman's terms, is the foundation for authenticating end users. As it hosts the Directory Server which contains user profile information against which credentials are verified, a fundamental design decision made at the outset of the implementation was that we would leverage the enterprise Authentication capability and build a custom Authorization framework within the Marketplace. The Reverse Proxy capability also resides under the same umbrella and acts as an emissary between end user requests and server-side portal applications. Leveraging the enterprise security infrastructure, by way of physical infrastructure, processes, and services, has bootstrapped our implementation significantly. There has been some customization to allow for Marketplace-specific requirements, such as junctions which allow unauthenticated access to backend web applications and rolling refresh token windows. This decision has also helped us navigate Architecture and Design approval boards. There was a sense of comfort from long-serving Architects that this bleeding-edge API Marketplace, which could be a new channel of attack, was secured using trusted enterprise security standards.

Container Platform (Managed/Unmanaged)

Figure 5-2 shows the evolution of how applications have been deployed. From right to left you see three approaches, Traditional Deployment, Virtualized Deployment, and Container Deployment, which are fast growing in popularity.

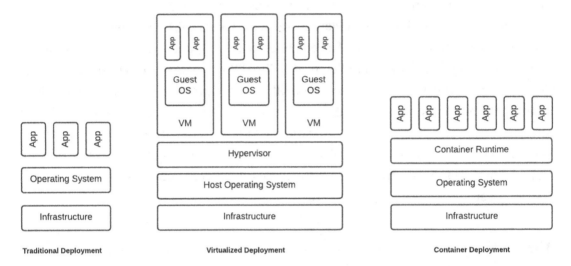

Figure 5-2. *Evolution of deployment strategies*

I have been fortunate to have experience with all the approaches in Figure 5-2. On one of my first projects, we were allocated a Windows server which ran on a physical machine in a datacenter managed by the organization. I can still recall eagerly taking a snapshot of the number of CPUs and memory and sending it to my university friends as bragging rights of the hardware allocated to my new project. Even when I had to drive through to the datacenter on the night of a production deployment to physically restart the server, I felt like one of the "Right Stuff" astronauts walking down the gangway on their next space mission. As the figure shows, all applications run directly on the Operating System, and if one of them threw a tantrum that caused high CPU or memory utilization, the others suffered.

A few years later, while on a project for a new middleware platform, we were allocated Sun Sparc servers, each with many CPUs with multithreading capability and a whopping 512GB of RAM. The server architecture whitepaper had a prized spot on my bedside table as NASA and JPL were probably using the same hardware to launch space shuttles. The beauty of using Sun Solaris was that the Hypervisor was baked into the operating system, and we could carve up the machine into several logical Solaris

Zones (Virtual Machines), each with its own operating system and allocated a specific number of resources in the form of threads and memory. If an application misbehaved, the Solaris management software would contain it and prevent it from impacting other zones. I found myself jockeying a spreadsheet containing the details of Solaris Zones which was used for various environments and components of the stack.

I prided myself with the detail of the spreadsheet, and to the annoyance of the rest of the team, referenced each zone by IP, like some old friend whom no one else knew. As I was responsible for the Platform build, I scripted as much of the installation as possible – but eventually had to resort to running custom commands on different zones, sometimes to resolve cluster issues, sometimes to resolve missing dependencies. Again, I chalked up these interventions as my part in a Herculean effort to keeping the platform up and running. Little did I realize back then that I was also responsible for creating a "snowflake environment." Each zone in the environment was different from the rest. I now take solace that even if my provisioning script did create identical clones, each of the zones would have invariably moved out of sync due to operational changes made on some, but not others.

Virtual Machines (VM) are a move in the right evolutionary direction – they allow better use of the underlying infrastructure. The drawback is that the VMs are heavy on resources, VM configurations could invariably move out of sync, and they also encourage vertical scaling of infrastructure which is not tenable over time. That is, the physical host machine can only scale to a maximum level which limits the number of VMs it can support.

For our Marketplace implementation, an early decision before I joined was to use a Container approach. My first experience with containers was Docker, and as I ran through a tutorial shown in Listing 5-1, I was blown away with the simplicity of the concept and sincerely wondered which rock I lived under when the technology launched in 2014.

Listing 5-1. Simple Docker configuration

```
FROM node:14

# Create app directory
WORKDIR /usr/src/app

# Install app dependencies
COPY package*.json ./
```

```
RUN npm install

# Bundle app source
COPY . .

EXPOSE 8080
CMD [ "node", "server.js" ]
```

Like the Hypervisor is the enabling element for Virtual Machines, the Container runtime enables Containers. There are many great resources which provide details regarding how this is achieved by Hypervisors and Container runtimes. My personal definition is that a container is a specific definition of a software configuration, which is referred to as an image. As shown in Listing 5-1, the definition specifies a base software element, to which you add custom deployments and commands to be executed. All instances which are created from that image will be the same. Instead of working from the OS level, it allows you to focus on the Application level and associated dependencies.

Consider the difference between a Virtual Machine and Container in the context of baking cakes. For the Virtualized approach, the chef is provided with a full kitchen – different cooking utensils, all appliances, and a full pantry to choose from. Invariably, the chef will only use a subset of utensils, appliances, and supplies. For the Container approach, the chef is provided with only what they need to deliver a cake – specific utensils, ingredients, and possibly only an oven. The Container approach also forces deployment teams to make changes at a code/configuration level. If a library or package needs to be included, the container image configuration must be updated. Container instances are purposely transient. Images are also lightweight, and as they do not need a full OS to run, they require a fraction of the underlying infrastructure. The result is that it is possible to run more containers on infrastructure as compared to Virtual Machines. A further benefit is that this allows horizontal scaling of infrastructure. Cheaper, albeit less powerful hardware, can easily host several container instances due to their lightweight footprint.

A Managed container platform, like Kubernetes, provides capability like self-healing which restarts failed containers and checks health of containers before advertising them to clients. It also provides automated rollouts and rollbacks. To be completely transparent, our early project team was in unchartered territory regarding containerization – let alone having to build a *Kubernetes* Managed Container platform *on-premises*. I can still see the hopeless expression of an exasperated project manager, eager to meet the sprint objective – when the resident DevOps engineer gave feedback of "*we don't know what we don't know*" for the resolution on an issue during the Container Platform build. Our frustration with internal organization governance and security restrictions grew exponentially as we experimented with Cloud PaaS services, which could be provisioned in minutes, but could not access internal systems. The first iteration of our Platform was a single pod on a single node – which had to be restarted periodically. A small victory – but for our project team, that was a small step for man, but a giant leap for DevOps!

We have since had two major iterations of the Managed Container Platform, and through our progression, now have a far better understanding and appreciation of what *Kubernetes* offers. It is easy to become enamored with the appeal of Containerization, especially a platform like Kubernetes. I have observed the power of Infrastructure as Code and have suffered delusions of grandeur by the possibility of creating "Genesis scripts" which can terraform entire environments in minutes. What jarred me out of my reverie was that, in the context of an API Marketplace, the Managed Container Platform is an *enabler* of the application platform. I have since come to the conclusion that the true power of a Managed Container platform, like Kubernetes, is that it fades to the background and allows you to focus on the application. As a full-stack engineer, it is essential to understand the elements and function of a container platform and how a request journeys from ingress to service to pod. The management of our on-premises Kubernetes platform has since been transferred to an enterprise DevOps team. This will further transition to a managed Cloud service. Kubernetes as a Service offerings abstract complexities of infrastructure management, network fabric configuration, and help teams to easily achieve complex objectives such as setting up persistent volumes.

Microservices

I may be heavily biased – but I consider our microservices layer to be the magic ingredient of our Platform. To be fair, microservices are underpinned by Containers. My view is that the Container is a Best *Supporting* Actor, while a microservice is the *Best* Actor. I did not always feel this way. Having spent most of my career in established integration environments, components such as an Enterprise Service Bus (ESB), Application and Process servers, all deployed across complex cluster configurations, were deeply ingrained when I joined the project. My opinion at that time was that integration built without these elements was simply not of an enterprise-grade – possibly as I previously worked at a software OEM. If we cut out the microservice layer, it would alleviate the burden of establishing an on-premises Container platform, and we could use conventional integration mechanisms to connect to backend services. Traditional meant safe and I could go back to the integration playbook I had perfected throughout my career.

I still recall the discussion with the project sponsor, when I attempted to remove microservices from our platform. I made an impassioned argument to rather use the integration software, which I pitched as a powerful cannon, which underpinned the API Gateway, and which was well established in the enterprise instead of the peashooter microservice approach, which was probably *before* bleeding-edge. As Containers were a key objective, I suggested we use them – albeit in a less critical role. In summation, I highlighted that the peas of the peashooter were NodeJS – which I regarded as a "web language" instead of an integration one like Java. I was quite impressed with the case I had amassed against microservices and reassured myself that we would pursue the technology under less intensive project timelines. I was stunned when the verdict returned was Not Guilty. The rationale provided was that the microservice layer would afford the platform a high degree of flexibility and, more importantly, speed. This is one of the most accurate predictions I have observed in my career.

The microservice layer has bestowed onto our Platform an unprecedented level of control and versatility and is pivotal to our success. Ideas which are casually tossed around in the morning are running components, ready to be demonstrated, by the afternoon. This has enabled our mantra of fixing forward, which, may at first, seem unorthodox. If testing or operational issues are encountered, we do our best to remediate instead of rolling back. I was extremely reluctant to use NodeJS as I felt it lacked the structure and performance of a language like Java, which I was extremely familiar with. After working with NodeJS for some time now, that reluctance has dissipated, and the lack of structure allows our team the ability to ship code at light speed. On the surface, JavaScript appears simple, but a firm understanding of its Event Loop and asynchronous nature has allowed us to build a platform which can easily handle high volume, low latency requests. Not all days are great, and there are times when the flexibility, like an incorrectly defined variable not caught during the build, can cause issues.

NodeJS is fantastic and serves the needs of our platform. It is not mandatory for the platform you will build. It is important to consider your organization's standards regarding development languages and developer and operational skill level. That is, if the organization uses .NET primarily, implementing NodeJS is tantamount to injecting a virus into the enterprise. It is important to keep in mind that the programming language supports the concept. Any programming language, strongly typed or not, can be adopted. It is not so much a question of *what* you use but more of *how* you use it.

As we built our API Marketplace within an established enterprise, we often found ourselves between the pressure plates of a well governed API Gateway and a risk-adverse, "if-its-not-broke, don't-fix-it" IT capability. Microservices are our shock-absorbing mechanism which buffers the impact and allows us to deliver on extremely aggressive project timelines.

We dive deeper into the microservice architecture later in this chapter.

Database

A database is an essential element of any platform, as it is used to persist transactions, more so for ours as it enabled a stateless microservice architecture. Our initial approach was to run the database on the Container platform. This featured prominently on the initial design submitted to an internal Solution Alignment Forum. Unfortunately, our DevOps druid skills were not strong enough to conquer persistent storage volumes on our Kubernetes cluster, and we instead adopted a new design strategy that our Kubernetes cluster would not have any persistent storage. I hope that this position inspires a reader out there to write a book on the "Dummy's Guide to Persistent Storage on Kubernetes" and I promise to buy a copy.

However, this decision was made after intense discussion and deliberation. The deciding factor that helped to settle the matter was that database management would never be a core function of our team. We could easily build a database container, but making it highly available and fault tolerant would make our container cluster configuration much more complex. Our Platform now uses an Enterprise provided service, and from observing the various areas of database management, I have no doubt that we made the right decision. To clarify, our team owns the data. The Enterprise service team owns the database.

Integration Strategy

As the following figures reflect, our microservice integration strategy has evolved over time. I find it remarkable that, at the outset of a specific phase, an idea or approach seems so fantastic that you cannot wait to roll it out to every component in the stack. As the sun sets on this approach, the reverse ideology kicks in as the team piles up technical debt items to move to the next approach. I consider the evolution of ape to man in the same light as I survey our integration methodologies over the years. In our defense, the benefit of hindsight affords this lofty perspective. This also offers some solace as our current integration strategy is likely to evolve as we discover a more optimal solution.

Figure 5-3 shows the integration approach used for our first generation of microservices, which underpinned our MVP. The team took a purist view of a microservice, and the principles of encapsulation and isolation were so enshrined that each component was assigned to a different developer. The result was that each developer built and embedded their own integration logic into the microservice they were assigned. From a post-mortem perspective, this is definitely a face-palm moment. In the heat of a MVP, with a geographically distributed development team and each developer working hard to stay off the bottom of the food chain to meet their sprint objective, this is a very probable scenario. It came to light much later that the platform one developer integrated into to retrieve a list of accounts was the same another developer invoked to retrieve mapping reference data.

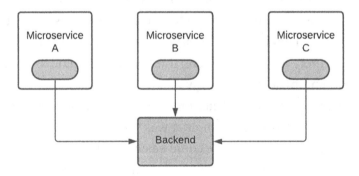

Figure 5-3. *Embedded integration logic*

The one benefit was that the team met the MVP objective. Unfortunately, that is where the benefits stop. Code duplication, varying integration approaches, larger and heavier deployments is enough reason to make any good integration team hang their head in shame.

Figure 5-4 shows the next stop on our evolutionary journey. Back then our codebase was not as large as it is today and in a moment of inspiration, I consolidated all integration logic into a shared library. I was especially pleased with my efforts as the shared library would allow in-process communication between microservice and backend integration logic. Not only would this solution be super performant, but it would also eliminate the horror of code duplication. I was so enamored with the shared library concept, I dubbed it a "framework." The home for this prized asset was a git submodule, which every microservice referenced.

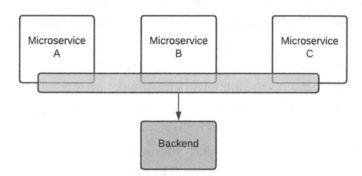

Figure 5-4. *Shared integration library*

Unfortunately, as the number of microservice developers on the team grew, the framework grew more and more fragmented. The submodule concept also resulted in each microservice referencing a specific variant of the framework. If a developer needed a new integration function or operation, they would simply pull down the submodule, add the new logic, and embed that version in the microservice. The git administrators and aficionados reading this are probably rolling their eyes wondering how this could ever happen. Again, with a geographically distributed team, with developers of varying skill levels and agile delivery targets, even good developers can do bad things to achieve a deliverable.

To this day, I still shudder when I open code elements from this era which have not been migrated. We have since come up with a remediation plan. The git submodule umbilical cord has been severed and each microservice has a local copy of the shared library. This may be a reason for you to chuckle as our bid to rid our kingdom of the evil of code duplication was not successful and its failure is multiplied by each microservice with a local copy of the "framework." Some development teams may argue that duplicated, yet isolated integration code components are not a bad approach, particularly in an agile environment – as it allows compartmentalization and components to be deployed independently and without the burden that updating a shared element could unerringly break components dependent on it. This could also eliminate the need for regression testing as only the host microservice would need to be tested. Other microservices would continue, untouched by the change.

As a developer, I am of the firm, possibly dated, belief that if a code element is written more than once, it must be re-written as a single element to serve multiple consumers, albeit with a different interface. A duplicated framework, with copies embedded in each microservice is akin to a catastrophic, world-ending event by my classification. Just as an alien race on a planet fast running out of resources to sustain its inhabitants would send out exploratory probes for a new home, our Research and Development team sought out new integration approaches as the framework fragmentation threatened to slow down our delivery and return our platform to the dark ages of custom integration logic per microservice.

Figure 5-5 illustrates the solution which now underpins our platform integration strategy and ensures our evolutionary survival. The basic premise is that the integration component is extracted, externalized, and only accessible via a well-defined interface.

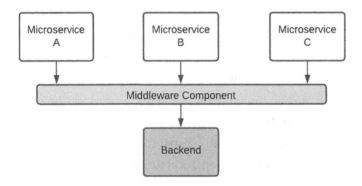

Figure 5-5. *Dedicated integration adapter*

This has led to the creation of a new category of microservice in our platform, which we have labelled as "middleware components." The various taxonomies of microservices in our platform are discussed later in this chapter.

The inherent benefit is that this reduces code duplication and results in a leaner, more streamlined microservice deployment. That is, instead of packaging a version of the framework inside the microservice, the framework functionality is externalized and accessed via an interface. Unfortunately, this opens the door to a potential performance drawback of out-of-process execution. The solution we use to minimize this impact is Google RPC (gRPC), which is discussed in more detail in the following section.

Google Remote Procedure Call (gRPC)

In all honesty, when the suggestion to use gRPC was raised, my knee-jerk reaction was to shut it down as quickly as possible. I equated RPC with the dark days of Microsoft Component Object Model (COM)/Distributed COM(DCOM) and complex Common Object Request Broker Architecture (CORBA) configurations. Although I adore the concept of distributed components, my experience with getting it to work was painful. I did not want to subject our platform to that complexity as it would increase operational overhead exponentially. So, I chose to stick with the safe path, which was most travelled. Essentially microservice communication would be achieved using good old HTTP. After all, we had our hands full with variable elements like an on-premises Kubernetes cluster and I shuddered at the thought of adding in a new, and at the time, relatively unproven technology element into the stack.

It was only 6 months later when I ran through a basic tutorial that the penny dropped that gRPC had the potential to revolutionize our platform architecture. A few minutes after starting the tutorial, I stared at the screen in disbelief as a client request from one terminal window magically and, most importantly, easily appeared in another. The technology has many virtues which I shall extol shortly. The one which I appreciate the most is its simplicity. At the heart of gRPC is a simple service definition which uses protocol buffers to define the request and response objects. gRPC takes care of the complexity of communicating between components, different languages, and environments. The *.proto* definition is the only shared component between client and server. This also presented us with the opportunity, which we have not used to date, of using different languages in our stack. This is made even easier through the availability of client libraries for most languages. gRPC is the key technology which allowed us to transition from a Shared Integration library (Figure 5-4) to the use of Dedicated Integration Adapters (Figure 5-5). Due to its use of a later HTTP standard and its transfer protocol, gRPC is far more performant than REST.

There are four types of Remote Procedure Calls (RPC):

1. **Unary RPC**: A client sends a single request and gets a single response. For example, the client requests the current time from the server. Most of our platform components use this style of communication. My suggestion is to start here first and, if the need arises, explore the other mechanisms on demand.

2. **Server streaming RPC**: It is similar to unary RPC, except that the server returns a stream of messages in response to a client's request. For example, to download a binary document from a server, the client initiates a request for the file, which is split into chunks on the server and then streamed to the client which is reassembled for processing. We use this mechanism to retrieve documents from an Enterprise Content Management system.

3. **Client streaming RPC**: It is also similar to unary RPC, except that the client sends a stream of messages to the server instead of a single message. For example, to upload an image to a server, the file is split into chunks which are then sent in a stream to the server which reassembles the image for processing. We use this approach to upload images for Optical Character Recognition (OCR) processing.

4. **Bidirectional streaming RPC**: The client and server can read and write messages in any order. For example, the image could be processed by different Optical Character Recognition (OCR) engines, and responses from each engine are returned in separate streams.

gRPC is a prime example of how technology can be simplified to encourage mass adoption. I also consider this specific journey as a stark reminder to have an open mind to new concepts and approaches and to fight pre-conceived notions to evolve our platform architecture. I have since apologized to the annoyed engineers who initially suggested the use of gRPC and have rightfully attributed its discovery and introduction to them. With that being said, I retain the claim for "weaponizing" the technology and taking it from a R&D construct to an operational environment.

The Power of Port-Forward

As our Business Logic components could leverage several integration microservices to fulfill a specific function, it became increasingly more challenging to assemble the solution. DevOps Continuous Integration (CI) pipelines can be leveraged for code deployments to the server. CI processes are great for transitioning between environments, but for initial development tasks, I consider using a CI pipeline like having a conversation with someone on a remote planet. You say something, wait some time until the message is received and has been replied to before you continue. As an impatient developer, I demand the ability to make and observe changes immediately. This can only be achieved using a local development environment.

My first pass at establishing this was to start up each microservice locally, in a separate terminal, each on a different port. It took a fair amount of time per development session to set this up, but the upfront time investment saved hours as I would not have to wait for the CI pipeline. I was fairly proud of this setup and patted myself on the back with each terminal tab opened and microservice started.

A pro tip from a fellow developer jolted me to the harsh reality that I was working harder, not smarter. The solution was to use the *port-forward* capability of the Kubernetes command-line tool, *kubectl*, to start a local listener which would route the request to a gRPC pod running in a Kubernetes cluster. This concept is illustrated in Figure 5-6.

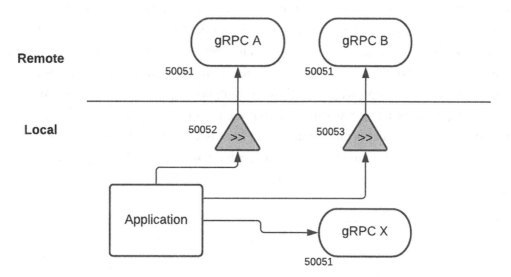

Figure 5-6. *Port-forward connectivity*

This allows the developer to build a solution using a blend of local and remote components based on the following strategy:

- Remote gRPC microservice pods (A, B) are listening on port *50051*. This is possible as each execute in separate container instances.

- Local gRPC microservice (X) listens on port *50051*. As this is running on my local machine, no other local process can use this port.

- Local *port-forward* processes listen on port *50052* and *50053*, which routes the traffic to gRPC A and B, respectively.

- Application is configured to use service A on port *50052*, service B on port *50053*, and service X on *50051*.

Taxonomy

Not all microservices are created equal, and, over time, we have created different categories of components. From previous roles as a Technical Architect, I prided myself on creating well defined, layered architectures. Each component fit into a specific layer and, like a military chain of command, a strict protocol was enforced – a component was only allowed to receive requests from the immediate layer above and could only relay requests to the layer below. Although the Architecture diagrams were great, they did not translate well from a development and execution perspective. Integrating into a new backend, adding or updating business logic required changes to various layers which slowed down delivery and increased operational overhead. Adding in new elements into the architecture also caused significant angst and architectural conjecture when solutioning.

Based on the battle scars of trying to compartmentalize components into layers, we have deliberately adopted a fairly "loose" architectural pattern. Like our team organogram, we have a flat structure and do not have a hard and fast rule that only certain types of components can interact with another. The relationship between components, as illustrated in Figure 5-7, has evolved organically. The key focus is on functionality and one of the core principles is reusability.

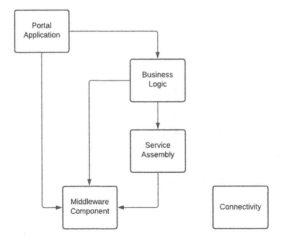

Figure 5-7. *Microservice taxonomy*

Our platform has the following categories of microservices:

- **Middleware**: The key objective of these components is to encapsulate integration to a backend platform. The microservice abstracts REST, SOAP, on-premises, or Cloud-based services and presents a standard, GRPC-based interface to the consumer. This allows us to implement changes, such as moving to later versions, without impacting consumers of the microservice – as long as we maintained the service contract (gRPC proto definition). All access to a backend or supporting system must be done via a middleware component. An example of this is database access. In contrast with our first generation microservice architecture, which allowed any component access to the database, only specific middleware components may integrate to our datastore. This affords us the bragging right of being able to switch database providers as well as from a document to relational database easily. Credentials and configuration for backend systems, across various environments, are contained and isolated within a specific middleware component. We also do our best to maintain a neutral service contract and do not allow "bleeding" of backend data structures to consumers. A key function of this component is to parse, process, and transform system-specific responses into a neutral gRPC response.

- **Connectivity**: This type of microservice is used as a protocol communication bridge. The component is geared to accept a request in Format A and convert that to Format B. For example, we use a Connectivity component to consume messages from a Kafka topic and prepare it to be written to a datastore. These components are generally event-based and are optimized for high-throughput, low latency processing.

- **Service assembly**: This is a "higher-order" microservice and is an example of organic evolution of our integration platform. While solutioning a new requirement, the team identified that certain pieces of logic were repeated in more than one Business Logic microservice. This presented a unique challenge as this was not backend integration logic but conflicted with our mantra of eliminating code duplication. To resolve, we used the same process as we did for backend integration. That is, we extracted the repeated logic, isolated, and externalized it as a new component, accessible via gRPC. A classification for this type of component would be centralized Service Orchestration. The key rule is that only one "Service Assembly" can be used for a particular request. This is to minimize the performance impact of communications between microservices.

- **Business logic**: This microservice is responsible for orchestrating the downstream components to achieve a specific business function. If the requisite work is done upfront and downstream middleware and service assembly elements are constructed correctly with the right interfaces, it is remarkable how fast these components can be composed. With that being said, do not over-engineer the interfaces of supporting components. A good friend used to joke that the Common Data Model of some organizations were so elaborate that if aliens landed in the year 3000, they would have no trouble interfacing. My personal take is that this adds unnecessary complexity to an interface in the hope of making it reusable. Chances are quite high that a new consumer will find the interface too complex to use and bypass it altogether. Rather start with a minimal interface and extend when necessary. If you adopt this approach, it will be necessary to tweak/update the interface of supporting components to achieve a new business function. Auditing is generally achieved from this component as information regarding the "business transaction" is recorded. This is also the layer you want to tap for Business Activity Monitoring. For example, a Business Logic component can trigger a "business-level" event for the creation of a Customer Account whereas the middleware components can send "system-level" events for provisioning requests in supporting systems.

As much as I would like to claim that this structure was our aim from the outset, it has evolved organically. In all honesty, there has been many developer man-days lost as elements have been written and re-written. With the base structure now established, new elements introduced into our ecosystem are quickly categorized and harvested. We have a fairly flexible architectural vision underpinned by key principles which ultimately result in a relatively uniform deployment.

Platform As a Service

The Platform as a Service (PaaS) concept shown in Figure 5-8 resonates across our Platform deployment, and I would like to spend a little time to elaborate.

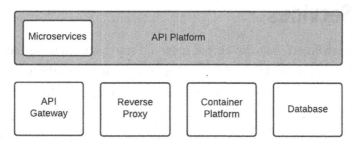

Figure 5-8. *Evolution of deployment strategies*

As mentioned earlier in this chapter, the technology we adopted at the start of our implementation was two to three years ahead of the rest of the organization. Our position in the Digital practice and our goal of establishing a new Platform afforded us this opportunity. As the enterprise, slowly but steadily, caught up, their ability to understand, incorporate, and manage the new application elements increased. I am also unashamed to say that their ability to support it, in an operational environment, surpasses our own. The reason is *Focus*.

As an API Marketplace team, our primary objective is on delivering an API product. Although commissioning a database, for example, might be the flavor of a particular timeframe, we may not give the database the true, long-term attention that it needs. Our dedicated Enterprise team does have that focus and has a wider view across the organization of similar efforts and is better positioned to negotiate a consolidated license agreement, for example, with the software vendor. The same approach applies to almost all the supporting elements in our software stack. The agreement between the Digital practice and the Technology Group is that the latter is better positioned to support software elements on an enterprise level.

Again, in all honesty, letting go of some of these elements has been difficult. In the same way a parent would nurse a newborn baby throughout the night and watch proudly as the toddler took their first steps, we did and still feel the same for elements in our environment. Late nights spent digging through cryptic configuration files, trying to understand why requests were not routed correctly, then proudly monitoring the platform fielding the first production traffic. Again, what has helped us relinquish control of these elements is the realization that they were going to a better home, one where they would receive the necessary attention and support. One better equipped to handle their needs with experienced subject-matter engineers and a well-planned future.

Platform Services

Developers are snowflakes. As a developer myself, I say this with the greatest of respect. Each developer is unique, and the odds are that if we were to ask three developers to build a logging solution, we are quite likely to get four different solutions – there's always that over-achiever who wants to impress by submitting more than one option. From a creativity perspective, this is fantastic. From a support perspective, this is a nightmare as uniformity and structure in an operational environment is a mainstay. Platform services are an essential mechanism to bridge development and operational worlds by providing shared libraries or packages to achieve the following:

- **Logging**: In an API environment, logs are as valuable as nuggets of gold. A challenge of working with containers is that logs are written to the local file system of the container. If the instance is restarted, which is extremely likely or if there are multiple instances of a container, finding logs becomes quite difficult. A key function of the logging platform service we have crafted is that log entries are routed to an Elastic Logstash platform, which are then indexed for searching and analysis.

- **Auditing**: This is likely to be as welcome as documentation by most developers. Good auditing is essential for customer support and reporting. Key business level events, such as payment transactions, must be audited to meet organization forensic requirements. An audit utility function or library provides a mechanism for all developers to audit easily and more importantly, consistently.

- **Error handling**: Having a central location for error processing is incredibly useful from an operational perspective. This provides the capability to handle events consistently, to upgrade or downgrade specific conditions, and to trigger alerts to support personnel. More advanced capabilities could also include complex event processing which allows a higher-level error condition to be triggered based on a sequence of events within a specified timeframe. A further benefit is that it allows consistent return messages in the form of HTTP status codes, error codes, and messages to consumers. If we consider the potential for fragmentation if each developer has to implement their own responses to errors, this would be one of the first platform services to be implemented.

- **Property management**: Property management and the ability to update runtime configuration is one of the most important, yet under-rated platform services in a stack. As an example, consider an API endpoint for a backend platform. As the consuming application would progress through various environments from development to test to pre-production to production, there is likely different endpoints for the backend. This would have to be updated for each environment. It would be poor form if the endpoint configuration was configured statically. A more elegant solution is the ability to specify the configuration at runtime. Note that there are varying degrees of elegance – configuration data can be specified in a Kubernetes config map. As your deployment could consist of several microservices, each with its own config map, this could result in configuration data scattered across config maps. Endpoints are just one example. Credentials, timeouts, and tax percentage values should also be configurable at runtime. By providing developers with a platform service, it indirectly affords the operational team a consistent mechanism for property management.

- **Tracing**: If you have spent time supporting an integration platform, you know that the Holy Grail is the ability to trace a transaction from entry, through the stack, to the backend platform through to exit. Let me assure you that in a microservices architecture, a transaction could make several hops for fulfillment. The ability to retrace the steps of a transaction is a critical element of the API platform. There are off-the-shelf Application Performance Management (APM) products which help to trace requests using probes and injecting trace information at runtime. These tools are great for application performance tuning and determining system outages but is not a silver bullet for transaction tracing. A good tracing and logging strategy is essentially the golden thread which will help operational teams follow the path of a transaction through the platform.

Deployment Architecture

We tried an assortment of combinations of the above elements to determine the most optimal configuration. This is possibly one of the most rewarding elements of our deployment architecture as the Lego brick approach allows us the flexibility to assemble the stack in various formations. Since inception, we have been tethered to on-premises infrastructure and systems. In the sections below, I detail a roadmap and a key objective to move to Cloud infrastructure and managed services. Each iteration adds support for the next and we have tested and pushed the organizations boundaries a little further on each deployment. It should be noted that high levels of tolerance and patience from our Enterprise Information and Network Security teams were key to our success.

Launch Configuration

Figure 5-9 illustrates the Launch Deployment Configuration which underpinned our MVP. Like kids let loose in a candy store, we threw caution to the wind and used as many technology elements as possible and routed requests through as many hops as needed to get to the destination. If an enterprise policy did not allow firewall access for a specific system, we adopted a rebound approach until we found an alternative. While this will certainly work with a tenacious team, the end result is not as optimal as it could be.

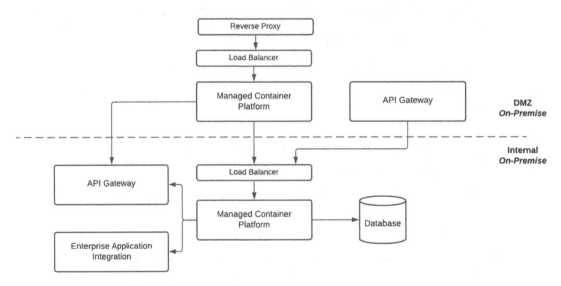

Figure 5-9. *Launch configuration*

If building an on-premises Kubernetes cluster was not enough of a challenge, we opted to build two – one in the internal network and another in the Demilitarized Zone (DMZ). Our organization's DMZ can be compared to a prison colony on a remote planet. Access is only allowed via a "jump box," which is essentially a remote desktop connection. If you're lucky, you can get one of two sessions, else you must wait until you can hijack a session when an incumbent user takes a bathroom break. I can still recall the look of desperation when a new DevOps engineer discovered he would not have GUI access to run his install scripts. In our DMZ, like a real prison, there are different levels of security. Back when we started, Containers and Kubernetes were deemed to be extremely dangerous, and a new zone, even more restricted than the rest, was purpose-built for us. We learnt of this when we attempted to connect elements *within* the DMZ. The focus session to troubleshoot the connectivity issue was similar to commands issued on a submarine – requests were relayed from Tester to Facilitator to Network Engineer to DevOps Engineer and all the way back. As painful as the experience was at times, it was also a tremendous learning opportunity as it afforded lessons to understand the organization's network topology and more importantly, how to navigate it. Configuration detailing the nodes across which requests would be load-balanced and ports for firewall access was essential to make the solution work and outsourcing it to infrastructure designers, while possible, would take days, if not weeks to complete.

The approach we chose was to roll up our sleeves, and complete the first pass internally, then review with a designer who would correct and teach us how it should be done. From a professional perspective, we forged good relationships with infrastructure project managers, designers, and supporting teams through this engagement. By working closely with these teams, we gained a better understanding of internal processes, the reason for their existence, and the sheer amount of pressure supporting teams in the Enterprise are under. Our annoyance with the internal teams for the seemingly long resolution times soon turned to compassion and respect for their effort and ultimately embarrassment of our petulant behavior. Instead of railing against the processes and governance which we felt slowed us down, we chose to understand and work with it. To its credit, the organization has also worked to streamline its operation to respond with more agility to get solutions to market. This experience, although a humbling one, was one of the most rewarding as it required the building of relationships with supporting teams to achieve the deployment objective.

A factor which accelerated our delivery, and which still does today, was permission for direct, albeit via a load balancer, access to our microservices from the API Gateway instance in the DMZ. The enterprise standard is that all internal APIs are to be accessed via the internal Gateway. This would have resulted in definitions published twice, internal and external. It would also have a performance impact as the request would have to traverse another stop. The multi-node Managed Container platform hosted a single Authorization portal container application in the DMZ. Justification for this elaborate deployment was that it would help withstand the high traffic when the platform launched. I still chuckle when I think back to our initial outlook and the design decisions made based on emotion rather than reality.

As-Is Configuration

Figure 5-10 reflects a deployment configuration of a much more mature and responsible team. Gone were the heady days of achieving an MVP, and we were far more in touch with reality regarding the technology elements of our platform and the supporting enterprise systems. We were also extremely fortunate to have two seasoned DevOps Engineers join our team, who actually "knew what we did not know." With their experience, a far more stable and enterprise-ready Kubernetes cluster was quickly established – the third iteration.

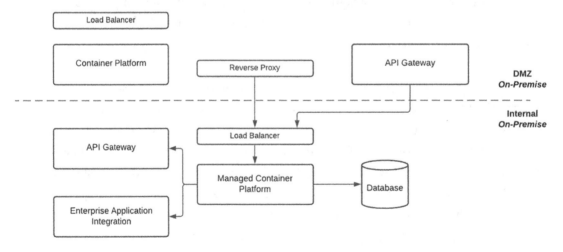

Figure 5-10. *As-Is configuration*

One of the first questions raised regarded the need for a full-blown Kubernetes cluster in the DMZ. They patiently explained, as a parent would to a child who wanted ice cream before the main meal, that a simpler Docker Container platform deployment could be used to achieve the same objective. Their contribution to the evolution of our DevOps platform could be compared to a far more advanced alien race assisting cavemen who had just discovered fire. This, too, has been a great lesson. If you are going to embrace new technology, be it for a short-term MVP or a long-haul transformation project, be sure to resource it with the right skill level or consider a subset of the technology or not using it at all. Observing a master ply their craft is truly something to behold and our platform soon had a working pipeline, and the team was soon issuing commands via instant message to characters from Tolkien's Middle-Earth to release code elements.

One of the most significant developments of this deployment was permission from Network Security to allow internally hosted web applications to be exposed by a Reverse Proxy in the DMZ. This milestone decision allowed the migration of the single web application hosted in the DMZ Container Platform to the internal Kubernetes cluster. This has optimized delivery as internal pipelines and network connectivity can be leveraged and support simplified as the container and associated logs can easily be accessed. We have chosen not to decommission the DMZ Container Platform and are currently using it to host external applications that are not core to the Platform. Applications which leverage the API Marketplace capability but fulfill a third-party objective, for example, to synchronize Account transactions, are residents of this platform.

To-Be Configuration

As challenging and rewarding as finally establishing an enterprise-grade on-premises Kubernetes platform has been, the team has reached the conclusion that this exercise is much like keeping a lion as a pet. The platform demands constant attention and dedicated support and if not controlled can gobble up an inexperienced handler. Figure 5-11 reflects the plans for the next step of our deployment architecture. We envisage running the various elements of the stack using Cloud infrastructure and platform services. Given that components such as the API Gateway is a shared instance, this will inevitably be a phased migration. Supporting elements, such as code repositories and DevOps pipelines, also must be migrated to the Cloud.

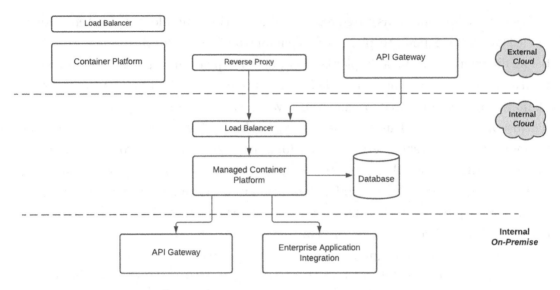

Figure 5-11. *As-Is configuration*

For a startup of smaller organization, using Cloud infrastructure or platform services is a relatively trivial task. This iteration has revealed that this lies on the other end of the difficulty spectrum for an established enterprise. There are various considerations, such as connectivity from an on-premises component to Cloud and back to on-premises. The ultimate aim is to use a Cloud provider Managed Kubernetes Service which would abstract the underlying infrastructure requirement and allow us to focus on the microservice as a container.

Simply put, we would pack up a container and have it hosted on a Managed Container Platform. The managed service would take care of any security patches, upgrades, or infrastructure scaling required. Scaling is a key factor as we would not have to maintain the physical hardware or virtual machines as we currently do. As much as we look forward to the move to Cloud, we are doing our best to keep our expectations under control. If the lengthy, and sometimes bumpy journey to get to Cloud is anything to go by, residing and operating in a new environment may present a whole new set of challenges. I hope that the learning and growth is as rewarding as our previous iterations.

Summary

Establishing the platform architecture for an API Marketplace has presented a tremendous learning opportunity for our team. We realized that reading a blog post detailing how Netflix deploys and operates applications only scratches the surface when the team has to do it themselves, within a significantly different organizational context. It allowed us hands-on exposure to elements like Docker for containerization, gRPC for inter-service microservice communication, and Kubernetes for container management.

We consider deep technical components like ingresses, services, and pods as offspring we have hand-raised and nurtured. Like parents with a newborn, the journey has also been challenging. We have had to weather severe bouts of cholic when we looked wearily at each other and wondered if we would make it through.

Equally, there have been moments of pride, when the platform took its first steps as we scaled the number of pod replicas and breezed through a performance test. Our platform, like a baby, has matured and is now entering a new phase of existence. The benefit of time affords us a much better understanding of its operation, strengths, and weaknesses. There is still much to be improved and optimized which is the reason I consider an API Marketplace to be a living, breathing organism. The African proverb "It takes a village to raise a child" sums up our experience as it would not have been possible to have achieved this objective without the help and support of the Enterprise.

In the next chapters, we discuss how the Platform Architecture is used to support the API products of the Marketplace, from Design to Development to Operations.

CHAPTER 6

Security

Establishing an API Marketplace can be like setting up an embassy for your organization in a foreign and hostile territory. Although your intention is noble and your aim is to help third-party providers leverage your products and services, it exposes the enterprise to a range of new attack vectors every day. The stakes are incredibly high when precious customer and other sensitive data are at risk. The mantra that everyone is responsible for ensuring the safety and integrity of the platform is not to be taken lightly. Any breaches across any of the API products could lead to negative public sentiment, impacting other products, the Marketplace, and the greater organization.

Security is not simply the access mechanism to the API. It is important to consider it as an element which permeates each layer of the platform – from a technical, people, and process perspective. Fortunately, there are well-established patterns and security standards which can be followed as a guideline to direct your implementation. It is also a fine balancing act as it must be tailored to the requirements of your organization without impacting developer adoption.

In the sections which follow, I will cover the security topics which may be applicable to an API Marketplace implementation for different products, audiences, and stages in their lifecycle. As covered in our earlier chapter on Regulation, there may be variants of these standards for specific industries. We will examine the Open Banking variation in more detail.

The dynamicity of the ever-changing security context is one which makes an API Marketplace more challenging and interesting as it demands constant learning and adaptation to stay safe. We are incredibly fortunate as there is an incredible amount of literature, offerings, and perspectives available in this regard. Knowledge is critical to understanding the landscape and to stay safe.

© Rennay Dorasamy 2022

R. Dorasamy, *API Marketplace Engineering*, https://doi.org/10.1007/978-1-4842-7313-5_6

Cross-Cutting Concern

Let us consider how security impacts various domains in an API Marketplace implementation.

- **API**: The nature of the product determines the API access mechanism. If it requires end-user consent, it will be done in a Business-to-Consumer (B2C) context. If the aim is to allow system integration, it will be achieved in a Business-to-Business (B2B) context.

- **Network**: As the call traverses the various elements in your platform stack, how can it be monitored, tracked, and interrogated? Will it maintain customer identity as it reaches the backend, or will it assume a system one? Should your platform be firewalled from the rest of the enterprise which would add significant administrative overhead but provide the benefit of fine-grained access control?

- **Application**: Even with the best security implementation, vulnerabilities in the application code may be exploited. There are hair-raising accounts of unauthorized access to customer data and systems which have been compromised through ways the technical team never thought possible.

- **Container**: This deployment strategy is extremely popular due to its modularized approach. It is important to determine if the base image could be compromised. The strategy for the configuration and management of credentials must be well defined at an enterprise level to prevent ad hoc and loose implementations. The context in which the application executes may appear trivial – however, root user or write access to a file system may unwittingly yield to security backdoors. The same rigor that applies to traditional deployment must be applied to containers.

- **Infrastructure**: Does your solution run on on-premises hardware or do you deploy to Infrastructure-as-a-Service (IasS) or Platform-as-a-Service (PaaS) public cloud solutions? If the latter, then new security policies and governance must be defined to maintain solution and platform integrity.

- **Process**: Consider the seemingly simple objective of providing a third party with credentials to access an API. Will this be achieved by sharing the details via email or possibly a password-protected document? This may result in a comedic chicken or the egg scenario as we need to determine how to share the password for the document containing the credentials. If the credentials are generated through human intervention, it is already compromised. Any decent security policy also demands that credentials are regularly changed – how will this be achieved – especially if dealing with a large number of third-party providers.

- **Operations**: Does your support personnel have credentials for access to backend systems? If the immediate answer is a resounding *No*, will this be an impediment to resolving support queries? Developers may unwittingly leak sensitive customer data, such as account numbers, through seemingly harmless log statements which ripple through to operational support tools.

The intention of this section is not to scare you into shelving your plans for an API Marketplace implementation until you can fully guarantee every aspect of security. The aim is to highlight the various dimensions across which security must be considered. Again, this will be tailored to the technical landscape and requirements of your enterprise, and each platform will undoubtedly be unique in their implementation.

An approach that has worked exceedingly well for ours is to actively seek out regular and rigorous review by teams from other domains – Information and Network Security, Architecture, and Shared Enterprise Services. In all honesty, the feedback was not always positive, and we had to refactor our solutions to mitigate. I can assure you that the integrity of the result has certainly been worth the effort.

In the following sections, we will deep dive into the tip of the iceberg – API security. This is just one of the many perspectives through which we need to consider a Marketplace implementation. Understanding that security impacts almost every aspect of your platform will help the technical team establish foundational elements and core practices in the right way to prevent rework later.

API Security

The access mechanism for your API product is intrinsically linked to the type of consumer and the nature of the solution. It can be considered in much the same way as access to your home. Depending on where you live, there may be a security guard at the entrance of your gated community to allow only residents in, your front door might have a heavy-duty lock which only you and your family have a key to, while locks on internal doors are probably never used. In the following sections, we will review security approaches in the context in which they may be best applied and the associated audience.

Open APIs

These interfaces typically provide reference or publicly accessible data. Examples include locations of service stations, country codes, or weather information for a specified location. Although the API may not require a security mechanism at all, it is best to use, at a minimum, a **Client ID** and **Secret** as illustrated in Figure 6-1. This has the benefit of understanding who is consuming your API – by way of a required registration to receive credentials. The *client identifier* can also be used to provide different service levels and, importantly, to restrict access to a rogue consumer without impacting others.

Figure 6-1. *Open API security pattern*

There may be a wide audience for this type of product. From developers learning how to consume APIs to established service providers looking for reliable source of reference data.

Business to Business (B2B)

The aim of these APIs is to allow system-to-system integration. Examples include interfaces to determine stock availability, placing an order to purchase a product, or sharing enterprise data with affiliates or partners. Traditional mechanisms to achieve this type of integration required custom, purpose-built interfaces and dedicated network infrastructure, in the form of leased lines, between consumer and provider. As a result, there was significant cost and time impact for the upfront provisioning. Although this can be achieved by configuring a Virtual Private Network (VPN) between the parties which uses public network infrastructure, it can also be achieved through the use of a security **certificate** to simplify the integration pattern as illustrated in Figure 6-2.

Figure 6-2. *B2B security pattern*

The certificate and associated passphrase provides an additional layer of security as it is directly linked to a specific consumer and is an essential element in the handshake to set up the Transport Layer Security (TLS) connection. The certificate may be issued by the API host organization or may be provided by the consumer to be registered with the host. Due to the sensitive nature of the API, the audience for these types of solutions is typically well-known partners or established third-party providers.

Business to Consumer (B2C)

In this type of scenario, the consumer requests permission to transact on behalf of an end user or to access their data. The end user provides direct instruction to the provider to allow or deny that request. This interaction is illustrated in Figure 6-3. A popular example is accessing a partner site using your social media (Google or Facebook) credentials to establish your identity. Fortunately, there is a widely accepted industry standard, in the form of OAuth 2.0, which provides specific details on the choreography between end user, consumer, and provider.

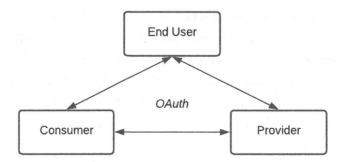

Figure 6-3. *B2C security pattern*

The magic ingredient of end-user consent makes it possible to offer these APIs to a wider range of third-party providers. Even with stringent security standards, an unscrupulous third-party provider, once admitted into your ecosystem, has opportunities to elicit additional customer data (one approach discussed later). It is extremely important that third parties are screened and vetted to meet the due diligence criteria set out by your implementation.

In the following section, we will dive into the detail of the OAuth process and discuss some of the supporting background processes and variations to allow you better insight into its operation.

OAuth

Simply, OAuth is an open-standard framework that provides applications the ability to *secure delegated access.*

To understand how it works, consider the following scenario:

- My favorite online diagram service, Lucidchart, requires me to create an account – as shown in Figure 6-4.

- To create an account, I could have stepped through the traditional registration process by completing an online form providing my name, email address, and setting a password. Lucidchart would then send an email with a link to confirm I am the rightful owner of that email address.

- Lucidchart also allows me to login using my Google account *if* I allow it permission to verify my profile with Google.

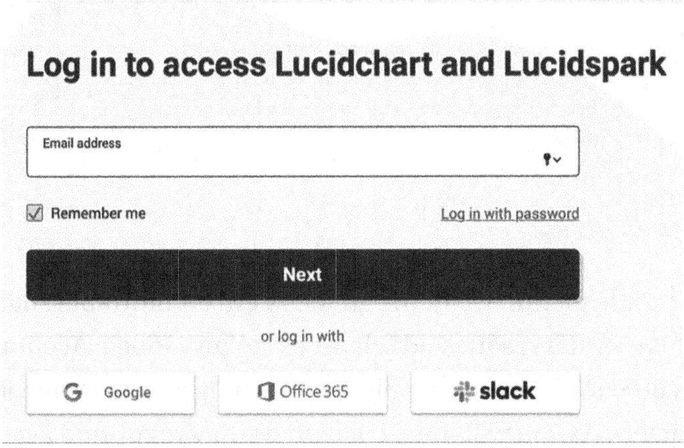

Figure 6-4. *Lucidchart Login*

OAuth is the standard that facilitates this process to allow end users to confirm identity and provide third-party applications restricted access to their data.

Actors and Scopes

Let us identify the actors or participants in this scenario, in order of appearance:

1. I am the *Resource Owner* as I am the holder of the Google Account.

2. Lucidchart is the *Client* as it is the application that requires access to my profile.

3. Google is the *Resource Server* as it stores my profile on its servers.

There are a few key concepts I would like to touch on. Although Google holds my profile data on its infrastructure, *I* am the owner of the data. The traditional practice that customer data belongs to the host organization has been reversed, and control has been returned to its rightful owner – the end user.

The *scope* indicates the extent of data that I would like to share with third parties. In the context of the above scenario, Lucid only requires my name, email address, language preference, and profile picture from Google as shown in Figure 6-5.

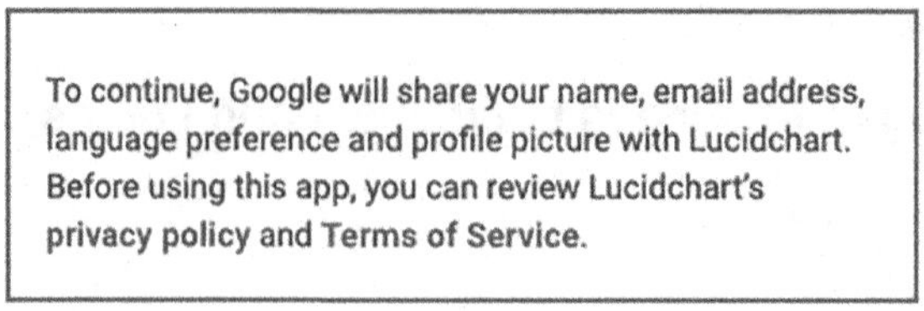

> To continue, Google will share your name, email address, language preference and profile picture with Lucidchart. Before using this app, you can review Lucidchart's privacy policy and Terms of Service.

Figure 6-5. *Limited access*

Although my profile picture is not the greatest, I'm comfortable sharing this information. Had Lucidchart requested full access to my Google Account – I would have been more than a little reluctant as I would be providing access to my personal email, calendar, and contacts. As you will note, Lucidchart only requested access to information it specifically needed, nothing more. Within an OAuth context, this is the limited scope or permission that I, as the *Resource Owner*, am happy to approve.

Before you move on, be sure to solidify the concepts of *actors*, roles they perform, and *scopes*. Consider other scenarios, such as OAuth in a banking (or relevant to your industry) context to identify the actors, roles, and scopes.

Application Registration

An important background process that is often missed in OAuth literature is the interaction between the *Client* and *Resource Server*. The *Resource Server* may not be the owner of my data but as a responsible service provider and as part of its due diligence process, should only release data to verified parties. Any application that uses OAuth to access its APIs must have authorization credentials that identify the application to the *Resource Server's* OAuth server. The *Client* will register an application with the *Resource Server*, providing details regarding where the request will originate from and where users should be redirected to.

A quick recap of this step:

1. The *Client* must register an Application with the *Resource Server*. The purpose of this step is to establish the *client* identity and allows the *resource server* to track access requests.

2. The *Client* provides details regarding where the request will originate from and where the end user should be redirected to. This is important as it limits potential man-in-the-middle attacks. As you will note, the redirect URI is used for a number of interactions.

3. At the end of this process, the *Resource Server* will provide
    credentials to the *Client* in the form of a *Client ID* and *Client
    Secret.*

In some API Gateway products, once an application is created, access to API
products is achieved through a process of a subscription.

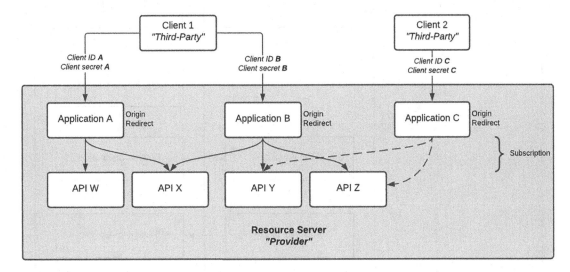

Figure 6-6. *Client-resource server interaction*

As illustrated in Figure 6-6

- One or more C*lients* (third party) may register one or more
  Applications with a *Resource Server* (provider).

- Each Application has a subscription to one or more APIs.

- Each Application must specify (one or more) redirect URIs, and may
  also provide (one or more) origin URIs.

- An Application is issued a set of credentials – in the form of a *Client
  ID* and *Client Secret.*

- Based on organizational policy, access to specific APIs may only be
  granted to authorized Clients. As illustrated, *Client 2* does not have a
  subscription (access) to API *W* and *X.*

Figure 6-7 outlines the Application Registration process.

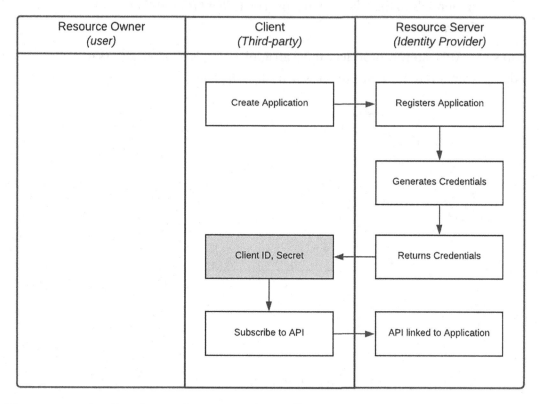

Figure 6-7. *Application registration process flow*

1. The *Client* creates an Application, providing details such as email, owner, and contact, metadata such as the solution name, redirect URI, and client certificate (if necessary).

2. The *Resource Server* registers an Application with the information provided, and credentials, in the form of a *Client ID* and *Secret*, are generated.

3. The credentials are returned to the third party. At this time, the third party has a *Client ID* and *Secret*. It is possible to change configuration data of the Application – such as the redirect URI. However, the *Client ID* may be fixed. Many API Gateway implementations only provide the *Secret* at registration, and it will be regenerated if lost.

4. At this time, the *Client* subscribes or links the Application to specific API products published by the *Resource Server*.

Note   Parts of the above process may be achieved via self-service or manual intervention.

- Some Marketplace implementations may only provide credentials, even to the Sandbox environment, to verified consumers.

- Application creation and subscription, in the Live environment, may be done by the Product Owner to restrict third parties to specific products.

Grant Types and Access Tokens

Now that a *Client* has registered an application and has credentials, there are different ways to get access. In the OAuth framework, this is referred to as a grant type. There are many grant types for different use-cases, as well as a framework for creating new grant types. As an example, a *Device Code* grant type may be used to sign on to an online service from a television set which may be input-constrained.

It is important to highlight that in an Open API or B2B context, the *Client ID* and *Client secret* may be sufficient to access an API. In a B2C context, *Client ID* and *secret*, in a process defined by the *grant type*, are used to retrieve Access Tokens which are the credentials used to access protected resources:

Client Credentials (ID/secret) + Grant Type ➤ Access Token ➤ API

A typical Access Token contains the properties shown in Table 6-1.

Table 6-1. *Access token properties*

Field	Presence	Description
access_token	Required	Access token string
token_type	Required	This is the type of token, typically just the string "Bearer" indicating that any party in possession of this token may use it
expires_in	Optional	The duration the token is granted for
refresh_token	Optional	If the access token expires, then this is used to request a new Access token
scope	Optional	Indicates the scope of access granted

In the following sections, we will dive into the process for retrieving an Access Token for the following grant types:

- Client Credentials
- Authorization Code
- Refresh Token

Client Credentials

Figure 6-8 details the Client Credentials process flow.

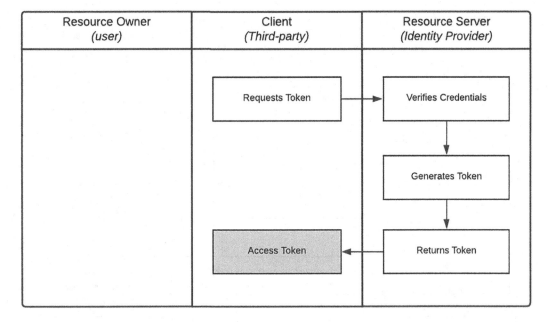

Figure 6-8. *Client Credentials process flow*

1. The *Client* initiates the request for an *Access Token* providing

   a. Credentials: *Client ID* and *Secret*

   b. *grant type* of `client_credentials`

   c. Scope: resources that the *Client* wants to access

2. The *Resource Server* will locate the Application referenced by the *Client ID*, verify that the *Secret* matches, and if subscribed to the requested APIs (specified in the *scope*), will return an *Access Token*.

3. At this time, the third party has an *Access Token*. Note that the token may have a specified period of validity, typically 3,599 seconds.

Authorization Code

Figure 6-9 details the Authorization Code process flow.

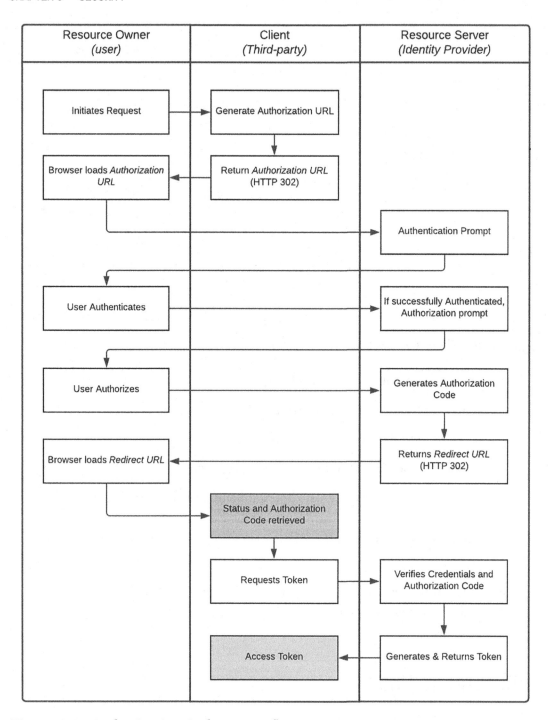

Figure 6-9. *Authorization Code process flow*

1. The request is initiated by the *Resource Owner*. As detailed in our earlier scenario, *I (Resource Owner)* requested to access Lucidchart *(Client)*, using my Google *(Resource Server)* profile.

2. The *Client* constructs an Authorization URL providing

   a. Credential: *Client ID* (only) – to indicate where the request originates from.

   b. Response type of *code* indicating that an Authorization Code is required.

   c. Redirect URI: Determines where the user should be redirected to after they complete the Authorization flow. Note that this **must** match the redirect URI configured for the Application.

   d. Scope: Identify resources that the *Client* wants to access on the user's behalf.

   e. State: This is used to maintain state between the authorization request and the authorization server's response.

3. The *Client* then redirects the user, by way of a HTTP 302, to the constructed Authorization URL. This is a pivotal step in the process as it requires direct interaction between *Client* and *Resource Server*.

4. The *Resource Server* verifies the *Client ID*, *redirect URI* and *scope* requested, and if valid, prompts the *Resource Owner* to confirm identity (Authentication) and provide consent (Authorization).

5. The *Resource Owner* authenticates themselves and authorizes the *Client's* access to the requested resources. From our scenario, I would provide my Google username and password and allow Lucid access to specific elements of my profile.

6. Upon successful Authentication and Authorization by the *Resource Owner*, the *Resource Server* generates an *Authorization Code*. If not, an *error* indicating the reason for failure is used instead.

7. The *Resource Server* appends the *Authorization Code* or *error* to the *redirect URI*, along with the *state* parameter and redirects the user, again by way of a HTTP 302, to the *Client*.

8. Upon redirection to the *Client*, the status of the Authorization request is determined – an *Authorization Code* if successful, an *error* if not.

9. If successful, the *Client* initiates a request for an *Access Token* providing

    a. Credentials: *Client ID* and *Secret*

    b. *grant type* of `authorization_code`

    c. *Authorization Code*

    d. Redirect URI: Must match what is configured for the Application

10. The *Resource Server* will locate the Application referenced by the *Client ID*, verify that the *Secret* and redirect URI matches, and if a valid *Authorization Code* is provided, will return an *Access Token*.

11. The *Access Token* returned will contain a *refresh_token* property.

12. The *access_token* can be used to make calls to APIs – to which the registered Application is subscribed to.

Refresh Token

As an Access Token is generally valid for short periods of time, typically an hour, the Refresh Token *grant type* is used to access resources for extended periods. This also saves the end user the inconvenience of having to re-authenticate and re-authorize once the Access Token expires. It is important to note that in some scenarios, such as a once-off Payment, tokens may only be used within a specific period (even shorter than the *expires_in* value) and only once.

To prevent perpetual access, it is important to fix the duration for the refreshing of tokens. As an example, tokens may only be refreshed for a maximum period of 6 months, starting from the issuing of the first Access Token – after which the end user will have to re-authenticate and re-authorize the access.

Figure 6-10 details the Refresh Token process flow.

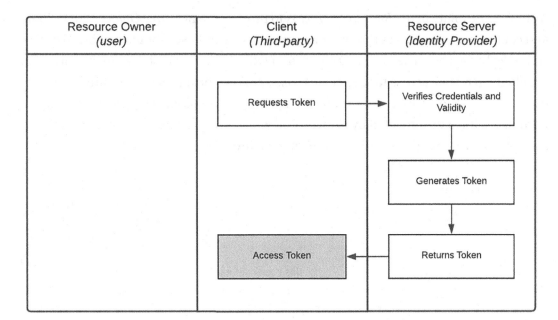

Resource Owner (user)	Client (Third-party)	Resource Server (Identity Provider)
	Requests Token	Verifies Credentials and Validity
		Generates Token
Access Token		Returns Token

Figure 6-10. *Refresh Token process flow*

1. The *Client* initiates the request for a new *Access Token* providing

    a. Credentials: *Client ID* and *Secret*

    b. *grant type* of `refresh_token`

    c. Redirect URI: Configured for the Application

    d. *refresh token*: Which was returned as a property in the last Access Token generated

2. The *Resource Server* will locate the Application referenced by the *Client ID*, verify that the *Secret* and redirect URI matches, and if within the refresh validity period, will return an *Access Token*.

3. At this time, the third party has an *Access Token*. Note that the *access_token* may have a specified period of validity, typically 3,599 seconds. The *refresh_token* is valid for a longer duration.

4. The new *Access Token* returned will also contain a *refresh_token* property which may be used for the next refresh request. Note that this can only be used once.

135

Permission Revocation

A key responsibility of the *Resource Server* is to provide the *Resource Owner* with visibility and control over previous authorizations granted. The end user should be able to easily view *who* has access, *when* it was granted, and *what* can be accessed. More importantly, the ability to revoke access for a specific *Client*. This is typically achieved through a user administration portal. Continuing the Lucidchart scenario, I can use the Account Administration page provided by Google, find which third parties have access to my account, and remove the access – as shown in Figure 6-11.

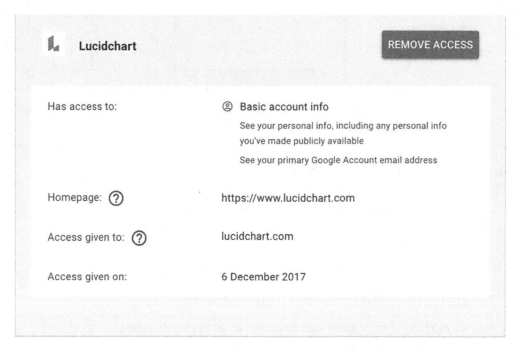

Figure 6-11. *Permission administration*

Some third parties may also provide end users with functionality to revoke access or unlink an account. The *Client* (third party) initiates a call to the token revocation endpoint of the *Resource Server* as notification of this event and to invalidate the authorization and associated token:

- Credentials: *Client ID* and *Secret*

- *refresh token*: Which was returned as a property in the last Access Token generated

Variation: Open Banking

The OAuth standard provides a great foundation for delegated access for most security contexts. Confirming customer consent in an Open Banking context requires a custom or tailored approach for one or more of the following reasons:

- It requires fine-grained access to end-user information. For example, a customer may allow a third-party access to only specific bank accounts.

- Due to the dynamic nature of the data, a custom consent mechanism is required. Continuing the above example, once the customer is authenticated, their accounts can be retrieved and displayed in a custom view for authorization.

- A two-stage mechanism is essential to verify that the third party executes the exact instruction or *intent* of the customer.

Central to this process is the concept of an *intent*:

1. The *Client* registers an intent with the *Resource Server* indicating what they would like to do.

2. The *Resource Owner* authorizes the intent while also specifying the exact resources which may be accessed which is recorded in the intent.

3. Prior to execution of the request from the *Client*, the *Resource Server* confirms the request matches the original intent and resources authorized by the *Resource Owner*.

To achieve the above, a combination of the *Client Credentials* and *Authorization Code* OAuth grant types, as illustrated in Figure 6-12, are used. This shows how the elements of the OAuth standard can be assembled for a customized implementation.

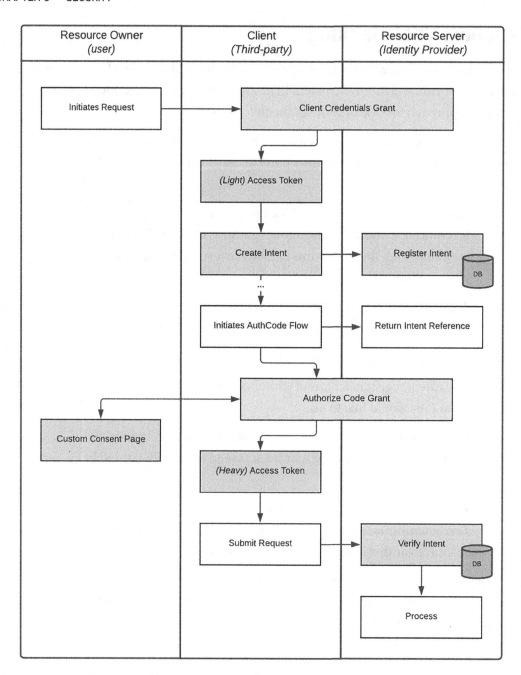

Figure 6-12. *Open Banking variation of OAuth flow*

A quick overview of the process:

- The *Client* uses the *Client Credentials* grant to confirm its identity and ability to access to specific API products and receives an *Access Token*. We refer to this token as a "light" token.

- The *Client* then registers an intent with the *Resource Server* using the light token and receives an intent identifier as a reference.

- The *Client* includes the intent identifier in the Authorization URL and initiates a customized *Authorization Code* flow.

- This allows the *Resource Server* to locate the original intent when it receives the request from the *Resource Owner* redirect.

- A custom consent page may be constructed around the type of intent registered allowing the *Resource Owner* finer control over which data is shared.

- For example, to make payment, a list of accounts can be provided and a specific one selected. As the interaction is directly between *Resource Owner* and *Resource Server*, the *Client* does not get access to sensitive data.

- On successful authorization, receipt of the *code* and final leg of the *Authorization Code* grant, the *Client* retrieves a new *Access Token*, referred to as the "heavy" token.

- The reason for the "heavy" classification is that the token is intrinsically bound to the intent. Subsequent requests to the *Resource Server* with this token are processed using the intent as a reference.

- The *Client* uses this "heavy" token for API calls to the *Resource Server*.

- Subsequent refresh tokens, if allowed, are also linked to this intent.

As you will note from the above, while there are additional steps in the flow, the use of an intent affords additional security by

1. Allowing finer-grained control of resources

2. Providing a second policy-enforcement point when the *Resource Server* compares the instruction to intent before processing a *Client* request

Vulnerability

As you may have observed, the *Authorization Code* flow is underpinned by redirects achieved using HTTP 302. Although important in its function, it provides an opportunity for attack and is one of the biggest threats to the integrity of the process. There are undoubtedly complex mechanisms of intercepting and redirecting network packets or creating fake DNS records which experienced hackers could use to exploit a redirect. As my career has been largely been dedicated to development rather than hacking, I present a far simpler way in which a dishonest third party could phish or compromise an end user's credentials in Figure 6-13.

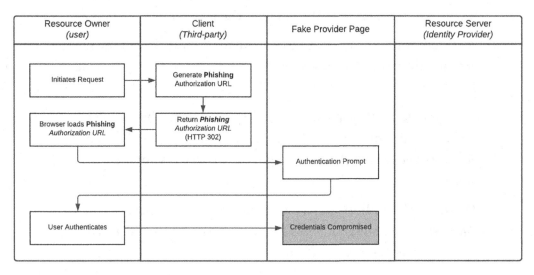

Figure 6-13. *Credential phishing flow*

As the diagram indicates, as part of the *Authorization Code* flow, the *Client* can maliciously redirect the end user to a fake provider page, which could easily be constructed to appear like that of the *Resource Server* – and also be hosted on a domain which closely matches the original. The end user would then be inputting their credentials into a compromised site. The technical acumen required to achieve this is elementary web development and hosting knowledge and considerably lower than having to understand the TCP/IP stack or DNS. It is important and interesting to note that the potential remedy to this attack is a *process* update to verify the integrity of third parties before allowing them to participate in your ecosystem.

OWASP

The Open Web Application Security Project (OWASP) is a non-profit foundation that works to improve the security of software through its community-led open source software projects, hundreds of chapters worldwide, tens of thousands of members, and by hosting local and global conferences.

Security Top 10

The Top 10 API Security Risks identified by OWASP [`https://owasp.org/www-project-api-security`] lists the following:

- **Broken Object Level Authorization** (API1): APIs tend to expose endpoints that handle object identifiers, creating a wide attack surface Level Access Control issue. Object level authorization checks should be considered in every function that accesses a data source using an input from the user.

- **Broken User Authentication** (API2): Authentication mechanisms are often implemented incorrectly, allowing attackers to compromise authentication tokens or to exploit implementation flaws to assume other user's identities temporarily or permanently. Compromising a system's ability to identify the client/user compromises API security overall.

- **Excessive Data Exposure** (API3): Looking forward to generic implementations, developers tend to expose all object properties without considering their individual sensitivity, relying on clients to perform the data filtering before displaying it to the user.

- **Lack of Resources and Rate Limiting** (API4): Quite often, APIs do not impose any restrictions on the size or number of resources that can be requested by the client/user. Not only can this impact the API server performance, leading to Denial of Service (DoS), but also leaves the door open to authentication flaws such as brute force.

- **Broken Function Level Authorization** (API5): Complex access control policies with different hierarchies, groups, and roles, and an unclear separation between administrative and regular functions, tend to lead to authorization flaws. By exploiting these issues, attackers gain access to other users' resources and/or administrative functions.

- **Mass Assignment** (API6): Binding client provided data (e.g., JSON) to data models, without proper properties filtering based on an allow list, usually leads to Mass Assignment. Either guessing objects properties, exploring other API endpoints, reading the documentation, or providing additional object properties in request payloads allows attackers to modify object properties they are not supposed to.

- **Security Misconfiguration** (API7): Security misconfiguration is commonly a result of unsecure default configurations, incomplete or ad hoc configurations, open cloud storage, misconfigured HTTP headers, unnecessary HTTP methods, permissive Cross-Origin resource sharing (CORS), and verbose error messages containing sensitive information.

- **Injection** (API8): Injection flaws, such as SQL, NoSQL, Command Injection, etc., occur when untrusted data is sent to an interpreter as part of a command or query. The attacker's malicious data can trick the interpreter into executing unintended commands or accessing data without proper authorization.

- **Improper Assets Management** (API9): APIs tend to expose more endpoints than traditional web applications, making proper and updated documentation highly important. Proper hosts and deployed API versions inventory also play an important role to mitigate issues such as deprecated API versions and exposed debug endpoints.

- **Insufficient Logging and Monitoring** (API10): Insufficient logging and monitoring, coupled with missing or ineffective integration with incident response, allows attackers to further attack systems, maintain persistence, pivot to more systems to tamper with, extract, or destroy data. Most breach studies demonstrate the time to detect a breach is over 200 days, typically detected by external parties rather than internal processes or monitoring.

Recommendations

To address the risk of Excessive Data Exposure (API3), we use the following guidelines:

- Detailed review of the responses from the API to confirm it contains valid data.

- Always filter sensitive data on the server.

- Avoid the use of generic methods such as *toJSON()* and *toString()*. Instead select specific properties to return.

- Implement a schema-based response validation mechanism to define and enforce data returned by API methods, including errors.

- Keep interfaces as simple as possible. Provide only as much information as required. Use versioning to extend the API if needed.

Most API Gateways provide out-of-the-box functionality to enable resource and rate limiting, often with fine-grained control for different Quality of Service per consumer. This should be leveraged to mitigate the Lack of Resources and Rate Limiting (API4).

To prevent Injection (API8), there is a clear separation of roles between logic orchestrating microservices and integration components as detailed in *Platform Architecture*. This measure limits the possibility of API input being used directly in database queries.

The intense Security Review process, discussed next, helps significantly in identifying and resolving potential issues.

Security Review

Security reports generated by application scanning tools sometimes run into tens or hundreds of pages. Apart from having to reassure nervous Delivery Leads that the issues are not as bad as it appears, it often feels like we're running through a gauntlet. What helps immensely is the realization that it is far better to find an issue during internal testing which can be fixed, rather than reading about a security breach of your API on your favorite technology news site. Our detailed and uncompromising process is outlined in Figure 6-14.

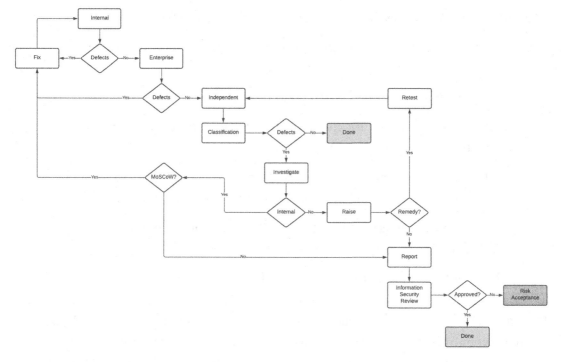

Figure 6-14. *Security review process*

Some quick highlights:

- Security tests are conducted by three teams, hailing from different competencies. From previous experience, we learned that we could cut out 80-odd pages of a security report with a stricter input validation strategy. To identify issues like these and to prevent our Delivery Lead unnecessary anxiety, security tests are first conducted by our internal Quality Assurance team before we request the Enterprise Security team to review. Thereafter, a test is scheduled with an independent, external security consultancy.

- The security report provided from the external test is reviewed and reclassified by Information Security – with severity typically being bumped *up* a level. That is, medium to high and high to critical.

- To assist prioritization of fixes, issues or defects found are classified using the MoSCoW (Must have, Should have, Could have, or Won't have) method.

- Issues identified may also fall outside the team's domain of control – such as configuration updates needed on shared enterprise components. In these cases, we still retain ownership of the issue while it is being investigated and resolved by external teams.

- The reclassified security report is owned by the Marketplace team, and both internal and external resolutions and updates are incorporated into the delivery cycle.

- Security tests are often re-run once updates have been applied to confirm resolution and identify new issues which may have been introduced with the fixes.

Summary

In this chapter, we started by taking a wider view of the importance of Security in an API Marketplace implementation. As noted, it touches on every domain and due attention and importantly respect to this purpose is critical to the integrity and longevity of your implementation. We then narrowed in on API security and considered three integration patterns. The first is Open APIs which are generally accessible but require credentials for tracking and controlling third-party access. Business to Business (B2B) APIs are used for to achieve system-to-system integration and limited to a smaller, more familiar audience. Using certificates as a security mechanism may simplify the network requirements for this integration pattern.

Finally, we discussed the most popular and widely used, Business to Consumer (B2C), pattern. With this pattern, an end user provides consent for a third party to initiate a request on their behalf or to access their data. To understand how this can be achieved using industry standards, we delved into significant detail of the OAuth process. With a firm understanding of actors, scopes, grant types, and access tokens, we reviewed supporting processes such as Application Registration and stepped through the Client Credentials, Authorization Code, and Refresh Token grant types. The ability to revoke permission is extremely important and is a non-negotiable requirement for any implementation.

We then covered a variation of OAuth which is used for Open Banking and observed how the intent plays a pivotal role in this approach. A way to compromise end-user credentials was also discussed, and I would encourage you to continue actively seeking out other opportunities for exploit. This would allow your team to pre-emptively address these issues – the resolution may be an update to process instead of technology.

We examined the Open Web Application Security Project (OWASP) Top 10 API risks and suggested how some of these could be addressed through smarter design, careful development, and leveraging the capability of the products in our stack. Finally, we ran the gauntlet of our iterative Security Review process which slowly but surely helps to identify and resolve gaps in our armor.

Over my career I have been extremely fortunate to have worked with highly skilled individuals who are as passionate about security as I am about integration. I would encourage you to seek out these tomes of knowledge, sit at their feet, and listen attentively and humbly while they will undoubtedly point out the flaws in your implementation and use their sagely advice to make your platform battle-ready. Due to the nature and area of operation of an API Marketplace, it will be under constant attack.

CHAPTER 7

API Design

Crafting the interface for an API is an activity that can be considered from a number of perspectives. For a Developer, it is fairly trivial as the set of inputs and outputs are well defined and if not, can be easily added later in the process. For an Enterprise Architect, this is a burden akin to Atlas propping up the world on his shoulders as the interface should be well thought through, be reusable by multiple consumers from the present and future, and should be able to withstand any tectonic shifts from the backend provider. For the API Product Owner, the interface should be clean, clear, and easy for Third Parties to consume. Regulators would define an interface which caters for a wide range of consumers which would require sophisticated documentation drawn up by ex-NASA Apollo engineers.

At one end of the spectrum, Design is an extremely important phase of the development lifecycle, and the gravity of making the right decisions can result in analysis paralysis. Additional pressure is introduced into the system when the product will be consumed by external third-party providers as changes or updates cannot be contained. In an active API ecosystem, a poorly designed interface can result in low developer adoption and possibly reputational damage to the product and the Marketplace.

At the other end, the API, although important, is simply a means to an end, and getting a specification out as quickly as possible will ease pressure from a demanding consumer. This might result in a custom interface which will satisfy just the one consumer, but that injustice can be addressed later – with more time and energy.

The APIs in our Marketplace have been built from multiple perspectives and at various points in the spectrum referenced above. This is a process that we are still refining and optimizing. In this chapter, I will share our experience, learning, and pitfalls to allow you more insight into our Design process. These can be adapted to your Marketplace implementation. From a convention perspective, I refer to the interface consumed by an external party as the northbound interface and the backend interface consumed by the Marketplace as the southbound interface.

© Rennay Dorasamy 2022
R. Dorasamy, *API Marketplace Engineering*, https://doi.org/10.1007/978-1-4842-7313-5_7

Design Strategy

Before we embark on the discussion regarding *how* to define APIs, let us pause briefly and consider the following question:

What VALUE does your API add?

Try to answer this as honestly as you can – there is no right or wrong response as it ultimately comes down to the requirements from the enterprise. Is the organization's intention to establish a presence in the market and this is simply a tick-in-the-box exercise to publish an API? In this case, the implicit value that could be added is that the organization meets regulatory or compliance requirements. Or is the objective to create more API products than a rival organization – with the preference on quantity for increased bragging rights rather than quality. In this case, your Marketplace appears closer to the top right quadrant of a popular survey. Perhaps this is a pilot initiative with a single confirmed consumer with the requirement that the APIs will be used by a larger audience later. Value in the short-term is to enable a single consumer and in the medium-to-long-term, multiple consumers. It could also be a genuine response to establish your organization as a Platform provider to enable a new digital channel for third-party providers to leverage the capability of your enterprise to build and launch their applications and services. This could result in long-term value for the organization as it would create a new revenue stream.

It is vitally important to reflect on this question as it essentially drives the strategy behind your API design. For example, regulatory requirements may have forced your organization to expose APIs for third-party consumption. The first iteration of your Marketplace could be to meet this objective by a regulatory deadline. The strategies outlined below, which will be used to build your API products, are driven by the objectives of the API Marketplace. Having a firm understanding of where trade-offs have to be made will help to shape the identity of your APIs, its adoption, and areas of improvement for later iterations.

Top Down, Pre-defined

These are standard APIs which all organizations must adhere to. The Payment Services Directive (PSD2) is an example. The advantage to the consumer is that the integration solution is built once and can be reused across different providers. The advantage to the provider is that the interface is pre-defined and only the implementation needs to be added. The challenge with this type of integration lies in the mapping between the northbound (external facing) and southbound (backend) interfaces. As the northbound interface is designed to be as general as possible, there are typically a wide range of inputs and myriads of combinations.

From our experience in implementing a PSD2 interface, we found that the southbound interface belonged to a niche mainframe application which has been loyally serving specific needs of the organization for many years. Our unenviable task was synonymous to patching hundreds of fine fiber-optic strands on one side to tens of vacuum tubes on the other. At the end of a mapping exercise to bridge the two interfaces for this type of integration, I generally feel the same way when I find extra components at the end of a pre-packaged product assembly. The way to establish confidence that the mapping has been done correctly is to rigorously test the solution and have the backend provider confirm requests are received and processed correctly.

A further drawback of this type of interface is that the organization loses its unique identity. Consumers would rightfully argue that a unique identity for each provider would significantly increase their development timelines. From the perspective of a provider, standardization makes it difficult to stand out from the crowd. Your API product simply becomes a new endpoint in the directory of providers. The mainframe solution, although archaic, could have some marvelous functionality which a third party could have leveraged. Unfortunately, this ray of sunshine would be covered by the blanket of uniformity thrown across the interface.

Bottom Up

Most northbound interfaces are driven by their southbound counterparts. In contrast with pre-defined APIs, these are products forged in the image of backend functionality. The unique, beautiful rays of functionality sunshine, mentioned in the previous section, that would otherwise be smothered by a standard interface, can shine brightly for the world to see and consume. The challenge that now presents itself is in determining which pieces of functionality and data to expose. In addition, special caution must be taken to avoid bleeding data structures from the southbound interface. That is, external consumers should not be impacted by subtle changes from the backend provider.

From an honest review of our API catalogue, there are a few which I am not entirely proud of. These are also absent from our Developer Portal. There will come a time during your Marketplace journey when the API production line cannot keep up with consumer demand. As much as I consider this to be an enviable position to be in, this can sometimes result in poor short-term decisions with long-term consequences.

I clearly recall the discussion with the Product Owner regarding an API urgently required by a key Marketplace consumer. The team had been working flat-out, and there was no capacity to harvest the API, especially within the prescribed timelines. The weary decision reached was that we would publish a version 0.00001 of the API. What this translated into was essentially a passthrough interface. Our proviso, which allowed us to retain a shred of pride in making such an abysmal decision, was that this API would be revised at a later time.

As most delivery teams know, most solutions that reach the operational environment are almost impossible to reverse. As luck would have it, the data model of the backend platform is one of the worst I have seen in my integration career. The consumer of the API published from my platform probably feels the same way about the interface I have published to them as I feel about the interface I have consumed. The challenge with creating API products like these is that it becomes the responsibility of the team to own and maintain for the duration of the lifecycle. Even if a new version is created, it is extremely unlikely that the consumer will be able to update their integration to the new interface if it is stable.

To avoid this situation from arising in your platform, it is important to have strong support from project sponsors who can shield the team from consumer pressure. As our platform gained more maturity, we have been able to handle requests of this nature in a better manner. Our current delivery process would require the re-prioritization of solutions currently in development or possibly a later scheduling of the required functionality. An upfront "No," although unpopular, may result in a better long-term solution. Having a defined process into our demand pipeline has also resulted in consumers planning more efficiently, which has resulted in a significant drop of last-minute requests.

Consumer-Driven

This type of design strategy generally starts with requirements from a single consumer with a key directive that the interface should be designed to support multiple consumers in the future. Our platform was recently tasked with bridging the divide between a new, externally hosted digital platform and core, internal enterprise capability. At the start of the project, the Marketplace team took solemn oaths to build northbound interfaces that would be reusable for other third-party providers. Evidence of our commitment to this goal can be seen from our API naming conventions and standards. It was designed in a way that would allow easy consumption by other parties.

The impetus provided from this mission objective has resulted in southbound integrations to almost every backend platform in the organization. When backend providers challenged us, we stepped aside and let the momentum of the digital platform juggernaut roll over them.

We soon realized that juggernauts are not delicate creatures as they also impacted our delivery process. As our team received more and more consumer specific business requirements, we struggled to maintain the sanctity of a generic, reusable interface. We attempted to stand firm and clearly signaled that the changes would impact the reusability and extensibility of the API. The logical left side of my brain agreed with the decision to make the change as, at the time, there was only one consumer. The emotional right side was gutted as this would result in us reneging on our promise of creating a reusable product.

We attempted to mitigate the spread of this contagion by first isolating payloads, then operations, that would be consumer specific – with the view of rehabilitation at a later point in time. Unfortunately, we have not been successful, and the current prognosis is amputation of specific APIs in our catalogue. This may seem a tad dramatic, and I hope you recall the analogy when you have a similar experience.

The key message that I would like to impart to you is this – if your journey starts with a single consumer, choose your battles carefully. As illustrated in Figure 7-1, be sure to abstract any key backend southbound integration into reusable integration components. For your northbound interfaces, determine which can be isolated and split these off into generic interfaces. As an example, Reference Data APIs are prime candidates as a generic interface. Rather than designing for future consumers, who may never turn up, pay the necessary respect due to your primary consumer by publishing a specific API that will satisfy their requirements.

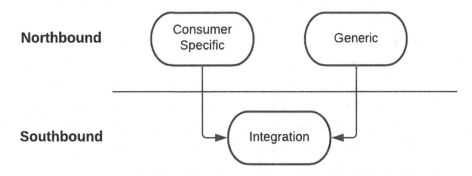

Figure 7-1. *Consumer-specific integration approach*

What helped me reached this conclusion is that without demand from this specific consumer, we would not have *any* API product to start off with. I would like to impart some sagely advice – don't boil the ocean by trying to reach the target state on your first move. Allow your platform the latitude to have consumer-specific interfaces with the view of creating generic and reusable integration components for later use. That is, instead of building a single product and slicing and dicing later, build multiple, segmented products from the start.

Build Your Own

If the Top-Down strategy provided a readymade interface you had to implement, the Consumer-Driven approach was driven by single user's requirements, and the Bottom-Up approach was influenced by backend systems, there was not much to design from an interface perspective. The Build Your Own strategy is one which allows the API Marketplace team full autonomy in defining the vision and purpose of an API. In much the same way that an artist creates a beautiful sculpture from a block of stone, chipping away the rough edges until the finished product is achieved, you too will undertake the same process. There will be no rigid regulatory bodies, demanding single consumers or outdated legacy backends to shield you from the ire of developers who have trouble consuming your API.

With that being said, the blank canvas to create your own beautiful mural of an interface is a rare opportunity and a brass ring which should be seized with both hands. What has worked for us as a team is a rigorous and thorough review process. We sometimes refer to this as the "Apple Design" review. Fans and critics of Apple would both agree that the end user product is both functional and elegant. This is not achieved by osmosis but is the result of numerous stringent design reviews and iterations. The same must apply to your API product. Accept at the outset that there will be numerous iterations and large amounts of rework. Friendships and alliances should be temporarily set aside, and the target should be set at nothing short of excellence.

During a recent API design review, there were a number of suggestions for improvements and questions raised regarding functionality and usability. After the first round of review, the direction agreed upon was to use a generic, open approach which would allow easy extensibility, but would require greater developer education. I was fairly pleased with this strategy as it mapped well to the middleware, integration components which were already in construction. To be honest, we were far along in the development process, with the API Gateway implementation almost complete, when a question was raised regarding usability.

I won't lie – going back to the drawing board, especially as the colors of your mural are starting to dry, is tough. It is only natural to want to defend the current position. What helped was the realization that the new direction of the end product would result in a simplified approach and greater developer adoption. I was lucky – we caught this midway through development. There will be API products which might launch but will need to return to the drawing board. This must be ingrained in the team culture – the need to rework, refine, and optimize until the final product is perfect.

It should also be highlighted that running the gauntlet of the design review process helps to solidify principles regarding the product definition. These principles proved to be essential supports when we received a challenge from a backend team regarding additional input elements. As much as the API can change, be ready to defend the identity of the product you have created. In short, if you firmly believe in a particular strategic direction, do not be afraid to stand firm.

Considerations

There are many factors to consider when designing an API. Some, to be considered early in the process, will be used as a filter to separate the wheat from the chaff. Others will be used to understand the form and function to ensure the delivered outcome can achieve the desired capability. Stages could be explicit, such as detailed performance requirements, or implicit, such as the navigation of architecture design reviews of your organization. In the following sections, we consider some of these factors, our experience and methodology during the design process to filter, understand, and build better APIs.

Viability and Feasibility

This is one of the most vital but potentially, difficult considerations, during the design process. Central to this is the realization that not all APIs are suitable products for a Marketplace. When an opportunity for a new product arises, the Product Owner, supported by the Engineering team, must perform due diligence by responding to one or more of the following questions before work formally commences.

- Is the product in compliance with enterprise risk, security, and data privacy policies?

- Is there demand from third-party developers for this product, and/or is it something an external provider can use?

- What are the dependencies on downstream systems and what are the timelines?

- What is the development effort and complexity to build the product?

- Will the forecasted explicit or implicit revenue model sustain the product throughout its operational lifecycle?

The output of this process is not necessarily a binary one. As part of understanding the product, the team may shape it to enable better viability. Dependencies on downstream systems and timelines could be mitigated through the use of a phased or iterative rollout of the product. It may also be prudent to engage third parties regarding the potential adoption of the product to determine demand. If the product leads to future potential opportunities, it could be funded in the short term from an operational perspective with the long-term view in mind.

An API product, although digital, is similar to a physical one. Before work commences on the build, the team must have at least a high-level view of the time, cost, and effort to create and operate it.

Requirements

Agility is one of our current team's greatest strengths as we are able to respond, pivot, and maneuver in light speed, in comparison to other parts of the enterprise. Unfortunately, it is sometimes our Achilles' Heel as we do not pause to consider the wider context of the problem statement. Our mitigation to this threat, learnt through some tough lessons in the operational environment, is to bolster our demand process with a clear definition of the API requirements. It is still possible to maintain an Agile approach, but it is necessary to have a clear view of the playing field and context of engagement.

This clarity can be achieved through Functional and Non-Functional requirements. The very mention of this terminology is likely to result in a shudder from fellow developers as this is synonymous with the traditional, sometimes hallowed practice of Enterprise Architecture. Before you skip to the next section, consider the amount of rework if you design and build a path for a solitary cyclist and a caravan of 18-wheeler trucks arrives. Conversely, consider the development effort wasted for the reverse scenario.

Based on our experience, the following are some of the questions we now consider before providing resourcing, development, testing, and delivery timeframe estimates:

- **Performance**: What are the anticipated volumes for the interface? What are the response times and associated service levels of supporting systems? This has a direct impact on the scaling of our platform infrastructure as a high-throughput API could require additional hardware capacity.

- **Availability**: In the event of a supporting system not being available, should the request be queued and retried at a later time or should an error be returned to the caller? If the request should be retried, the API Marketplace platform requires capability to handle asynchronous requests.

- **Maintainability**: Which operational team will field end user queries? What is the support process regarding tracking an operational issue across support teams?

- **Onboarding**: Who will deal with onboarding, due diligence, commercial legal agreements of third parties wanting to consume the service?

- **Reporting and historical data:** What are the key metrics to be reported on, frequency, and availability of reports – from a publishing and historical perspective?

- **Business rules**: As a new channel into the enterprise, we strive to keep business rules out of the Marketplace. Ideally these should be maintained centrally as backend logic instead of being duplicated in channel logic. If it cannot be hosted centrally, what are the business rules, level of complexity, frequency of change, and timelines required for change?

It should be highlighted that these are *some* of the areas we consider when building a new API. For some solutions, when working with a known backend, we consider just a subset. In the spirit of agility, we also commence backend integration in parallel to allow us to hit the ground running once the requirements have been established and a high-level design is formulated.

Caution should be advised when providing delivery estimates, even with the proviso of revision as any estimate is likely to be considered as binding – especially in a high-pressure environment. Another mitigation strategy, possibly easier to achieve during the early phases of your implementation, is to launch an API under the ambit of a "beta" banner. This allows some flexibility for rework if required. There must be a firm timeline for this phase as a prolonged testing phase might scare off external consumers of your API.

Documentation

A key element, instrumental to the success of an API product, is documentation. I cannot emphasize this enough. Unfortunately, from several years of development experience, documentation is generally tacked on at the end. The greatest API product cannot and will not achieve its potential without the requisite level of documentation to support it. Just as the lines of code reflect a developer's legacy, documentation that details the use of the API represents a legacy the team will impart to future consumers. Details regarding the API such as behavior and operation, parameters, inputs, and outputs should be included in the definition, also referred to as the swagger, of the API. The relationship between documentation and definition is symbiotic, and both should evolve, preferably at the same rate and importantly, simultaneously.

This is a feat easier described than achieved and is one of the activities which must be undertaken by the team rather than a single individual. As a Developer, I really enjoy coding. An area of coding I sometimes consider a boggy marsh as it slows me down is naming a variable or operation. The reason for my angst is that I want the name to make good sense and to resonate with a future maintainer of my code. The same can be said for documentation. The member of the team shaping the definition may be able to provide only a few terse words or phrases to describe it. As the definition is reviewed, the documentation must be peer reviewed, updated, then sent on for Engineering Lead and Product Owner review and feedback. If team resourcing permits, this task would be best achieved by a Technical Writer.

As highlighted in an earlier chapter regarding *API Consumption*, there are different types of consumers of the API product. Technical documentation will satisfy the needs of a Developer. Details and guidelines regarding the commercial use and application of an API product are essential for a business audience. It is also necessary to market and position an API to bring it to the attention of external consumers. The various types and levels of documentation must be considered during the design phase of an API product.

Governance

Governance is another topic that could scare the agile developer. However, it has immense and wide-reaching benefits to the APIs the team will build, and the Marketplace will host. It should be considered as early as possible in the development lifecycle and continuously. I am sure you will agree that there are very few things as disheartening as seeing a project or initiative, which you have invested significant time and energy into, shelved due to non-compliance. Within our organization, the Enterprise Architecture (EA) team is tasked with ensuring solutions are designed and built in accordance with a specific direction for the enterprise.

Our relationship with the EA capability went through a metamorphosis, inversely proportional to the maturity of the platform. Let me explain this statement. In our MVP phase, we did our level best to skirt around Governance and Enterprise Architects. The primary reason was that the Marketplace initiative, not to mention the underlying technology, was so far from what the organization typically did that we were afraid that we would arrive to work one morning and find out desks cordoned off with bureaucratic red tape. I clearly recall our first submission at the Solution Alignment Forum where our approach to get partial approval was to label the initiative as "Research & Development." That is, we were allowed to continue, but only under laboratory conditions and strictly warned to return for further approval.

Over time, we discovered that the insight and advice from the Architecture review process allowed us to navigate other areas of delivery more efficiently. For example, having approval to use a document-based datastore afforded us the use of an enterprise service.

We learnt and continue to learn how to navigate the Design Review process more efficiently. The key principles are respect and humility. Respect for the process – the governance structures which might seem arduous to delivery teams but is there to protect the enterprise. Respect for the Enterprise Architects – at times, the questions and feedback seemed completely out of context, but in hindsight has saved us a considerable amount of time in the operational environment. Humility is one of the most important attributes which is at the heart of our Governance journey. The ability to process feedback and make the necessary changes will ultimately result in a platform which is in alignment to enterprise standards.

Through a process of maturity and awareness, the project now allocates sufficient time for thorough preparation for a Design Review. In addition, we have enlisted the assistance of a Lead Architect, who acts as a journeyman for the submission, streamlining it as it navigates through a number of internal updates and reviews from key Enterprise Architects prior to the date of presentation. This has also assisted our project team and Marketplace to establish a deeper connection with the enterprise.

Access Mechanisms

There are many ways in which the API may be accessed. SOAP (Simple Object Access Protocol) and REST (Representational State Transfer) are both web service communication protocols. There are also exciting options like GraphQL which are available. The approach should be determined by the type of consumer or client accessing the API, programming language, environment, and application requirements.

Your Marketplace would be well equipped to have a number of options available and the ability or flexibility to choose the best at design time. A large portion of public APIs are REST APIs. I would suggest the first APIs published in your Marketplace are RESTful as there are several resources and reference sites to benchmark against. In this section, we discuss and contrast the different access mechanisms.

SOAP

SOAP exposes components of application logic as services rather than data. It is programming language, platform, and transport agnostic. As an established World Wide Web Consortium (W3C) standard, it has pre-built extensibility in the form of error handling and automation. It is highly extensible through other protocols and technologies.

In addition to WS-Security, it supports WS-Addressing, WS-Coordination, WS-Reliable Messaging, and a host of other web services standards. If you need more robust security, support for WS-Security offers additional assurances for data privacy and integrity and provides support for identity verification through intermediaries rather than just point-to-point, as provided by SSL. Another advantage is that it offers built-in retry logic to compensate for failed communications. This comes at a cost as it is a more heavyweight choice for web service access and as it uses a complex XML format, it tends to be slower.

REST

A RESTful API is an architectural style for an API that uses HTTP requests to access and use data. Objects in REST are defined as addressable URIs, and are interacted with using the built-in verbs of HTTP – specifically, GET to read, POST to create, PUT to update and DELETE to delete, etc. The core concept is that everything is a resource. As it is built in close alignment to HTTP, it can be used practically anywhere on the web and is commonly used when exposing a public API over the Internet.

REST allows a greater variety of data formats and coupled with JavaScript Object Notation (JSON), is generally considered easier to work with due to a smaller learning curve. It offers better support for browser clients and does not require expensive tooling to work with. As a more efficient approach, it is generally faster and uses less bandwidth than SOAP.

GraphQL

GraphQL is an open-source query language for APIs, developed by Facebook in 2012 as a data-fetching API. It has grown in popularity as it was open sourced in 2016. A graph refers to resources that are more complex and relational. Fetching complicated graphs requires round trips between the client and server. As a result, REST APIs often result in over/under fetching. Over fetching is when more data is fetched than required, whereas under fetching is the opposite, when not enough data is delivered upon fetching.

GraphQL is instead established around schema, queries, and resolvers and rather aims to improve upon REST by allowing the client to ask for a specific piece of data, not just the entire block. There is no need to process a long stream of data – you only get what you ask for. And what you ask for could be compiled from several different REST APIs. REST works well in the context of a thin client, such as a web application hosted in a browser as a major part of the processing is done on the server. GraphQL leverages the capability of a more powerful client, such as a mobile device which hosts an Application.

Patterns

An API product is similar to an iceberg, with only ten percent protruding above the surface of the water, and a massive portion beneath. Third parties will only see the polished, published interface and associated documentation. The core of the product, which might be more intricate, lies in the implementation. There are a number of approaches for building the product and the following is by no means an exhaustive list. As your Marketplace matures and evolves, you will add your own variant which will serve the unique needs of your organization. It is easy to become entangled with classifying a product into a specific pattern. Try to avoid this pitfall. As a digital platform, the products do not necessarily conform to classic architecture convention. This is what affords the platform agility and flexibility. In short, allow a product to color outside the lines.

Synchronous

Our first microservices were built using a Digital Integration framework which was geared for integration into a single backend as illustrated in Figure 7-2. Back then, it was completely plausible that there was only one backend to integrate to. After all, the pure definition of a microservice is an atomic unit of function. In the early phases of the platform, this pattern served most of our needs perfectly. This approach is also a great starting point for most API platforms.

Figure 7-2. *One backend*

As requirements from the Consumer-Driven approach became more complex, it became necessary to string together calls into different backends. This was done under the banner of a tactical approach with the long-term aim to move this logic into dedicated middleware services. To make extremely aggressive project delivery dates, we added more logic to our microservices and found ourselves with implementations detailed in Figure 7-3. Based on several years of integration experience, this type of implementation gives me severe vertigo.

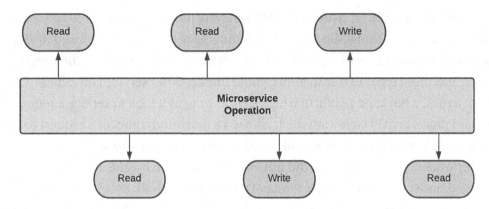

Figure 7-3. *Complex business logic*

If this sequence flow had a single write operation, it may meet the minimum criteria to be allowed to continue to exist. Unfortunately, there are further write operations in this process flow. To the more lenient developer or architect, this may be an acceptable approach. My concern with this approach is in maintaining the consistency of a transaction across the process flow. If the first write works and subsequent writes fail, the transaction or request is in an inconsistent state. In traditional middleware platforms, this is where message queues and rollbacks are critical to ensure transactionality. My firm stance is that this type of integration logic is best maintained in an environment which has the necessary tools and services to support it.

Unfortunately, the tactical approach yielded far better delivery times than the strategic one, and pseudo-transactionality has been achieved with storing transient state and replaying requests. My advice is to never allow your microservices to reach this level of complexity as you're building a house of cards. I refer to this type of microservice as a Monolithic Microservice. Avoid it at all costs.

Asynchronous

We were initially fortunate as the backend platforms we integrated to responded within milliseconds, seconds at worst. As we assimilated different backends and added more business logic, we found the latency of requests steadily creeping up. For some API operations, it took more than a minute to complete. Do not waste time and energy railing against a mainframe application for taking minutes to provision a customer record. Although minutes to a digital platform is a lifetime, in a mainframe context, it is light speed.

This quickly became an issue as the API Gateway timeout was set at 60 seconds. It escalated into a significant issue when the custodians of the Gateway refused to allow us to increase the timeout – and rightfully so. An API Gateway is not geared for long running requests, and these types of transactions would impact other service consumers. Caught between a rock, a backend platform which took as long as it took to service a request, and a hard place, an API Gateway which allowed a maximum time for a request to be processed, we had to find a new way of execution for these use-cases.

Unfortunately, our constraints did not end there. Like an escape artist bound, submerged under water and under threat of an imminent shark attack, another parameter we had to deal with was network firewall restrictions. The microservice was not allowed access to a service outside the corporate network, without some elaborate reverse proxying through the API Gateway, which would double development time.

Without this restriction, we could have simply implemented an async-callback pattern shown in Figure 7-4. The caller initiates the request, passing a return URL which is invoked at the end of the process. If your microservice platform is not hosted in Alcatraz, this is a far more efficient asynchronous processing pattern as it allows an event-driven architecture.

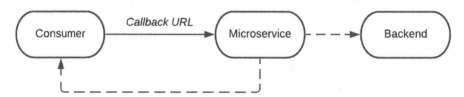

Figure 7-4. *Async-callback*

The solution eventually adopted is an Async-Polling approach as detailed in Figure 7-5. A *Callback Identifier* is returned to the consumer on an API initiation. The microservice continues processing the request and updates a datastore with the response upon completion. In the meantime, the consumer polls the microservice using a dedicated operation to determine if the request has been completed. Although not as elegant as a callback mechanism, the inherent benefit is that the microservice is not burdened with responding to the consumer. The responsibility shifts to the consumer to determine the transaction state.

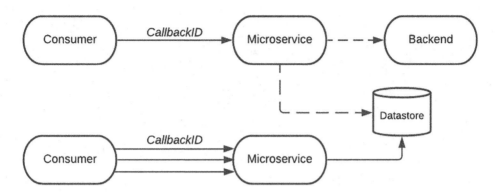

Figure 7-5. *Async-polling*

The Proxy vs. Tap Debate

Solution design to achieve an API product is never a dull affair in our team. As an example, consider the following scenario which has come up based on a recent API product requirement and, in full transparency, is the subject of significant debate within the team. As our API Marketplace is now considered an entry point for external third parties to access the organization's services, we were requested to host an API for a specific business requirement use-case. It is a niche function, which will only be accessible to specific consumers. As a result, it will not appear in the externally published catalogue of API products. Furthermore, the nature of the transaction is that it carries a highly time-sensitive customer request. That is, if the request is not processed successfully within milliseconds, it could result in potential revenue loss for the merchant consuming the interface.

The approaches to achieve this requirement are contrasted in Figure 7-6. On the left is our current approach which we have dubbed the "man-in-the-middle" pattern and on the right is the new "tap-and-go" strategy. Proponents for the tap-and-go highlight that as the Marketplace is not an integral participant in the transaction, an observer role should be adopted. As an observer, only information necessary for monitoring and insight should be extracted. Supporters of the traditional proxy approach highlight that this product should be implemented in accordance with the standard design philosophy.

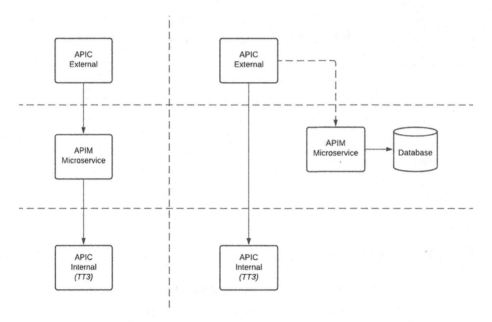

Figure 7-6. *Proxy vs. tap*

In true gladiator style, the team has elected to race both solutions all the way to the staging environment. This allows us the flexibility to choose the best solution as requirements for the API were clarified and as performance test results became available.

From a traditional application development perspective, this may appear to be extremely inefficient. I consider this to be one of the greatest advantages of our Marketplace. A flexible architecture coupled with a highly agile and capable team allows multiple solutions to be built and tested to determine the best approach to be used.

Lifecycle

The design process represents the embryonic phase of an API product which will grow, change, age, and ultimately expire. If we consider an API product in this way, it allows us the flexibility to evolve it and constantly make it better. Changes to the interface should be made carefully as these impact consumers of the API. There are other dimensions to consider, which can and should change. We consider some of these in the following sections.

Developer Experience

Feedback from actual consumers of the API is an incredibly vital input to the design process. An API product approved by backend teams, Legal and Compliance, and delivered by the Technical team with little end user value will stay on the shelf waiting for its best before date to expire. We unfortunately have API products in our Marketplace which fall into this category. While building the API, it can become easy to stumble into the trap of "if you build it, they will come." An early warning sign is difficulty in finding an actual use-case that an API would support. Step into a third-party consumer's shoes and critically evaluate how it would help you achieve a specific outcome. If you have trouble with this task, chances are that the third party will too.

Feedback from potential third parties should be solicited as early as possible regarding demand and adoption. This might be a challenge during early phases of the Marketplace as the developer community itself is still forming. Third-party adoption is also the first step in the process and the relationship requires constant attention. During the initial phases, assistance with understanding the function and use of the API can be achieved using documentation, guides, and tutorials. As uptake increases and the API gains traction, increased functionality can be added to the API product. As an example, an Insurance API product may start with providing a quote for personal insurance cover. A later iteration could include quote acceptance and policy issuing. Thereafter, other types of cover could be added. Revisions and updates to log claims could also be considered.

As this example illustrates, try to get a revision of the API product out as quickly as possible instead of waiting for the full product set to be available. Defining a roadmap of when features and functionality will be available is a plus but may not be a key pre-requisite. That is, if there is strong third-party uptake of the initial API revision, it may create momentum to convince backend enterprise teams to expose further functionality. It may be tricky but try to keep the product roadmap flexible – more popular or requested features should be allowed to bubble up to the top of the backlog. A key mantra, highlighted in the chapter on Consumption is – *without third-party consumption, there would be no traffic. No traffic, no revenue. Revenue sustains the Marketplace which exists to achieve the Vision.* Third-party and developer reception and feedback is a crucial element of the Design process.

Versioning

One of the greatest advantages of an API is that multiple versions can exist simultaneously. I will highlight at the outset that this is by no means a license for poor design. Care and consideration must always be taken when publishing an API. Versioning essentially decouples consumer and provider and allows both to continue on their own release trajectory. If the functionality from a specific version continues to satisfy the requirements of the consumer, there may be no need to move to a later update. Newer versions of the API also allow the provider to publish additional functionality which can be adopted by a subset of consumers.

Most API Gateways provide this capability natively, and the complexity of different versions is handled at this level in the stack. Minor revisions are updates to an API with no breaking interface changes, and on each deployment, all API consumers are automatically subscribed to the updated product. If there are changes which will require an update from a consumer, a new product is created which will require subscription and update of endpoint configuration.

It is also important to consider the changes to the Developer Portal and supporting documentation when adding a new API version. As the maturity of your platform grows, Release Notes detailing the change for every update – from minor to intermediate to major – should be published. This is also a signal regarding the transparency of the Marketplace to your external developer community.

An approach which has helped our implementations immensely is providing early access to new versions to only a subset of external consumers. This not only allows us to determine consumption behavior, but to also determine gaps in coverage – be it in API functionality, documentation, or understanding. Be warned that this is also a time-consuming activity as it is often a many to one effort. The many in this case is many members of the delivery team to the one external developer who could not consume the API due to a misspelt variable.

On a final note, I would like to highlight that the identity of an API should stay the same. Versioning should be used like different lenses of a telescope to adjust contrast and focus to bring the product into better view. If there is a significant difference or change in direction of the product, it may be prudent and more responsible to your consumers to create a variant or possibly a new product.

End of Life

A recent mail I received from a Development Manager of a backend team had me gob smacked. It read as follows:

> *Subject: Decommissioning <System> API v1 and <System> SOAP v5, v6, v7*
>
> *Message:*
>
> *Hello Everyone,*
>
> *We are planning to decommission old version of <System> SOAP and API versions in Prod on <date – in 10 days>.*
>
> *These are currently disabled in DEV, TST and QA for more than a month.*
>
> *Should you have any concern decommissioning of these versions, kindly contact myself and…*

My first reaction was one of panic as I frantically checked the latest code in our integration component to determine the versions our Platform consumed. This soon gave way to relief as I found we were fortunately using API v3 and SOAP v8, respectively. As the jolt of adrenalin dissipated, relief was replaced by anger. Although our platform was safe, for now, this was extremely poor service from a key southbound provider. Consider an application using an older version of the API in a production environment which did not have the need to test within the last month. If this application was in operational mode without a development capability, they would be in for a rude awakening in just 10 days!

This was extremely callous and irresponsible behavior from the provider. If there was a pressing need to retire the older versions of the interface in a short space of time, it is the responsibility of the provider to draw a list of consumers – from API subscriptions or security access configuration and then contact each one directly to confirm the older version can be retired. Sending an email announcing the retirement of an API version in 10 days is simply not an acceptable practice.

This is an example of the consequence of an API built off the cuff, possibly to satisfy a specific consumer requirement, without a defined lifecycle. The date of end of support/retirement of an API must be clearly defined at the moment of its birth, when it is published or when a new version is released. This follows the practice of any commercial software release. It is an indication by the provider of their commitment to support the product until that specific time and allows the consumer to plan migration off that version. I believe that this demonstrates maturity and is the basis of trust which is a key foundational element of your API Marketplace.

Keep in mind that a third-party consumer is making a significant decision to use your APIs for their application, product, or service. There will most likely be funding for development at the start of their journey. By providing clear information regarding the timeline for availability of the API, the consumer can factor this information into financial, business, and development planning.

Design Guidelines

In much the same way that an apprentice gets more adept and skilled with experience and under the tutelage of a mentor, your team will fast become better at defining APIs. As part of this process, there are generally accepted guidelines and standards to be considered. These are platform and product agnostic and can be applied to almost any definition. There are great examples and references of API Platforms, from Twilio to Facebook to Google. These can be used as a guideline when defining the standards and conventions for your Marketplace. We consider a subset of these guidelines in the sections below.

Error Handling

Returning error information to a consumer is a key element of an API. HTTP status codes, as detailed below, are generally considered the best practice to return the execution result of an API call:

- **Success**: Successful processing of a request is indicated by a 2xx HTTP response code. The 200 OK code is most popular. Other codes such as 201 indicate creation of a resource, and 204 indicates that a request was successfully processed, but no results were found.

- **Client errors**: Client errors are indicated by a 4xx HTTP response code. Client errors indicate a problem with the client request, such as missing required parameters or an authentication failure. The issue must be fixed in the client application and submitted again.

- **Server errors**: Server errors are indicated by a 5xx HTTP response code and need to be resolved by the provider. This could be due to a downstream system outage. The client can resubmit/retry the request until it succeeds.

As a point of departure, you can start with the following and add on as required:

- 200 – OK

- 400 – Bad Request

- 500 – Internal Server Error

Status codes are intended to be consumed by machines. Messages providing more information regarding the error should also be included. Try to include as much detail regarding the issue as possible.

For example, if the request could not be processed due to a missing required parameter, specify the name of the parameter(s) which were missing. This will not only help the developer determine the root cause but also save your Support team from fielding a potential request for assistance.

Be careful not to bleed internal system information in the response message. For example, including a stack trace in your error message. This compromises your API as it exposes internal implementation details and could also be a potential security risk.

Filtering and Pagination

Always attempt to engineer the interface for performance. Ever increasing network and CPU speeds may result in the development of interfaces which could burden consumers by returning large datasets and providers with wide-ranging queries. From my time in an Operational middleware environment, I have learnt that the threads servicing requests are finite. As a request comes in, a worker from a pool of threads is assigned to process it. You need to do your best to ensure that the worker returns to the pool as quickly as possible to be able to service more requests. If all workers get busy, requests start to queue. Keep in mind that the consumer considers the request as active from the moment it is initiated. If a request is in a queue before it can be processed, it could result in timeouts to the consumer.

The DevOps engineer on the team is about to interject with the argument that a containerized platform can easily scale to manage high traffic conditions. This is a fair point but consider the scenario from the backend provider perspective. This provider may not have the luxury of a scaling containerized platform and could also be servicing requests from several other channels. A burst of requests from your Marketplace could result in high system load, failed transactions, and possibly system outages. As an API designer, one of your most important responsibilities is to not only protect your platform, but also supporting platforms.

The mechanisms to achieve this and increase performance is to specify request filters and paginate responses. Filters can help prevent broad queries from reaching downstream systems. Limits and offsets make it easy for developers to paginate objects. This will also lead to more predictable execution times as processing is not linked to the size of the dataset or complexity of the query.

Software Development Kit (SDK)

When fielding requests from third parties regarding our APIs, I often have to stop and consider the query from the perspective of an external consumer. As we get more involved in the technical detail daily, some aspects of dealing with an interface almost become mechanical, and complex concepts or functions could be assumed to be easily understood. An example of a mechanical operation is configuring a security certificate in a client application. This was a challenge the team overcame many years ago and any developer can easily access samples from our code repository. As much as we would like our developer community to be self-sufficient and familiar with resources like StackOverflow, our goal is to improve and accelerate the developer experience as much as possible. In further support of the external consumer, keep in mind that the technical team may only be a single developer.

One approach is to provide code samples and tutorials which painstakingly describe the process one step at a time. Another strategy is an SDK which wraps your API and can help developers significantly with assimilating your interface and provides the following benefits:

- **Simplify integration**: Complexities such as certificate configuration, timeouts, and exception handling can be abstracted by the SDK.

- **Uniform consumption**: Policies and rules regarding API usage can be enforced consistently by the SDK as it is the entry point. Client-side validation can also be included to buffer the API from poorly formed requests.

- **Native language support**: The SDK can be incorporated as easily as adding in a software package which can be used from native code. There is no need for a HTTP client and marshalling of the request and response. HTTP status codes can be returned as exceptions.

It should be noted that an SDK is not a silver bullet and the support and ongoing effort of maintaining client-side code should be clearly understood before pursuing this measure.

Summary

API Design is one of the most exciting but sometimes overwhelming domains in building a Marketplace. In this chapter, we discussed how the definition and objective of the APIs are influenced, implicitly or explicitly, by the organizational strategy. We highlighted key considerations to filter, understand, and support the design process. Access mechanisms – traditional, current, and future – SOAP, REST, and GraphQL, respectively, were also reviewed. Patterns regarding implementation, the lifecycle of an API, and guidelines were also discussed. The golden thread of the design philosophy is that the Marketplace is an extension of the organization and its APIs are a reflection of its identity.

The output of the Design phase is the API blueprint which is the input into the Development phase which is the topic of the next chapter. In a traditional waterfall approach software development lifecycle, these were two clearly defined and separated phases. Architects passed the baton to developers and returned to their ivory towers to ponder over the next perplexing business requirement. In an agile delivery approach, the designers are very much part of the delivery capability – in our project, the designers and developers are often the same people. This allows an iterative approach to overall delivery of an API product.

CHAPTER 8

API Development

Of all the phases in the software development lifecycle, Development is my favorite. This is when life is breathed into designs and postulations and hypotheses can finally be tested. Unlike other software domains, the complexity of implementation, in an API context, is shielded by the interface. As any seasoned integration engineer will confirm, the interface allows the team to maintain a poker face regarding the level of completion of development. On many occasions, across different projects, I have sometimes published an API with a wafer-thin implementation to either get off the critical path of a maniacal project manager or to shift pressure to the consumer by bluffing with a show of readiness for integration testing.

This phase is not without its challenges. There are often times during construction of the bridge between two systems that the realization slowly dawns that the complexity of integration is far greater than anticipated. Any seasoned integration engineer will also attest to the fear of not having the required information available at the point of connection. This can be compared to the moment when you're wrapping up a 10,000-piece puzzle and find 3 pieces missing. If this were not bad enough, this generally happens on one of those solutions with a wafer-thin implementation!

Throughout my career, I have found that the development rollercoaster never follows the same route. This is possibly the primary reason why I love integration engineering. From the initial cordial meet-and-greet with representatives from an external team to the techno-jargon exchanges between developers, to the flurry of heated exchanges between teams to resolve issues, to the required diplomacy with network security to unblock firewalls, leading to the adrenalin rush of the first system handshake and finally to the relief of seeing it work in an operational context – there is always a variation that keeps it exciting. In this chapter, we delve into the detail of a number of key areas which support the development of an API.

© Rennay Dorasamy 2022
R. Dorasamy, *API Marketplace Engineering*, https://doi.org/10.1007/978-1-4842-7313-5_8

API First, Tech Second

Early in my career, I found myself enamored with Java. Specifically, Java Enterprise Edition (JEE). I dreamt of beans – Enterprise Java Beans (EJBs) – and welcomed hour-long discussions with like-minded friends and colleagues, debating the merits of stateless over stateful session beans and feeling quite pleased with the parallel processing capabilities of message-driven beans. Several role changes later, I realized that I had set my level of focus to maximum magnification which did not allow me to see the bigger picture.

Simply put, the primary objective for an integration requirement is not *how* it should be done, but *why*. This may be a tough message for development teams – but an API consumer simply expects a response to a request. The consumer is not really interested in the detail of the implementation – it does not matter if the request has been processed using the latest Artificial Intelligence (AI) cloud product or using a mainframe from decades past for processing. The main objective is a consistent and reliable interface.

With the plethora of technology options available today, it is extremely easy to go down a rabbit hole trying to find the most optimal and possibly bleeding edge way in which to implement a solution. In a budding API Marketplace, particularly in a digital context, this position can very easily become the norm. As much as I enjoy tinkering with new tech, I strongly advise restraint when solutioning. It is always important to remember that the technology serves to achieve a purpose.

A favorite example is implementing an interface to retrieve reference data. To make this seemingly mundane task a little more interesting, an eager developer may attempt to cache responses. The strategy starts off with a simple in-memory cache which will work well in the context of a single instance. But what about multiple instances distributed across different nodes in a cluster? Should the cache have data persistence which will require technology like Redis, or is it memory-based which will require Memcached? As this is the first caching implementation, where should the solution be hosted? On-premises or maybe cloud? What about a cache invalidation strategy? How and when can we get rid of stale data in the cache? Although a valid objective, you can see how the focus of the API has shifted from the *retrieval* of reference data to the *caching* of data.

I have observed on many occasions how secondary and non-essential objectives have impacted and slowed down the delivery of requirements as these tasks have become embedded into the solution. In an agile environment, the goal is to publish a minimal, functional solution as quickly as possible. Note the difference to a wafer-thin implementation which is essentially an interface with a mock response.

Returning to the reference data requirement, the first iteration to get out the door as quickly as possible, is the pure retrieval of data. By exposing an API which responds to a request, even with high latencies, the consumer can get a feel for the integration – from interface specification to the data returned. This strategy should be followed even if the requirement for improved performance was specified at design time or later during performance testing. Given a choice between better performance or faster development, a project manager under aggressive delivery timelines is likely to choose the latter. A middle ground to the performance requirement may be the implementation of a cache on the client side.

This philosophy borrows heavily from the motto of Facebook:

Done is better than perfect.

Resist the temptation to optimize an interface early in its lifecycle. Start simple and iterate. Focus on the main tasks such as mapping from source to target. *Identify* areas of improvement, such as caching for performance, paging, and filtering. Also be sure to consider other areas, which may not be as exciting to develop – such as security, validation, and error handling. With a functioning API, even in the Development environment, prioritize requirements with help from the Product Owner and the Engineering Lead. From years of experience, I am quite certain that security, reliability, and consistency would be chosen over performance. Be sure to keep the objective of the API in focus at all times.

Team Structure

Contrary to popular belief, development is more than a lone developer banging away at a keyboard in a semi-dark room. Borrowing from an African proverb that it takes a village to raise a child, it is a team effort to deliver an API. The product is more than just lines of code but is dependent on the following roles during its journey from design to implementation.

Delivery Lead(s)

Delivery leads are responsible for coordination and scheduling of activities to build the product. This is a challenging task and requires careful coordination across several streams, as illustrated in Figure 8-1, to ensure timelines can be met. A significant amount of diplomacy is required as external teams and systems may provide critical dependencies and each element must be carefully orchestrated to minimize delays.

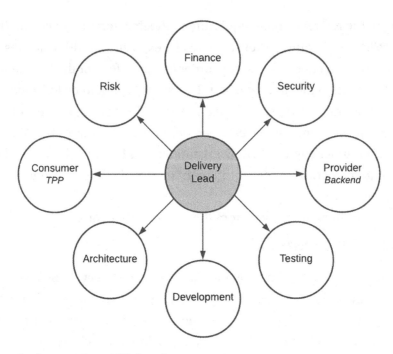

Figure 8-1. *Orchestrating API development*

Let us consider how some of the external entities take part in the development process and the responsibilities of the Delivery Lead:

- **Provider**: Will supply specifications of existing interfaces, timelines of development of new interfaces, and availability of subject matter experts to field developer queries. Any delays from the backend could impact development and testing activities.

- **Consumer (third-party provider)**: Will request specifications of the API product and timelines regarding the availability – either in a Sandbox (discussed in a later chapter) or Live capacity, and work with the Product Owner to coordinate onboarding activities such as screening and approvals to pre-empt administrative delays.

- **Finance and reporting**: Forecast timelines for product delivery and potential cost recovery from external teams, manage the budget for API delivery and operational support of the product being built, and provide regular reporting to project stakeholders regarding delivery and to manage expectation regarding timelines.

- **Development**: Ensure a smooth, uninterrupted path for developers by providing approved designs and backend interface specifications when development begins, access to subject matter experts for speedy resolution of queries, and access to enterprise resources.

As there could be a number of APIs in development at any point in time, the Delivery Lead has insight across multiple products and may prioritize the delivery of one product over another. For example, if a more urgent API requires additional developers, the teams may have to be rebalanced.

A valuable lesson, from years of project experience, is that there is a limit to the number of people you can throw at a problem. That is, some tasks take a specific amount of time and cannot be delivered faster with additional team members. It is essential that the team management understands and appreciates this concept as the adage of too many cooks spoil the broth could very easily come true as time could be lost by time lost bringing new members up to speed and splitting tasks could result in dependencies and budget over-runs.

As there are several balls to juggle, a strategy which has worked remarkably well for our implementation was to divide the Delivery Lead roles among individuals having commercial or technical focus. This allows us to have a person dedicated to chasing commercial objectives such as Finance and Risk and another person focused on closing out technical targets such as approvals from Architecture and Security. There are areas of overlap which reduces a single person delivery – the technically inclined Lead can draw on assistance from the Project sponsor, and similarly the commercial Lead is supported by the Engineering team if his counterpart is not available. This dynamic duo, as I like to refer to them, ensures that all requirements of the delivery spectrum are considered which keeps our project in equilibrium.

Developers

Integration development, by its nature, is generally fast paced as the interface between two systems is often on the critical path for overall project delivery. Whereas traditional project timelines generally run into months, our delivery targets are sprints, which could be a week at minimum, two weeks at maximum. The driver is that third-party consumers, generally working in hyper-speed paced environments, also have faster release cycles making time to market a critical factor.

Our philosophy to handle the rapid delivery cycles is to iterate on an API product in each release. That is, instead of waiting three months for a big-bang rollout, we provide basic functionality and update on each deployment. This does add some complexity to development as fixes or updates to a previous version may be required while work is underway on a new version.

There are many facets to consider as part of the Developer journey. Let us consider a few, which I consider key to success.

- **Ownership**: A significant portion of our development team are full-stack engineers. Niche skill developers may be necessary from time to time, but a developer should have the ability to solve problems outside their immediate area of expertise. As an example, a developer may suggest changes to an API definition and provide the swagger updates for review. Critical to ownership is *timely* communication. As development may span a range of systems and personnel, such as an API Gateway, microservice and datastore, communication is key for successful delivery. In a delivery cycle measured in weeks, losing hours waiting to report an issue at the next team meeting could result in missing the target date. Members of the team are strongly encouraged to attempt to resolve blocking issues on their own if possible and to escalate for assistance if they cannot. Granted, there may be some challenges such as accessibility to backend subject matter experts which cannot be overcome. In these instances, the team culture should be to pivot – make an assumption and continue, pause the activity, and move to a non-dependent task or send a message to the rest of the team indicating availability to assist with another task.

- **Unit testing**: In an agile, fast-paced delivery environment, good and proper unit testing may be one of the sacrifices made to achieve aggressive delivery timelines. I have observed over many implementations that the proverbial "can" is kicked down the road and developers hope that any issues will be identified and resolved during later phases of quality assurance. It is important that the team makes a global and conscious decision regarding the level of unit testing. In most instances, *reduced* unit testing is due to delivery pressure. Project stakeholders must understand that unit testing is a vital element of the development process and take accountability if this is short-circuited in lieu of faster delivery. This could also be mitigated by confronting the issue head on instead of ignoring it. That is, an early iteration could have basic functionality, released under a beta banner. A planned release, later in the cycle, could focus explicitly on testing and quality assurance. This strategy could alleviate delivery pressure – get a version out the door as quickly as possible but with a firm commitment to harden the solution before full rollout.

- **Documentation**: Another sacrifice made to appease the Delivery Gods is deferring proper documentation. To be honest, even the benefit of time may not result in good documentation from a developer. In a traditional, waterfall-driven project, not a single line of code would be written until the technical design was drafted. In an agile, digital delivery environment, prototypes are up and running before requirements are even fully captured, and there is always the possibility that solutions and implementations could change all the way up to and including production deployment. As a result, developers are sometimes loath to document their development as it is fluid and could change over its lifetime. One option is to accept this position and adopt a strategy that the documentation is "in the code." Another option is to create a simple template on a team collaboration wiki which requires minimum, but key information such as mapping rules between source and target systems. It is important that the development methodology be geared accordingly to support the selected strategy. Review and approval of documentation by a Team Lead should be a key requirement for the gate to transition to the next delivery phase. Without the necessary checks and balances in place, it allows the possibility of low quality or no documentation.

Each team will have their own variant of development practice tailored to the host organization. It is extremely important that all stakeholders, internal and external, are aligned and for developers to manage expectations regarding the level and quality of solution delivery during planning sessions. If timelines are reduced, all members of the team should be aware and accept that elements such as testing and documentation will have to be revisited. Instead of ignoring these issues, address it at the outset and plan accordingly, as a team. A key to the success of our implementation is that development is a team effort.

Quality Assurance

This is one of the most vital pillars of support in our delivery process. As a signal of importance, the QA or test engineer can exercise a veto to stop a release. As delivery objectives are aggressive, developers tend to test in a vacuum and primarily on happy-path scenarios. Integration testing is possibly the first time the solution is tested across different systems and in various contexts.

As part of the testing effort, the solution must be subjected to various levels of scrutiny, from standard to error to exceptional scenarios. Standard, functional and error conditions can be simulated by providing a range of valid and invalid inputs. Simulating exceptional scenarios may require bringing down connectivity components to backends to determine application behavior. A vital input of scenarios and conditions to be tested may be provided by the Operations team from experience with regular production releases.

As we have evolved our testing capability significantly over some time, we now also consider the following sub-domains:

- **Security**: During a recent application scan conducted by the Information Security team, we received a blistering report of close to 100 pages. From review of the report, we found that improved validation of a single input field would address 70 pages of the report. The remaining issues had been previously identified for other APIs and discussed. Based on this learning, we made a team decision that the security scan will be run internally as part of the testing review and approval process. This will allow the team to address any issues pre-emptively. It is important to note that this is not the end of our security review. Before a new API product is approved for release, the Enterprise Information Security team enlists an external service provider to conduct a detailed security assessment to determine if there are any vulnerabilities.

- **Performance**: Part in jest, part serious – stress testing in an integration context could become quite a stressful activity as it would require participation from downstream service providers. Performance testing of API Marketplace components should be done regularly in a loopback or environment with mock backends.

Testing with backends should also be scheduled, at a minimum every quarter. This will ensure all the elements in the end-to-end value chain can withstand load from peak events like Black Friday.

- **Automated testing**: Unfortunately, this presents a unique catch-22 for testing teams. Automated testing will undoubtedly save a considerable amount of time, especially for regression testing activities. In a frenetic environment, with multiple testing efforts underway, automated testing efforts are generally delayed. Automated testing must become part of the team culture as its execution is a core element of the Continuous Integration (CI) / Continuous Delivery (CD) process. This is the primary reason why organizations such as Netflix can release often to production.

Delivery Approach

Our Marketplace came into existence at a time when the organization had made a conscious decision to shift to a more agile delivery approach. A new Way of Work was quickly established, and it was not uncommon to find business units which had previously operated along more traditional lines huddled around a Kanban board for the morning standup. Our delivery philosophy has always been based on Agile principles, and we have adapted and tailored our approach over time to meet unique requirements.

The initial strategy for the Marketplace was more tactical. The primary objective of the team was simply to launch an API Marketplace with the hope that third-party providers would come. As a result, delivery targets and sprint objectives were technically focused which kept the team busy but did little to establish much needed roots for the platform.

A dedicated Product Owner was assigned to the initiative, and attempted to shift focus, but was often overwhelmed by a stubborn technical team. Fortunately, the platform was identified as an enabler to a much larger organizational objective which mandated more process and structure operationally and more direction and focus commercially. This has necessitated better planning and use of time, development capacity, and budget to achieve strategic objectives for the Marketplace.

The following sections detail our process, which is still evolving, for the handling of requirements as it enters the Delivery phase of its lifecycle.

Defining the Strategy

At the start of each new quarter, the project executive meets with the senior members of the team to

1. Provide a view of organization-wide initiatives and objectives. As there are many ongoing enterprise and divisional projects, this provides insight into how the Marketplace fits into the bigger picture.

2. Review progress over the last quarter and gauge the position of the platform on the planned roadmap for the financial year.

3. Identify potential risks and areas of improvement to streamline solution delivery and operational capability.

4. Define goals for future quarters and to prioritize objectives with inputs from all domains of the team.

The aim of these sessions is to define, at a high level, strategic objectives for the coming quarter in alignment with other external initiatives. It is also highly collaborative and seeks to find the middle ground to allow planned initiatives to continue without interruption but to also steer the Marketplace to be in a good position for future opportunities.

In subsequent planning sessions, which are scheduled more frequently and described in the next section, these outlined objectives are used as a compass to ensure our bearing is correct and the platform is headed in the right direction. The team ethos also allows for an update of the objectives if required. That is, if the organization requires a shift in focus to deliver a requirement of more business or customer value, the leadership of the team will reconvene to determine how it can be achieved.

Planning

During early phases of the implementation, planning was an all-day affair, with the full team in attendance. The aim was to provide visibility to all members of the team regarding upcoming requirements, and to solicit feedback and sizing of tasks. The intention was noble, but the result was that the team generally lost a full day from a sprint and often still had to investigate tasks outside the session to provide estimates. As part of our current process, a high-level Impact Assessment (IA) is compiled by the Engineering Lead at Design time with ad hoc assistance from the team to resolve any technical queries. The IA provides an indication of time and resourcing required, from which a cost estimate can be determined.

As actual development time is precious, we try to use as little as possible by requiring the technical team to join sessions only if necessary. To achieve this, the Planning effort is split into two rounds.

In the first round, the Platform Executive, Product Owner, Delivery, and Engineering Leads meet to discuss the delivery objectives for upcoming sprints. This must align with the quarterly strategic targets. Requirements are also prioritized, and there is an initial indication of which developer will be assigned to which task.

With this view in hand, a second session is scheduled with the team to provide the goals of the next sprint. In most cases, this is not the first time the team has been exposed to the requirement as their input was considered as part of the Impact Assessment activity. The sessions are focused as the objectives are clearly defined and developers do not have to endure prolonged prioritization and strategy debates. During this session, the Engineering Lead also provides a detailed breakdown of the solution and a clear definition of done. It may be very possible that a requirement is split into phases and the team has insight into this decision. Members of the team can voice concerns regarding the objective and to highlight risks and possible issues with the upcoming work. This allows the Delivery Lead greater visibility into the upcoming deliverable and to initiate steps to mitigate potential risks and delays.

As detailed in Table 8-1, there may be several initiatives active, in various states, at any given time.

***Table 8-1.** Ongoing delivery in an API Marketplace*

Stream	A	B	..	N
Design	Done	Done	Blocked	In progress
Architecture	Done	Done	Blocked	In progress
API gateway	Done	Done		
Microservice	In progress	In progress		
Quality assurance	On hold	On hold		
DevOps				
Change management				
Post rollout support				

The concurrency of tasks is carefully managed by the Delivery Leads and although it may add administrative complexity, affords the team flexibility to pivot to a new stream if one lane becomes blocked due to delays from design approval or backend readiness. This is a bane for Release Management as the Marketplace cannot forecast months in advance what will be deployed to Production but is one of the greatest capabilities of our team.

Squads

Over the lifetime of our Marketplace, there have been larger initiatives which did not fit into this rapid delivery mold. Initial attempts to bundle these initiatives resulted in a team size of close to 30. As a result, sprint ceremonies such as planning, standup, and retrospectives took a significant amount of time and were an inefficient use of the team's valuable time. Taking inspiration from Amazon's "two-pizza team" rule, which states that teams should be no larger than can be fed by two pizzas, we split the team into squads.

The definition of a squad is a self-organized, cross-functional team that has skills to deliver a product end-to-end, with limited input from others. The squad should be composed of people that can design, develop, test, and deploy the product.

We also consulted other teams which had experienced similar growth trajectories and leveraged their insight and experience. A key lesson learnt was the formation of a Platform squad which focused on advancing the capability and maturity of the base Marketplace and which would support ongoing Product development.

As illustrated in Figure 8-2, the Platform squad aims to evolve the Marketplace by focusing on initiatives such as the migration to Cloud, building Billing and Analytics capabilities which are leveraged by Products deployed to the Marketplace. The Platform squad is also long running but leaner, whereas the Product squads are spun up and down as required, with larger team sizes. This also allows more efficient scheduling of resources as teams are assembled on demand. Furthermore, the Platform squad is funded by an operational expenditure (OPEX) budget, and Products squads are funded by capital expenditure (CAPEX).

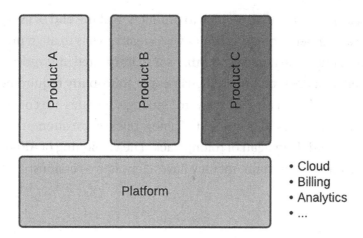

Figure 8-2. *API Marketplace squad*

Agile Methodology

Delivery is achieved in the duration of a sprint – which is a short, time-boxed period, minimum a week, maximum two weeks. As detailed in Figure 8-3, functionality is released in phases. The phased approach is based on a "Release Often" principle. We have found that solutions with a prolonged stay in Development tend to become more complex as changes from various requirements are made to shared components. A telltale sign of this occurrence is if the production and testing versions start digressing significantly. For example, production is on version 2.04 and test is on version 2.17. The greater the divergence, the more changes have been applied which increases the release risk.

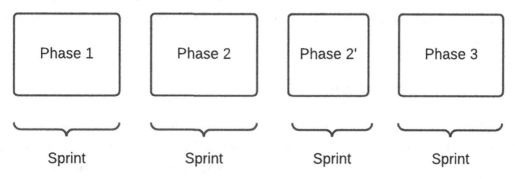

Figure 8-3. *Sprint approach*

From a release perspective, we deploy to production at the end of every sprint. As there may be a number of ongoing initiatives, a team goal is to align production and QA environments at least once a month. As also illustrated, the sprint duration may be shortened to address an updated business or third-party requirement. Faster delivery cycles also underpin our "fix-forward" strategy. If issues are encountered in an operational environment post deployment of a new release, we attempt to resolve the issue as quickly as possible instead of rolling back. The versioning of APIs affords us this luxury as the operational environment may have a few active versions.

DevOps

When I first encountered the term "DevOps" many years ago, I jokingly commented that many of the project teams I had worked on were doing this for some time – developers were writing code in production to fix issues. Now, armed with the experience of working with specialists, I understand and appreciate that this is a new and critical realm of the software development lifecycle. The *practice* of DevOps is now fundamental to the ongoing success of our Marketplace.

At the start of the implementation, it was an aspirational goal as the delivery team leveraged a manual deployment process. As discussed in previous chapters, the project was extremely fortunate to have the skills of experienced DevOps engineers for a period which accelerated our progress significantly. From observation of these masters plying their craft, I now consider DevOps engineering as infrastructure sorcery, which allows the creation of new worlds, in our case – environments, with a magical incantation, otherwise known as a Terraform script. The practice and benefit of this paradigm is detailed. In the following sections, I will focus specifically on how DevOps supports our development process.

Continuous Integration (CI)

At the start of the implementation, the Marketplace consisted of a few microservices – which could be counted on one hand. Everyone knew them well and each was authored by a specific developer. When the time came for integration testing, all members of our geographically distributed team joined audio conference calls, which sometimes lasted the entire day. The team would tensely watch on a screen sharing session as the appointed "Deployment" engineer would run through a cryptic sequence of commands to deploy the required code elements to the test environment, gasp in frustration as we found a missing configuration parameter, and finally breathe a sigh of relief when the test engineer gave an all-clear signal. This was the first iteration of our (manual) Continuous Integration process.

The process evolved, almost overnight, as the on-premises Container platform was rebuilt. As part of the rebuild, the deployment process also changed dramatically. Suddenly, pipelines were triggered on code commits which automatically built and deployed to the next test environment. Once functionality was confirmed in lower test environments, the developer would initiate a pull request which had to be reviewed and approved before the code change could be merged into the main branch. This action would also trigger a higher-function process which would deploy the component to a staging environment. The deployment process would not set it as the active version. An Instant Message (IM) had to be sent to a middle-earth wizard, Gandalf, a chatbot, who would then magically update configuration in the Kubernetes cluster to route requests to the new version. Gandalf only took instruction from specific hobbits on the team which maintained the sanctity of the release process and readily assisted by reverting to previous versions if an issue was encountered.

The deployment process was beautiful in its simplicity, shielded the development team from significant backend complexity, and introduced an explicit, repeatable, and reliable process to be followed for migrating code between environments. If the deployment or test failed due to a missing configuration parameter or code bug, it forced resolution at the source – which triggered the pipelines and process to resolve it. Our implementation was extremely fortunate to have been visited by time-traveling DevOps engineers from the future. Any time benefit was lost when they suddenly left, and the team had to support and update a seemingly complex release process.

The key lesson I would like to impart, from this experience, is to build your CI pipeline iteratively. Lay the foundation with the fundamental principle that there will be no manual deployments. Then put in a simple process and iterate. There are great open-source CI tools, such as Jenkins and Cloud offerings which can deploy to on-premises infrastructure.

Once you have established a simple, stable, repeatable process, slowly phase in elements such as versioning, chatbots, and automated tests. Automated tests are crucial to Continuous Delivery, which is discussed in the next section.

Continuous Delivery (CD)

At a point in our journey, an over-enthusiastic engineer added in several additional validations to the pipeline, which stalled the process. Developers are an industrious bunch, and the team found a way to sidestep the validations. The goal of adding in extra validations was noble and if followed to the letter of the law, would have resulted in higher quality code elements in the target environment. Unfortunately, and in all honesty, the team development maturity was not at the required level.

Anyone who has read the blog detailing the Netflix release process aspires to reproduce the same for their development environment. Frankly, the idea of checking in code and having it deployed to production 16 minutes later is a utopia we still strive for. It is important to remember that this process may have taken time to achieve, is possible due to the Netflix system architecture, and may have the support of the full enterprise. It has always been one of our key aspirational targets to have a streamlined Continuous Delivery (CD) process but be aware of the context of your organization. As an established enterprise, we must adhere to strict governance gates at each release phase. There are also external systems which we are dependent on which use traditional mechanisms, that is – manual deployment. Also, to be fair, required service levels for a financial institution may be far more stringent than Netflix.

My recommendation in this regard is to focus and optimize the phases of the CD process you can control. Any deployment to a production environment, let alone automated, is a massive responsibility and should be done with great care and consideration. An automated deployment process can only be achieved with commitment from the full delivery team. When a developer uses a new external code package, an enterprise security scan should be run as part of the build pipeline to determine any vulnerabilities. Developers must also include detailed unit tests as part of the commit, which is run as part of the pipeline. Code coverage tooling must be included to confirm adequate unit testing. The quality assurance team must create new automated test scripts, based on business requirement scenarios and not simply rehash the developer's unit tests. Upon successful completion of the automated unit and functional tests, the full team should be confident enough to approve the component for deployment. CD is even more about people and process than about the enabling technology.

Microservices

A recent post-mortem review of a batch synchronization solution, which had grown into a monolith to address operational issues, provides a great example of how a Microservice approach enables DevOps. Figure 8-4 provides a view of the As-Is approach on the left and the proposed To-Be design on the right.

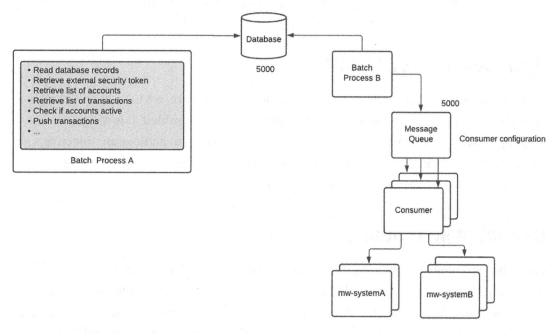

Figure 8-4. *Monolith vs. microservice*

There are several benefits of decomposing the solution into smaller components. From a design perspective, it allows a change from synchronous to asynchronous process execution by adding a messaging platform. More importantly, from a DevOps perspective, it shifts operational control and power away from the Developer to Operations. With the earlier process, the original developer of the solution was always required to discuss performance issues. The new approach allowed the DevOps team to scale the runtime solution without any development changes. Concurrency could be controlled through configuration by specifying the number of consumers of the message queue. Connections to source and target systems could also be scaled independently by adding in more replicas of middleware microservice pods based on defined service levels. So DevOps is not limited to automated provisioning of infrastructure and CI/CD pipelines – it is an important consideration of the detailed solution design.

DevOps is a *practice* and must become part of the team ethos and culture. It is a part of every step of the journey – we discuss Monitoring and Logging, another key supporting element of the Operational domain in a later chapter. From a team resourcing perspective, be sure to include one, possibly two, dedicated DevOps Engineer roles. Establishing and iterating the CI/CD process is an important foundational element, and a simple, basic process must be available as early as possible in the development lifecycle to prevent the possibility of manual deployments.

Application Development

As discussed in the chapter detailing our Platform Architecture, we have been through many iterations regarding the way our microservices are assembled. It is still an ongoing activity as we find new and improved ways in which to achieve an objective. The following sections detail our process and technology approaches to building implementations which support products of the Marketplace.

Development Guidance

From the experience of several solutions which have reached the operational environment, I would like to highlight the importance of keeping in constant contact with developers throughout the development process. Agile environments are fast, and this may sometimes result in chaos. Once the API design has been completed and the integration approach is defined, it will be handed over to the development team to build.

This is the point where the vision of the Engineering Lead must be clearly communicated to the developers to ensure the solution is built according to the correct pattern. I like to think of this process as "painting the target." It follows the military approach of an infantryman in the field shining a laser onto a target which a missile fired from hundreds of miles away can home in on. As teams are most likely geographically dispersed, sometimes across continents and time zones, take nothing for granted. A line between two boxes in a component diagram could be interpreted in a myriad of ways by a developer. For example, the connection could be made synchronously or asynchronously; it could be done via HTTP or gRPC.

The developer might not be aware of an available downstream integration another team had just built and might unerringly duplicate effort. Be sure to outline the definition of done at the outset and to take the time to have detailed solution implementation sessions at the start of the development process and at regular checkpoints during the sprint.

An approach which worked extremely well for one of my most challenging projects, even with a junior team was four standups, then a sit down. At the end of the week, midway through the sprint, we conducted a detailed review with the team to determine if delivery was on the right trajectory. These detailed reviews may even go down to the code level. Regular checkpoints ensure that issues can be identified earlier, and there is sufficient time to resolve. Without regular reviews, the issue will most likely be found in the operational environment. This is a key process which must be ingrained into the team's delivery methodology. Note that this is not micromanagement or mistrust of the developer but is a call for the senior members of the team to take more responsibility for the end delivery.

API Gateway

I consider this element in much the same light as a passport control function at an international airport. Each API Gateway product implementation, from various software vendors, may have a unique set of features and capabilities. For our implementation, we have made a concerted decision to leverage the standard, vanilla capability to allow easy migration in the future. A large driver behind this decision is that the Gateway infrastructure is a shared, enterprise service and customization could impact future upgrades or other tenants. The key principles of our API Gateway development are as follows:

1. **No transformation or protocol translation**: The key objective of the Gateway is to proxy a REST API. The swagger definition published to third-party consumers matches that of the microservice – direct mapping.

2. **Well-defined requests**: From my experience with SOAP, I attempted to sneak in an *<any>* type of request to speed up development. It turned out that generic payloads are viewed in very much the same negative light as *<any>* XML requests and my suggestion raised alert levels with the technical owner of the API Gateway and resulted in increased scrutiny for future requests.

3. **Lightweight**: API Gateways are not ESBs or Process Engines and do not have the same time tolerances. There are no long-running processes. Requests should be processed as quickly as possible. The enterprise timeout standard is 60 seconds, which is quite lenient considering that a popular Cloud provider API Gateway PaaS offering is a non-negotiable 30 seconds. Be sure to remember that the API is most likely supporting a customer's digital experience and millisecond response times are required to retain the audience.

4. **Security**: Specific third parties can be granted access to certain APIs by controlling subscription. Access to "Live" APIs can only be provided once the third party has been approved. There are several access mechanisms ranging from a client identifier and secret to token based access. Additional controls such as client certificates and jws-signatures can also be applied for more sensitive APIs. The biggest benefit to the development process is that this complexity can be handled by the gateway product and the downstream components are shielded.

5. **Rate limiting**: A great feature, which is key for an environment with many new third-party developers, is the ability to throttle requests. A third party could accidentally or intentionally trigger a large number of requests – which could result in a denial of service, impact other API consumers, or flood downstream systems. This can be prevented by specifying the number of concurrent requests and number of requests in a set timeframe. This is out of the box functionality which can be achieved with a configuration update rather than custom development.

Microservices

Figure 8-5 shows the key types of microservices in our platform, their interaction pattern, and the use of platform services. To provide greater insight into the internal microservice operation, I discuss the components in greater detail.

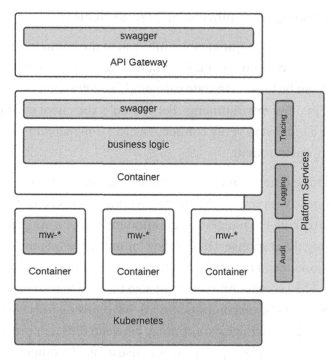

Figure 8-5. *Microservice architecture*

Middleware components are used to integrate to backend systems. These are dedicated components which are used as gateways to southbound platforms. The component encapsulates the integration logic and complexity and exposes a simple business interface for consumption. A middleware component can only connect to a single backend. A key principle is that cross-communication between components is not allowed. That is, one middleware component cannot call another. Figure 8-6 details the internal architecture of a middleware component.

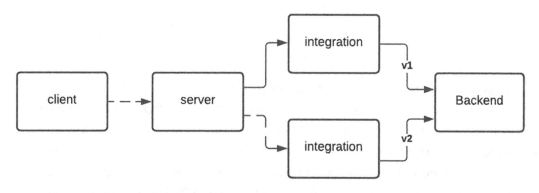

Figure 8-6. *Anatomy of a middleware component*

Working from left to right, the function of these elements is

- **Client**: This is used to initiate the gRPC call to the component. It is used during development and for unit testing. Using a *port-forward*, the client can be used to initiate calls directly to components deployed in other environments. For example, the client can be used to initiate a request to verify connectivity to a downstream system in the testing environment.

- **Server**: This element contains the "plumbing" to service the gRPC request. Responsible for unmarshalling, transforming the request, invoking the integration component, transforming and marshalling the response. During development, the response from this component can be mocked in the event of a backend not being available. The server component can also be used to route requests to different integration components. We have successfully used this approach to effect a migration strategy between different provider interfaces. The simple approach was to use an environment variable to reconfigure the route at runtime.

- **Integration**: The objective of this element is simply to interface with a backend system. For reasons of abstraction, there are no gRPC references in this development, and it can be tested directly from the command-line without any upstream dependencies. The component is responsible for handling various types of responses and error conditions which may arise during the request. Application-specific rules such as mapping of error codes or setting default values are also made within this component as a means of consolidation and isolation. It is generally advisable to have a dedicated integration component for a specific interface. This keeps code elements clean and allows easy maintenance.

Logic components orchestrate the process flow to achieve an API product implementation as illustrated in Figure 8-7. For example, an API product to retrieve a Customer profile could leverage a number of middleware components to assemble the response. The response from one system could be interrogated and transformed to construct the request for another. It is extremely important to differentiate between application and business logic. Routing a request to a middleware service to create a customer is an example of application logic. The process to create the customer record is an example of business logic. As the Marketplace is a new channel to the enterprise, it should leverage centrally owned and controlled business processes.

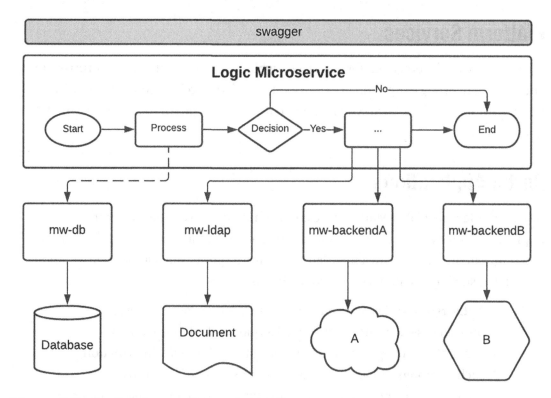

Figure 8-7. *Logic microservice orchestration*

The northbound interface of this component is typically the swagger definition which is published on the API Gateway. This simplifies the integration between API Gateway and microservice. Another key function of this component is policy enforcement. Depending on the nature of the API product, the microservice may perform validation and verification such as confirming end user consent before fulfilling the request. To streamline process execution, requests to middleware components can be initiated concurrently. A gRPC stream can also be used to optimize processing of requests. As an example, for Optical Character Recognition (OCR) of a document, we initiate the call to a middleware component which then initiates a request to a local enterprise service and to a Cloud vision service. Once the request is processed, a response is returned in the stream. If the first response received was not successful, the component waits for a second response in a best-effort approach to process the request. If the first response indicates successful processing, there is no need to wait, and execution continues.

Platform Services

All microservices leverage platform services, which are packaged as an enterprise library and imported during the build. As discussed in Platform Architecture, this provides a uniform "utility service" layer which allows consistent support and management of the microservices.

Portal Applications

A User Interface in an API Marketplace context may seem oxymoronic. From implementation experience, web applications are one of the mainstays of the platform, and front-end developers are a mandatory staffing requirement. Our implementation has built custom applications for the following use-cases:

- **Authorization**: The consent page, which is presented to the user, post successful authentication and as part of the OAuth flow is a custom portal application. This is used to retrieve user information, such as profile and account data, and present a richer consent screen. For example, instead of providing a simple permission screen to grant access to all account information, we present a detailed list of accounts and allow the user to select specific accounts which may be accessed by a third party.

- **Third-party onboarding**: As a digital channel, an aspirational goal for our implementation is to ensure the full experience is as automated and streamlined as possible. As discussed in Chapter 3, the platform must scale to handle large numbers of external consumers. To achieve this, a custom portal was required to facilitate the onboarding process, from requesting company registration documentation, to the acceptance of terms and conditions to the supply of banking information – based on the API product. It is key to note that the web application is an access mechanism and key to this objective is a well-defined business process flow.

- **Administration**: This allows an interface to the Support team to change runtime configuration data such as property values and endpoint configuration data. The benefit of providing a UI is that it ensures consistent, uniform access, which is secured, audited, and versioned – so changes can be tracked and rolled back if necessary. More importantly, it minimizes access requirements to supporting systems such as databases and configuration maps, in the case of a Kubernetes cluster.

- **Hosted applications**: This is certainly a unique use-case but is also a significant revenue stream for the platform. It is also an example of a pivot by the team to maintain delivery momentum. The squad delivering a strategic set of API products learnt that the pilot consumer would not complete development in time for rollout by Black Friday. As a delay would essentially result in missing this key event, the squad made a tactical decision to build and host elements of the application, on behalf of the third party, which leveraged the new APIs. The development effort required from the third party was significantly reduced and with well-placed redirects, the User Experience also preserved. The approach was so successful that it gave rise to a new deployment pattern. The benefit is that the hosted application can be reused by several third parties, broadens the audience as integration is significantly simpler, can also leverage internal services which might not have been externally published, allows our enterprise to shape and tailor the user experience, and increases user confidence as the end user is interacting directly with the enterprise.

Summary

In this chapter, we discussed a key development philosophy that technology serves to support delivery of the API. We also identified roles that contribute to this activity, implicitly by clearing blockers on the delivery path and explicitly by writing the code and examined our approach to planning and managing concurrent activities. Establishing a DevOps *practice* and adopting Continuous Integration/Continuous Deployment principles helps streamline the development process, adds more stability and predictability, and supports existing and new development resources. Finally, we delved into Application Development, strongly motivated for more communication and guidance during this process and considered core elements of our platform, and finally reviewed types and objectives of portal applications.

It is important to note that these approaches and processes took time to define and refine and are *still* evolving. It has been tailored to the requirements of our implementation such as a geographically distributed team and the use of shared enterprise capabilities. Personality traits of a customer obsessed, broad-shouldered Project Sponsor who constantly backs the team, Delivery Leads who set a high bar and hate missing deadlines, stubborn Product Owners who will not compromise, and Engineering Leads pedantic about leaving a legacy in code have also been instrumental in forging a formidable delivery capability. In the next chapter, we discuss the Sandbox environment, the role it plays in the API Marketplace ecosystem, and strategies regarding how it can be implemented.

CHAPTER 9

Sandbox

The Sandbox is a demarcated, carefully cordoned off space which allows consumers to test and use your APIs to get a feel for how they function. Of all the technical challenges, achievements, and breakthroughs over the lifespan of our API Marketplace, it was a revamp of the humble Sandbox which proved to be the tipping point for me to write this book. Our initial Sandbox strategy was relatively simple and catered for a specific spectrum of API products. As the platform grew, matured, and evolved, this construct and approach remained unchanged. In much the same way that a Jitterbug or Charleston step may function in today's dance era, it just seemed out of place. The team had recognized for some time that the approach needed a serious overhaul, but the priority was always bumped down in favor of other "more important" deliverables.

This was possible due to the unique combination of API products and third-party consumers within the platform ecosystem – as you will note from the strategies outlined below. However, a perfect storm was brewing which mandated a specific scenario to be tested and signed off before a key consumer could launch their offering. As fate would have it, this scenario cut clean through our Sandbox strategy and threatened not only to bring out one of our oldest Technical Debt skeletons from the closet but to also ask it to do the Moonwalk. The pressure from the commercial team to launch the solution to market was converted into momentum and impetus which brought upon not just the re-engineering of our Sandbox – but also a re-imagining of its purpose and function for our platform.

It is this unique synergy between engineering and imagination which is the core of our implementation – and hopefully yours. From observation of this unique trait yet again working its magic in and throughout our Marketplace, the call to at least attempt to capture its essence in this book became too loud to ignore. In the following sections, I will share my thoughts regarding Sandbox purpose, process, strategies, and ways in which to implement them.

© Rennay Dorasamy 2022
R. Dorasamy, *API Marketplace Engineering*, https://doi.org/10.1007/978-1-4842-7313-5_9

Purpose

I consider the following metaphors to best describe the purpose of a Sandbox – *kicking the tires, allowed to run around with scissors, try before you buy*. As you might imagine, making an investment or associated commitment to a specific API provider is a significant decision. For intra organization projects, the risk factor is minimal – project teams on both sides of the integration requirement have little choice and *must* integrate. For an API Marketplace implementation with pre-defined interfaces, consumers may be wary of having an expectation of a three-pin plug and finding a two-prong euro socket – and rightfully so.

One of the functions of the Sandbox is to mitigate this concern. From experience as an integration developer, I can assure you that reviewing an interface specification, even a well-documented one, is far different than initiating a request from code to an endpoint and receiving a response. Developers get a tangible opportunity to map a specification to function and importantly, can verify if the API is a fit for the use-case. "Fit" also needs to be understood from many perspectives.

Consider the following abbreviated interface definition:

```
...
paths:
 /customer
...
 parameters:
  -in: customerID
...
 responses:
  200:
...
```

Although the interface may satisfy the requirements for the third party, the *behavior* of the interface is also a key factor. Suppose the above function is made up of several queries to backend providers to compile the response and as a result, the overall latency of the call is greater than 30 seconds. This latency may have a significant impact on the end user's experience and may impact the decision to consume the operation. This may also result in a feature request for an operation which provides a subset of the data with a faster response time.

The Sandbox enables an engagement point for these discussions to occur. Its context, relation, and function relative to the "Live" environment are shown in Figure 9-1. As the diagram shows, a request that traverses the "Live" route eventually reaches a backend provider. A request processed in a "Sandbox" context is serviced by an element I refer to as a "*Virtualiser.*"

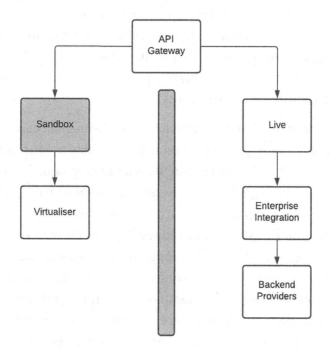

Figure 9-1. *Sandbox and live context*

Used tactically, the Sandbox provides a unique opportunity for the Marketplace team to publish an API product, for which an implementation does not exist. There could be several reasons for this:

1. It can be used to determine the level and extent of consumer demand for an API product. In our engagement with third-party providers, we have learnt that there is often a gap between intent and implementation – that is, consumers express interest in an API but do not follow through. The Product Owner can use a Sandbox product to determine *actual* consumption as an indicator of third-party commitment.

2. In addition, the hotspots or mainly consumed functions can help shape the product. Difficult or complex operations will naturally attract less consumption and can be easily identified for simplification or possible termination.

3. It can also be used by the delivery team to release the API in phases – where more popular operations are provided earlier. This helps alleviate pressure on the development team and allows more quantitative analysis when planning a release. That is – the Product Owner can clearly show hotspots, which translate into demand, for specific functionality.

It is extremely important that this approach is used with great caution. As I've mentioned previously – developers have a remarkable ability to sense a ruse and once trust has been broken, it is difficult to regain. With that being said, the approach is to stay one, preferably more, steps ahead of the consumer. Be open with the phase and objective of the API – consider the disappointment if a developer builds a solution around the product and the decision is made not to continue. Also, be clear on timelines. There is little more frustrating for a third-party developer to have vague or non-committal dates regarding availability of a specific product or feature in the Live environment.

It is also important to note that the "Sandbox" construct is maintained across Development, Test, Staging, and Production environments as shown in Figure 9-2. This decision has served to reinforce our commitment to ensuring that the Sandbox is fully tested and verified internally before changes are deployed for external consumption. In addition, the Production Sandbox environment is considered a *full-blown* operational environment. Changes and updates are subject to the same governance, and any support is provided on similar operational levels.

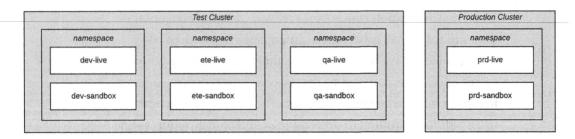

Figure 9-2. *Sandbox across all environments*

Process

The Sandbox is as important to the host organization as it is to the third-party provider. It plays a key role in our onboarding process and is used as a quality gate for many reviews. The first review is for the third party to showcase the application that will consume the APIs. This provides tangible indication of the use-case that will be launched to market. It will also demonstrate successful consumption of the API and its role in the application.

The second review is for functional testing of the third-party application. Calls originating from the consumer are traced through the Sandbox to confirm the accuracy of request payloads and destinations. For this reason, our Sandbox environment is fully representative of the Live environment, from an operational perspective, as it also has the same support tools and processes.

It is important to note the support requirement and context for the Sandbox environment. While the service levels may not be as stringent as Live and we may be slightly more tolerant of service outages, the audience to be supported is developers. This is typically the first port of call for the first application a developer will write, and although the detail may be provided in the documentation, various types of requests and approaches will be attempted as part of the API consumption process. Processes must be well defined for Developer support, and it is imperative that the Sandbox environment can withstand a barrage of ill-formed requests without keeling over and requiring support intervention. Given the use-case, automatically restarting failed components or stuck processes to ensure service availability may be an accepted practice.

As your Marketplace implementation matures, consider implementing a self-service capability to facilitate Sandbox access. Registration and sign-up should be seamless to allow development to start as soon as possible. Be sure to also highlight the onboarding process and use of the Sandbox environment to potential consumers to align expectations and provide an indication of timelines.

Sandbox Strategies

As our initial approach to the sandbox had not changed since the launch of the platform, we chose to use the re-engineering opportunity for maximum impact. Fair enough – there was an immediate need that had to be resolved urgently. But there were also a fair amount of other skeletons that we were keeping in the Sandbox closet that were not fond of any dance steps. With that being said, we were also careful to control the scope to stay focused on the task. Given the set of API products in our Marketplace, the first objective was to identify the potential use-cases:

- **beta**: Products being considered for further development or in the development process with changing definitions; important to track consumption usage patterns.

- **Backend Simulation**: Relatively simple "ping-ack" API, which are atomic in nature; preferably read-only operations; responds with a well-defined, standard response.

- **Shallow**: *Intercept-early* pattern for API products with orchestration across many backend systems; calls across one API product could impact others.

- **Semi-Live**: API products which allow controlled and limited access to a live backend system.

- **QA**: Access to the internal Quality Assurance testing environment of the organization.

In the following sections, we dive into more detail of each Sandbox strategy by examining the purpose it intends to fill, the approach, pros and cons which will drive its use, and finally, how it can be achieved technically. I would be especially keen to learn of any new or hybrid approaches you might have implemented for your platform.

beta

This strategy may be used for one of the following reasons:

- To answer the question – *If we build it, will they come?* As delivery teams may be lean to keep costs and overheads low, building the right product for the right audience is key to the overall success of the platform. It is essential to spend time and focus on products which are required and will be consumed when launched.

- To define and shape an API product. The ability to test and refine certain features could improve adoption and consumption in the long run. This could also be used to address complexity of interfaces long before a single line of implementation code is written.

- To buffer backend delivery from strong consumer demand in a cat-and-mouse game of *staying one step ahead*. Simply, implementation of the API may be falling behind – possibly due to internal development or external backend provider delays. This approach can be used to publish a working interface while the implementation catches up.

Approach

Tracking and recording of third-party consumption is essential for this approach as the value is in the analysis and insight from the data. Usage patterns should clearly indicate the consumers, APIs, and operations. The interpreted metrics could form the basis for discussion with users of the API to identify what worked and what did not.

As these APIs may still be in the "inception" phase, performance data such as latency of calls to backends may not be available. This must be considered as part of the API design – for example, it may be prudent to use an async call-back approach to compensate for possible long-running transactions.

Based on the nature of the API, it may be necessary to restrict access to a closed user group. For sensitive or strategic APIs, only specific third parties may be allowed access to retain institutional intellectual property and possibly competitive advantage.

Table 9-1 illustrates the pros and cons of this approach.

Table 9-1. *Pros and cons of a beta Sandbox strategy*

Pros	Cons
Rapid response from conception to implementation	Not representative of actual backend behavior
Quantitative measure to determine third-party consumption	Third-party interest may be low due to volatile or dynamic nature of APIs
Define and refine API products interactively with active feedback from third parties	Prolonged timelines from Sandbox to Live implementation may lose trust of third party
Ability to test and verify design approach and assumptions	
Used to buffer implementation delays	

Use-Case

This strategy would typically be used during early ideation and conception phases of API Product development. Can also be used to understand consumption patterns and to shape an API product. It is important that third-party expectations are managed accordingly since the API is a work-in-progress and subject to change and possible termination. May also be used as a mechanism to engender trust with select third parties through an "invite-only" access policy.

Design Considerations

As illustrated in Figure 9-3

- There may be no Live implementation.

- Static responses may be stored in files.

- Interactions are logged in the database for analysis and insight.

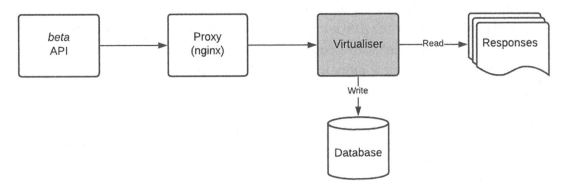

Figure 9-3. *Design of a "beta" Sandbox environment*

Backend Simulation

This is best used for *simple* APIs which satisfy *all* the following conditions:

- APIs which are serviced by a single backend provider.

- The API operation is typically a *read* function. There are no state changes to the provider and the operation is implicitly *atomic*. For example, an API which returns customer data.

- Responses from the backend provider are fixed or well-defined. Continuing the above example, the backend responds with (i) customer data, or (ii) a *business* error indicating the customer is not found or (iii) a *system* error indicating a technical failure.

Approach

The approach to create a Sandbox for these *simple* APIs is possibly the most *complex* as it is achieved by simulating the backend provider. The API call travels through all the elements of the Platform stack, blissfully unaware that it is executed within a Sandbox context. When it reaches the middleware component for interaction with a backend provider, the call is made to a "*system virtualiser*" which returns a pre-defined response if it can match a specific value in the request. Different responses and behavior from the simulated backend can be elicited by varying the input data. It is also possible to simulate system failures and varying latencies for more representative behavior.

Table 9-2 illustrates the pros and cons of this approach.

Table 9-2. *Pros and cons of a Shallow Sandbox strategy*

Pros	Cons
Call traverses the full application stack for more representative behavior	Full deployment of all components to Sandbox environment has a higher resource footprint
Responses can be configured or parametrized based on specific request data	Only suited to simple, read only operations
The nature of API product allows a quick turnaround time for implementation and updates	Static responses are used across all third-party consumers – no or limited customization
	Rigid or fixed response may potentially limit additional use

Use-Case

This approach is best suited for API products backed by a single provider for data retrieval or read operations. It also functions well in contexts which support static responses across many consumers. In our case, updates to the *system virtualiser* initially required development effort. As the Testing team were delayed waiting for developer availability, the Test Lead spent time understanding the framework and has since taken ownership of this capability. Scenarios are updated and added through the modification and creation of new data files. At the last check, I found the Testing team writing code to mimic a backend more accurately.

Design

As illustrated in Figure 9-4

- The *system virtualiser* is configured to return defined responses based on specific values in the request.

- Endpoint configuration of middleware components is updated to route to the *system virtualiser*.

- This requires a dedicated operational environment for execution. It does require a similar deployment strategy but does not require similar scaling as the Live environment as performance requirements would be lower.

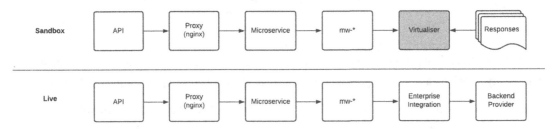

Figure 9-4. *Design of a Backend Simulation Sandbox environment*

Shallow

As you might recall, there was a specific scenario which brought on the update to the Sandbox. The early products in our platform were relatively simple. That is, there was typically a single backend provider which could be serviced by the *Backend Simulation* strategy. Over time, as more middleware components became available to integrate to backend systems, microservice orchestration logic gradually grew ever more complex to satisfy business requirements. This soon became a juggernaut which could not be stopped due to delivery targets and objectives. Before we knew it, some of our APIs were achieved with complex processes as shown in Figure 9-5.

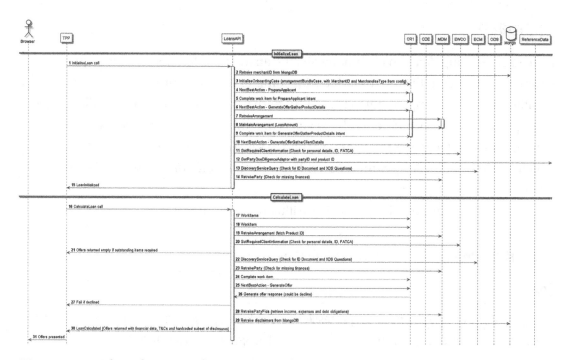

Figure 9-5. *Flow diagram showing complex orchestration logic*

Unfortunately, the request to create a Sandbox version arrived before we could fulfill our solemn promise to simplify the orchestration logic. The challenge with using the established *Backend Simulation* approach was that it needed complex data setup as a single transaction spanning multiple systems. What added to the complexity was the *write* operations for some of the steps. After many attempts, the team soon realized that the customization of the *system virtualiser* made it almost unsupportable and would be a nightmare to update.

In a typical *"think outside the box"* approach, the solution we discovered was at the furthest point from the source of the problem. By taking a step back and posing the question from a consumer's perspective, the primary objective of the Sandbox integration was to get better acquainted with our APIs. Essentially, the third party is simply looking for a representative response given a request. How this is achieved behind the abstraction afforded by the interface is not a Sandbox concern. By reframing the problem statement and considering it from a different context, the purpose of this Sandbox strategy is to allow third parties to test API products with complex orchestration logic spanning many backend systems, with potential write operations which cause state changes.

Approach

Instead of teaching skeletons to moonwalk, the answer was to intercept the request early *before* it entered the microservice with complex logic and process the request in a parallel, but *shallow* implementation. This pattern may appear to be very similar to the *beta* approach. The key difference, however, is that this was an API product with defined contracts we needed to maintain, and we had to satisfy the requirement of state changes which would be managed *per* third party. The technical solution is discussed in further detail later in this chapter.

The pros and cons of this approach are illustrated in Table 9-3.

Table 9-3. *Pros and cons of a Shallow Sandbox strategy*

Pros	Cons
Caters for APIs with complex business processes spanning multiple backend systems	Not fully representative of the Live solution as it is processed in a parallel flow
Ability to manage state per third party	Additional software components to maintain and support
The custom solution allows easy configuration and update to handle new requirements	
Smaller resource footprint as microservice and middleware components are not deployed	

Use-Case

This approach allows a neat and elegant solution to keep the Sandbox APIs aligned with the Live implementation. It also allows state to be maintained per third party to cater for more detailed integration scenarios. To elaborate – a *Shallow* approach would provide the same response in a *ping-ack* fashion. Using this strategy, third parties would receive updated datasets based on operations performed. It should be considered for solutions with medium to high complexity spanning two or more backend systems.

Design

As illustrated in Figure 9-6

- The request is processed in a parallel flow.

- Details of the Technical design for this approach are provided later in this chapter.

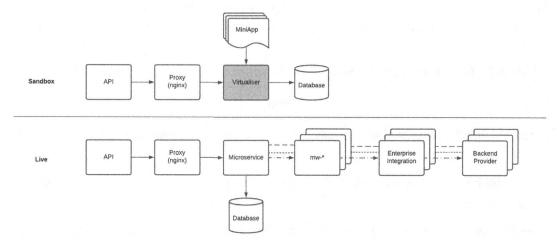

Figure 9-6. *Design of a Shallow Sandbox environment*

Semi-Live

The essence of this approach is that it connects the Sandbox environment to defined Live interfaces. As the distribution graph discussed later in this chapter shows, this is not a common Sandbox strategy. I have observed two use-cases which were highly dependent on a Live interface.

The first is the Twilio Messaging environment. Developers can send messages which terminate on a user's device. Twilio ingeniously allowed testing of the WhatsApp API by sending a specific keyword to a shared WhatsApp destination that links a mobile number to a developer's test account. Free credit of $20 in value is initially provided and additional credit can be added for further testing. This is a fantastic example of the ability to earn revenue from the Sandbox environment.

In the second instance, we found that it was necessary to connect to the Live security service to generate a token which would be used on subsequent calls in the Sandbox environment.

Approach

As fond as I am of this strategy, I am equally wary. I consider it as the opening of
Pandora's box and strongly advise caution regarding its use and potential abuse. The
approach can be implemented by simply updating endpoint configuration and routing
a request to a Live backend. Throttling of Sandbox API requests is critical as a third party
may unwittingly cause a Denial of Service by initiating a flood of requests. With a more
mature ecosystem, it may be possible to charge consumers for transactions.

The pros and cons of this approach are illustrated in Table 9-4.

Table 9-4. *Pros and cons of a Semi-Live Sandbox strategy*

Pros	Cons
More representative behavior of API requests	Opens the Live environment to a development audience
Hybrid capability saves time on simulating backend services	Requires additional support elements to regulate and monitor usage
Potential revenue stream by charging for controlled or restricted access to Live platforms	Introduces a security risk as the Sandbox is now an access mechanism to Live elements and services

Use-Case

The ability to invoke Live services affords a flexible, hybrid Sandbox capability which
must be carefully used and managed as it represents a potential security risk. It should
be used by exception, rather than the norm. There are great use-cases to support its
adoption – such as the Twilio messaging service previously mentioned. It is important
that the relevant systems and controls are put into place to manage and monitor its use.
It is best used to provide reference data, which is typically read only and can be openly
shared.

Design

As illustrated in Figure 9-7

- Specific middleware components which are configured to the Live backend providers are deployed to the Sandbox environment.

- The Virtualiser has access to these middleware components.

- Details of the Technical design for this approach are provided later in this chapter.

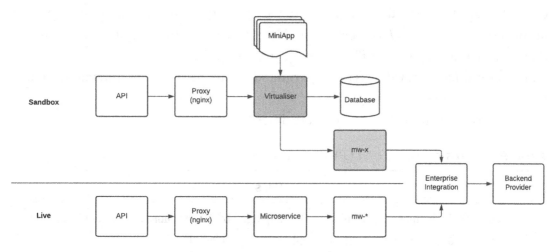

Figure 9-7. *Design of a Semi-Live Sandbox environment*

QA Live

We have found this to be the least commonly used strategy. It has special function and caters to a specific audience and use-case.

As previously mentioned, a foundational consumer of our platform is an internally developed application that is hosted externally and uses the Marketplace to access key enterprise services. Due to the nature of this consumer and the rapid pace of development, access has been granted to the Quality Assurance (QA) Test environment to verify end-to-end functionality before product releases.

Although the pattern was isolated to this specific use-case, we have found that for some APIs, testing in a "Live" context is sorely needed. In all honesty, simulating a backend or shallow interception strategy may not sufficiently cover all responses and use-cases of a backend provider. In these scenarios, the only way to get *true* representation is to integrate directly to the backend for the full transaction.

Approach

The internal foundational consumer helped trailblaze the path to allow access from an externally hosted system. Specific rules were added to the firewall to allow traffic from defined source IPs. Instead of connecting to the *Production Sandbox* endpoints, the destination was set as *QA Live*. Network and Information Security allowed the access due to the nature and high profile of the consuming application. In all honesty, access for other third-party providers is rarely permitted due to the sensitivity and nature of the testing environment.

The pros and cons of this approach are described in Table 9-5.

Table 9-5. *Pros and cons of a QA-Live Sandbox strategy*

Pros	Cons
Of all approaches, is the most representative of application behavior in a Production environment	Impacted by the availability of systems and data in the QA environment
No need to create a Sandbox version of the API – saves manpower	Adds additional load and traffic to shared components in the internal domain
	Development – new releases or patches may impact testing and needs to be scheduled carefully

Use-Case

There are very specific use-cases for this approach. The first is for consumers who are internal to the organization, have insight into organizational processes and information, and can tolerate varying service levels of availability and performance. The second is for those situations when it is not possible to create a Sandbox version of the API and when it is critical that the consuming application gets *full* representative behavior and responses during testing. In this instance, the access policy should only allow temporary access.

Design

As illustrated in Figure 9-8

- The request is processed in the Quality Assurance (QA) environment.

- This is a parallel implementation to Production.

- The approach fulfills the requirement to functionally test a solution end to end. It is important to note that the QA environment may not be scaled similarly to Production – there is a possibility that behavior could vary.

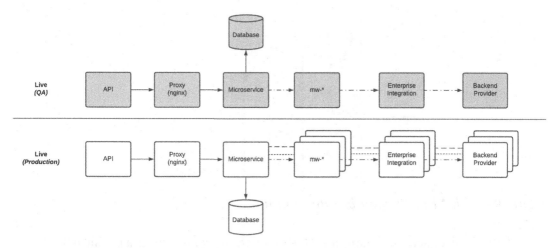

Figure 9-8. *Design detailing the use of QA as a Sandbox environment*

Third-Party Sandbox Access

A sample distribution detailing the third party to Sandbox access relationship for our platform is shown in Figure 9-9. The key factor which influences this spread is that not all third parties consume the same API products for one or more of the following reasons:

- The API products in ***beta*** may have smaller audiences – if only a subset of third parties are allowed access *or* if interest from potential consumers is low. Many third parties may only focus on stable, production-available APIs.

- Many will consume the simpler API products which use a ***Backend Simulation*** strategy.

- APIs are classified as complex if orchestration spans multiple backend providers and are great candidates for a **Shallow** approach. These API products generally fill a niche function which leads to lower third-party attraction and consumption.

- Only a few, select third parties may have access to API products which are backed with more complex Sandbox strategies – such as **Semi-Live** and **QA**.

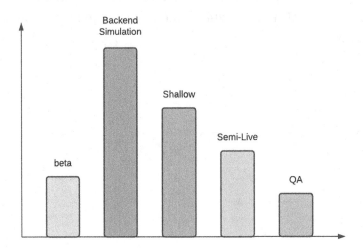

Figure 9-9. *Third-party Sandbox distribution*

I like to think of access to Sandbox APIs in much the same way as a physical bank branch. Anyone is allowed to enter the branch. Only bank personnel may enter the staff-permitted areas of the building. Of the bank personnel, only senior and authorized members are able to gain entry to sensitive spaces, such as the bank vault.

In much the same way, there are APIs and associated Sandbox environments, which only select and authorized third parties may access. This strategy may appear to be contrary to the approach of maximizing third-party consumption. The adage *"horses for courses"* comes to mind and there will be API products in your stable which are suited for specific consumers. Although it is possible to grant every third-party access to every API product, the organization may not have the temperament or appetite for *any* third party to access key areas or services – due to sensitivity of customer data and security restrictions.

I depict our access strategy in Figure 9-10 in a dartboard-like approach, starting with the lowest security and most open on the outside, to the highest and most restricted at the core or bullseye of the board. It is important to note that your access strategy may differ based on the API products and governance policies of your organization – you may choose to add, remove, or even reorder the sequence of layers.

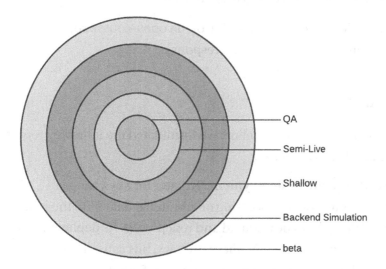

Figure 9-10. *Third-party Sandbox access*

Building a Virtualiser

Our first and only Sandbox strategy until the redesign was *Backend Simulation*. To achieve this, the team leveraged the *Mountebank* Open-Source project which allows a pre-defined response to be returned given a specific request. A custom application was deployed to our managed container platform. The application listened for requests on a specific port and only endpoint configuration for integration components needed to be changed to route to this service. For each new backend to be simulated, the application was updated to

1. Route the incoming request, based on a set of rules which includes the path, operation, parameters, and payload to a specific embedded JavaScript function.

2. With the context of the function known, the function teased out further information from the request using custom logic built specifically for that integration solution.

3. The function then used the collected information to locate a data file, deployed with the application – either in *json* or *xml* format.

4. Upon retrieval of the file, some elements were updated, such as the date and time to give a more representative response.

5. The updated response was then returned.

This approach leveraged the capability of the open-source solution to process the request and custom code to compile the response.

Requirements

Using this implementation as a baseline, we formulated the following requirements for the next iteration of the *Virtualiser*:

- **No code update or deployment**: To cater for any changes – request or response processing or additional data files, the custom application had to be updated and redeployed. As deployments had to be done within maintenance windows, this caused a lengthy delay. Our goal was to implement updates as configuration.

- **Runtime configuration**: As *Mountebank* config lived in files within the application, changes could not be done at runtime. We need changes to reflect immediately.

- **Accessibility and ease of update**: Given the complexity of rules and embedded JavaScript, initial setup could only be done by a developer and later changes, or updates could only be done by technically skilled members of the team who had a good understanding of the framework. Our requirement was that *any* member of the team could easily make changes.

- **Third-party specific**: As the third-party identifier was generally included in the call to a backend provider, a generic response was returned. We wanted the ability to return consumer-specific responses.

- **Application aware**: The custom application executed in its own context without any connection to our application architecture. As part of the redesign, the team threw in the kitchen sink with the requirement that the new version should be aware of internal constructs and be able to leverage those for routing and processing of requests.

Implementation Options

With the humility and maturity that comes with years of software development experience, we understood this was not a new problem, and many API platforms would have a similar challenge. There are great Commercial-Off-The-Shelf (COTS) offerings such as Computer Associate's Service Virtualisation product. Unfortunately, this would not only attract a license cost, but it would also require navigation of governance processes for new software acquisition – which would result in lengthy timelines.

The team evaluated and tested two impressive Open-Source projects:

- **Hoverfly** is a lightweight API simulation tool. Using Hoverfly, you can create realistic simulations of the APIs your application depends on.

- **Mountebank** is the first open-source tool to provide cross-platform, multi-protocol test "doubles" over the wire. This is the tool which underpinned our *Backend Simulation* strategy.

After much deliberation and debate, we based our final decision around the local configuration which was core to both tools. A key requirement was that changes could be made without a code update or deployment. Forking the projects and making it bend to our will was also an option – this would require significant customization and maintenance. Given our constraints and requirements, the route that we finally settled on was custom development. This would result in the fastest and possibly most efficient resolution.

Design Philosophy

We used Mountebank as a reference and established two essential elements:

A **predicate**, which is a condition based on the combination of input parameters which include the elements of an HTTP request and external configuration, listed in Table 9-6.

Table 9-6. *Predicate parameters*

Element	Example
Method	GET/POST/PUT/...
Path	/customer
Query	?x=1&y=2
Header	x-subscription-id
Body	{ name: 'Tom Sawyer' }
DB Config	Database record retrieved using x-subscription-id

Note the following customizations:

- A specific header value of *x-subscription-id* is used to retrieve a database configuration record which is used as a parameter for the predicate evaluation.

- Fuzzy logic to match on the key or key and value of a parameter – for example, if the *query* contained the key *x* or the expression *x=1*.

- As many predicates could match, the one with the highest number of matches is used.

A **response** is an action to be performed to generate a result. A response is configured based on the scenario being simulated as listed in Table 9-7.

Table 9-7. *Virtualiser responses*

Type	Description
Static	Constant, pre-defined data that does not change
Random	Regular expression to update specific elements of the response using configured variables such as the current datetime or elements of the input request
Code	Dynamically executed mini applications (script)
Proxy	Routes the request to a configured endpoint for processing

The dynamically executed "mini application" allows us the capability to respond to complex API requests. It enables *Shallow Virtualisation* by writing to persistent storage (disk or database) to maintain storage. It also allows *Semi-Live* by invoking Live services to construct a response. The application is stored as a script, which is interpreted at runtime. The script can be updated without deployment. The proxy capability provides an elegant mechanism to dynamically route the request at runtime for processing.

Sample Flow

Figure 9-11 and the sample configuration which follows provide more insight into the process.

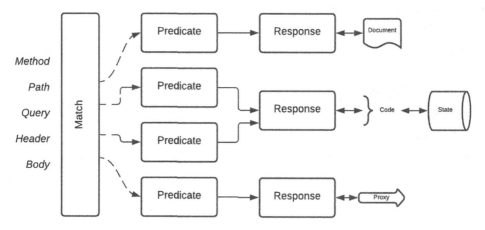

Figure 9-11. *Virtualiser process*

- When a request is received, we attempt to find all *Predicates* which match.

- There could be several matches for a specific request. The Predicate with the highest number of matches is used.

- The linked *Response* is then retrieved. Many predicates could be mapped to a single *Response*. This allows separation between request identification and handling.

- The *Response* could be generated using static data, code execution, or by proxying to a configured endpoint for processing.

- The code execution element or "mini app" can maintain state. This allows dynamic responses based on defined state.

The extract below is sample configuration for

- `http://`*`server`*`/sport/catalogue?categoryID=`*`nnn`*

- If the value of *categoryID* is not specified, any value *nnn* will match.

- If another *Predicate* configuration exists without specifying criteria for a *query* parameter, this will be used as there will be more matches.

```
{
  "method": "GET",
  "path": "/sport/catalogue",
  "api": "SPORT",
  "operation": "GetCatalogue",
  "response": {
    "query": [
      {
        "key": "product",
        "source": "query",
        "query": "categoryID"
      }
    ]
  },
  "query": {
    "categoryID": ""
  }
}
```

The extract below is sample configuration for

- `http://`*`server`*`/sport/catalogue?categoryID=` *`11329`*

- Once a *Predicate* is found, the *Response* it is linked to is found by using the `response` data. From the above configuration, it specifies that the `source` of the search criteria is the `categoryID` parameter – `{"product":"11329"}`

- The `action` parameter of the *Response* indicates that the payload to be returned is the JSON object in the `context` variable.

- This strategy allows different payloads to be returned for various categoryID values. It also allows updates to be made at runtime.

```
{
  "product": "11329",
  "response": {
    "action": "data",
    "context": { .. },
    "ErrorDescription": "OK",
    "TxID": "0c772fd1-4203-4390-bc51-8c74edf0e979"
  }
}
```

This Virtualiser design has been specifically tailored to meet the requirements of our Marketplace implementation. There are other extensions we have added to use the value of a header or query parameter to retrieve a database record from a specified collection and use those values for additional matching. This solution outlines a sample design. There are many updates and optimizations that you may apply for your Marketplace. If you have any ideas you would like to share, please keep me posted.

Summary

In this chapter, we covered the Sandbox – which is an essential element of any API Marketplace. We highlighted its purpose and the essential role it plays for a third-party provider to understand your APIs and allows you to get a better understanding of the consuming application. Several Sandbox strategies were discussed in detail describing the approach, benefits and drawbacks, the use-case each strategy was best suited for, and a high-level design.

I also provided a sample distribution showing which strategies were most used as well as a strategy for providing access. We finally dove into the detail and defined requirements for our custom Virtualiser which could be used to fulfill two Sandbox strategies. From requirements, we then considered implementation options, from commercial to open source, but finally chose to build a custom solution for maximum flexibility. We finally outlined the core elements of the custom solution and processed a sample request to get a better understanding of how it works.

The process of implementing a Sandbox environment is possibly one of the rare occasions in enterprise software development which allows significant more latitude for creativity and out of the box thinking. It could even be the pilot phase of your Marketplace implementation to gauge market demand.

In the next chapter, we dive into the realm of Operations which is potentially the domain your APIs will reside in the longest.

CHAPTER 10

API Operations

In contrast with other domains in the API Marketplace, which are hyper-flexible and able to pivot or change direction on a dime, our realm of Operations is far more structured, organized, and focused. The team runs on a strict regimen of process and structure and is the foundation of the platform. Any other approach would result in a rapid descent into chaos, and the implementation would quickly be classified under the banner of a prototype. As the platform is an enabling ingredient for greater third-party applications, any internal or supporting system failure is likely to trigger a ripple effect which would eventually cause a larger impact resulting in poor perception of the third-party consumer's customer-facing product or service.

As this domain typically falls under an operational expenditure (OPEX) budget, the knee-jerk reaction may be to keep costs down. Although our Marketplace may not be end-customer facing, there may be significant reputational impact and industry perception if the service levels are found to be flaky. As described in previous chapters, a big effort is to attract external developers to the platform. It takes even more effort to maintain the relationship and retain these consumers.

From experience, integration support has always been a challenging but rewarding role. Without a doubt, my greatest learning from design to development to truly understanding a solution and its underlying elements has been from time served in Operations. Parameters and conditions well-defined during development. Even with extensive testing scenarios and strenuous load tests, the environment may be fairly isolated. From a project early in my career, I can clearly recall a senior engineer reporting excitedly that he had run millions of transactions throughout the night on his notebook without an issue. When our solution finally made it to production, we spent countless nights over the next two years trying to resolve operational problems. The reason is that a production environment is vastly different and traffic load, supporting system availability, and unpredictable customer behavior should not be underestimated. It is for this reason that I am of the firm belief that solution architects must spend time in an Operational role to learn how to design more robust solutions.

© Rennay Dorasamy 2022
R. Dorasamy, *API Marketplace Engineering*, https://doi.org/10.1007/978-1-4842-7313-5_10

Unfortunately, fighting fire with fire by using a loose, tactical approach in a fast-moving, high-traffic, chaotic operational environment will most likely result in failure which could jeopardize the success and longevity of the platform. In this chapter, I discuss our previous, current, and aspirational operational standards, processes, and approaches to running a Marketplace successfully.

The Operational Universe

In all honesty, stabilizing our support capability has been one of our greatest challenges and is an ongoing effort. The project sponsor had foreseen the criticality of the platform years ago. Unfortunately, his sagely advice went unheeded as the team raced to build and deploy the platform with a mantra of – *"we will cross that bridge when we get there."* As the Marketplace was suddenly identified as a pivotal element to allow a new, externally hosted digital experience, to leverage internal, enterprise capability, the team found itself thrust into the operational spotlight almost overnight.

Like firefighters in training, with emergencies typically being called on to save a cat stuck in a tree, the team was ill-prepared when called in to deal with infernos of high-traffic and high-value transactions spanning several downstream systems which we had not dealt with operationally before. A term to reference this condition was "support surgery," and daily calls were scheduled to check if suggested strategies had taken hold and to adjust if not. With time and much effort, the team has established a firm support foundation through the improvement of the platform monitoring capability, definition of an incident management process, and better understanding and operational relationships with backend supporting systems.

A key takeaway from this experience is to put sufficient and, importantly, honest focus on support operationalization of a Marketplace as early in the project lifecycle as possible. In the following sections, we discuss key concepts and approaches which enable the operational domain and identify foundational elements upon which it is built – as shown in Figure 10-1.

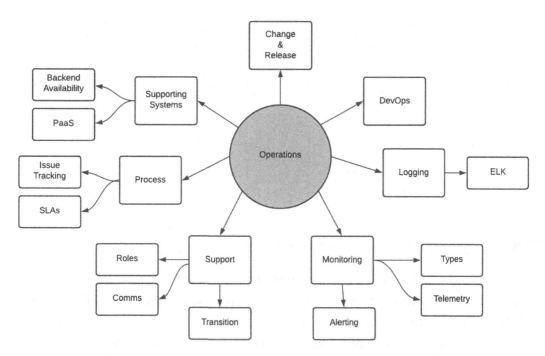

Figure 10-1. *The Operations sub-domains*

Change and Release Management

Traditionally, operational teams are not typically fond of updates as they introduce risk into the environment. What has worked exceedingly well for our implementation is a philosophy of frequent but small releases. As noted in the chapter detailing Development, there may be a number of concurrent streams running in a sprint that will deploy to production at the end of the sprint.

For major updates such as new API products, the release is generally made to production well in advance of any third-party consumption as shown in Figure 10-2. By providing a buffer between release and consumption, it allows the team an opportunity to verify functionality in a relatively unpressured capacity and to make any updates or revisions if required. From launching new functionality, we have often discovered, on the night of deployment, that additional configuration was required, and most often outside our sphere of control (such as firewall or network access). By deploying sooner, it has allowed our team to identify and resolve the dependency before we found ourselves on the critical path.

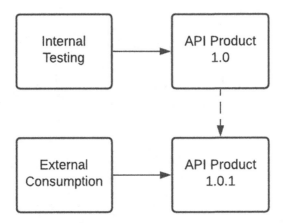

Figure 10-2. *First release of an API product*

For minor product iterations, as shown in Figure 10-3, API versioning is a critical element. As different versions of API products can co-exist, the decision as to when to migrate is left to the third-party consumer. This is done with the proviso that specific versions have a well-defined end of life. By providing well-defined release notes detailing the changes in later versions, we also provide a clear signal to our consumers that it may be in their best interest to move to the newer version – for reasons of improved security or stability or possibly additional functionality.

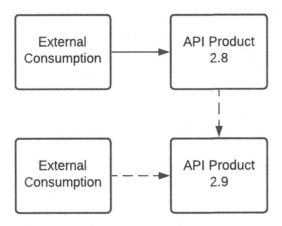

Figure 10-3. *Updates to an API product*

As shown in Figure 10-4, updates to internal, supporting elements such as microservices are generally minor and iterative. In the event of an issue arising from an update, the team will assess the cause, impact, and possible resolution. From a culture perspective, our preference is to minimize blame by not dwelling too much on the cause. We have found that blame results in fear which inhibits the team's agility. If an issue could have been identified during testing, it is taken as a learning for the future. More often, the issue is related to data or scenarios unique to the production environment which could not be replicated during testing. If the impact is significant service degradation, the change is rolled back immediately. A strong DevOps capability allows this to be achieved in a matter of minutes. This, too, is also a liberating capability that underpins the team's ability to deliver quickly. If the resolution can be achieved quickly and with minimal, preferably zero risk, the Delivery Leads, in consultation with the Engineering team, may make the decision to "fix forward."

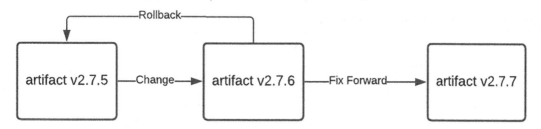

Figure 10-4. *Internal updates*

This is not a decision that is made lightly, and the practice, if left unchecked, could lead to the cardinal sin of "coding in production." Special caution must be taken to ensure that in-progress development is not accidentally included as part of the update. A well-defined code versioning strategy with release tags and branches is critical to support this. If used wisely and sparingly, the inherent benefit of fixing forward is that time is saved by not having to roll back the release which would keep the release pipeline flowing. Depending on the nature of the issue, impact, frequency, and resolution timeframe, it may be possible to implement the fix over a longer duration – which would minimize additional errors creeping in through last-minute updates.

The requirement for a more flexible change and release strategy for agile, digital solutions has been recognized by our organization, and significant effort has been put into attempting to adapt to it. This statement must be fully qualified as the quality gates have not been lowered – the processes have been streamlined to allow faster transition. It is still a work in progress, and there is some way to go before we reach the Continuous Deployment nirvana of Netflix – but with that being said, the service levels and potential fallout for a Financial Institution would be far higher than a video streaming service.

Figure 10-5 provides a high-level view of our Release "funnel." I like to think of it as atoms bouncing around in a space which gets progressively smaller until they eventually bounce out or must file in line orderly to move forward. At any given time, there are a significant number of requirements, fixes, or prototypes in development. Some prototypes may graduate to fully fledged solutions; others may be retired. The readiness of supporting backend platforms will also determine which requirements will transition to testing. Planning sessions, led by the Delivery Leads, will identify a potential implementation date for specific solutions, which are bundled into a production release. The goal is a release at a minimum of every two weeks. As soon as a view has been determined, the necessary change control artifacts are assembled, and Release Management is notified of the intention and date to deploy.

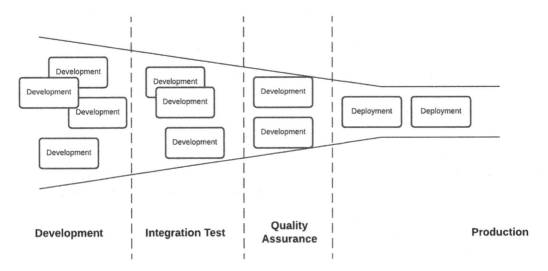

Figure 10-5. *The Release funnel*

The artifacts that are required for the release process include the following:

- **Implementation guide**: These are the set of instructions for the deployment of code assets and configuration required in the operational environment. With a well-optimized DevOps pipeline in place, this document simply details the components and versions to be deployed. It may be necessary to also document configuration updates to firewall rules and security access to backend systems. For more complex deployments which span different systems, this guide will detail a timeline and sequence of events for the release.

- **Testing evidence and QA sign-off**: Documented test execution and acceptance from the Quality Assurance team is a key input before a solution can be released. This is currently in the form of a document to meet existing criteria. As part of the Continuous Deployment (CD) intention of the team, an aspirational goal is to provide automated regression, functional and performance test results which provide assurance of the integrity of a solution.

- **Release notes**: Description of the changes to be deployed to the environment – be it new functionality, updates or optimizations to existing solutions, fixes or patches to resolve operational issues.

DevOps Practice

Like the humble sled, which was used to transport large and heavy objects during the construction of the pyramids in Egypt, the practice of DevOps is the pivotal element that underpins our operational environment, as illustrated in Figure 10-6. From years of experience in an operational domain, regularly pulling back platforms from a catastrophic demise by tweaking application server configuration or masterfully rebuilding systems on the fly by hand, and in so doing have been responsible for creating "snowflake environments," this has been both a humbling and insightful experience.

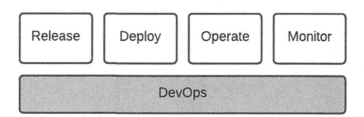

Figure 10-6. *DevOps foundation*

A well-instrumented operational DevOps process starts even before the first line of code is written. Code repositories, build pipelines, Continuous Integration (CI), and migration processes (detailed in previous chapters) all form part of the process which enables the DevOps practice from development, and which ultimately pervades into the operational domain. In all honesty, as a developer who has witnessed a pre-DevOps era, there are moments of frustration as a defined release process minimizes the opportunity for tweaks and quick updates. As an Engineering Lead observing a well-oiled, well-defined, repeatable, and reliable process with almost zero opportunity for tweaks and quick updates, I am immensely grateful.

A repeatable process is key, particularly more so in an agile, fast-moving environment as it enables rapid delivery with the ability to roll back if the need arises. The ability to roll back *reliably* and *rapidly* in an operational context should not be taken lightly. From years past, I can still clearly recall not only the disappointment and embarrassment of rolling back a release but also the apprehension as backups were used to restore a system and we waited to verify the rehydration process. The microservice construct also helps immensely as it allows fine-grained control to roll back or roll forward only ailing components. This ability affords our platform a safety net which provides a level of confidence in much the same way that it would allow a highwire act to push the envelope a little further.

As there are legacy elements in our platform architecture, not all systems have a DevOps capability. The organization is well aware of this, and each system has defined a roadmap to ultimately achieve this. For new implementations, such as the Cloud Container platform we have recently migrated to, this is non-negotiable. The environment is locked down with a "zero-touch" policy, and the only mechanism available to make changes is via a DevOps pipeline as shown in Figure 10-7. Firm and unrelenting commitment is possibly the only way to achieve this goal. If there is a loophole or backdoor available, it will be discovered and exploited by the delivery team.

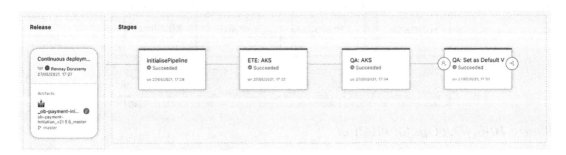

Figure 10-7. *DevOps pipeline*

Logging

From years spent in an integration environment, I consider logs to be the lifeblood of any middleware solution. Logs are the primary mechanism I use during development and support to get insight into the execution path of a request. There are possibly far more elegant ways of using debugging tools to watch values on the stack, but for me personally, a well-positioned *console.log* or *logger.debug* statement, acting as an informer, can lead to the criminal mastermind in a bewildering "whodunnit" tracing challenge.

As illustrated in Figure 10-8, there are various contexts in which a log may exist. During development, there is typically a single file or standard output (stdout) stream to tail. In a clustered environment, the number of logs is equal to the participating nodes. In a microservice, container-oriented platform, there is an explosion of logs, and a single request could traverse several pods, each of which is distributed across various nodes in the cluster.

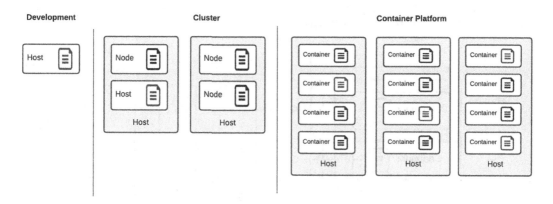

Figure 10-8. *Logging contexts*

Tracing a transaction can be compared to trying to find needles in many different haystacks. This is one of the lessons I've learnt in an operational domain that I always keep in mind during platform design. A key platform architecture principle is to have a unique identifier which is attached to a transaction from the point of entry and is used for every logging statement as its journeys through the environment. This seemingly simple strategy enables what I refer to as the "Holy Grail" in a distributed integration environment – the ability to trace a transaction across various components. With each component logging with a traceable identifier, half of the battle is won. It is important to always keep in mind that containers are transient – more could be created to handle load, then destroyed as the load dissipates or the container could be restarted due to an application exception. As logs are typically written to *stdout*, this could result in the loss of the log with the shutdown or restart of the container instance.

There are options to mitigate the loss of the log, such as mounting persistent storage which the container has access to. To minimize the complexity of the container environment, the team addressed the requirement at an application level with a solution detailed in Figure 10-9. All applications use a platform logging service, which has access to an application context. The context is populated with a wide range of metadata, such as the unique transaction identifier, name of the host application, and details of the client initiating the request. With a logging request, supplementary data is retrieved from the context, container and runtime, packaged into a simple JSON object which is then fired to a load-balanced endpoint via UDP, which minimizes any performance impact to the application as it is a fire-and-forget request. This is the entry point to an Enterprise Elasticsearch, Logstash, and Kibana (ELK) service.

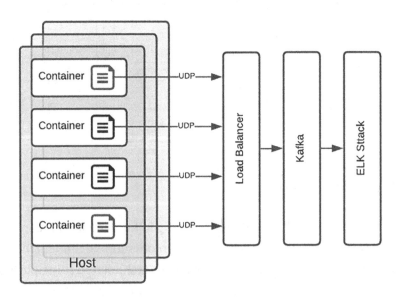

Figure 10-9. Logging strategy

A system-specific Kafka topic is used to buffer requests and prevent message loss as the capability is used by different platforms across the enterprise. This is another example of our decision to leverage enterprise services to minimize operational overhead which allows the team maximum focus on creating *API* value. The logging *event* is then ingested into the ELK stack, described in more detail in the next section.

The ELK Stack

ELK is the acronym for three open-source projects: Elasticsearch, Logstash, and Kibana. Elasticsearch is a search and analytics engine. Logstash is a server-side data processing pipeline that ingests data from multiple sources simultaneously, transforms it, and then sends it to a "stash" like Elasticsearch. Kibana lets users visualize data with charts and graphs in Elasticsearch.

A trait of a great application is easy adoption and operation by a wide range of users and the Kibana console, essentially the User Interface for the ELK stack and shown in Figure 10-10, not only meets this objective, but in my opinion, exceeds it exceptionally well.

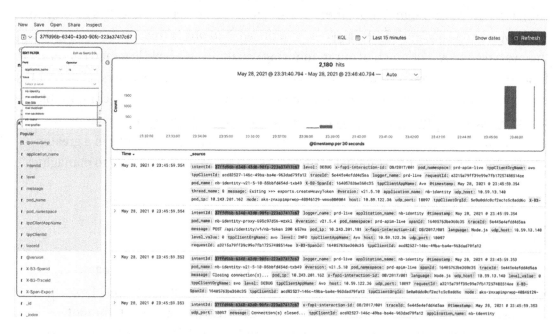

Figure 10-10. *Kibana console*

I have observed support engineers, sometimes relatively new to the team and having been through a handful of knowledge sharing sessions, expertly navigate the Kibana console to track down the cause of a request failure. By providing the unique identifier, Elasticsearch eliminates the difficulty of scanning multiple logs and almost instantly shows all entries which contain that reference, with a time-series graph which can be used to drill into a specific timeframe.

Kibana goes further by allowing the user to view only a subset of fields. Additional filters can be specified to narrow in on specific components. Kibana queries, in the form of Kibana Query Language (KQL), can also be executed to widen or narrow the search radius. The ELK stack is potentially the most important element of our operational environment, and if time and effort is invested into mastering its capability by all members of the team, it will most certainly yield great results across both development and support.

Monitoring

This area of operations follows the iceberg principle. On the surface, it appears relatively simple. Upon closer examination, there is a lot more than meets the eye. It is an ongoing journey, and on Day One of our implementation, we had only a fraction of the capability that we have today. For much of our monitoring capability, we have leveraged enterprise functionality which has resulted in lower costs from a software license perspective and a smoother transition for our releases as change management boards are comfortable that existing operational processes and tools are in use. In the following sections, we examine areas of monitoring and discuss how the sum of the parts results in a greater whole which allows our operational team to take a pre-emptive approach to managing the platform.

Environment Monitoring

Almost every Network Operations or Command Centre environment has banks of screens showing impressive dials and gauges which are constantly moving. From my perspective, this is the traditional mechanism of monitoring an environment. Line graphs, as shown in Figure 10-11, generally indicate CPU utilization or memory consumption. When pre-defined thresholds are met, there is generally a flurry of activity from the support personnel and a sigh of relief as the graph dips below the threshold.

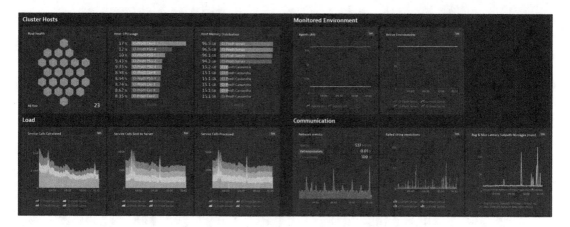

Figure 10-11. *Infrastructure monitoring*

The source of information for these metrics is generally an agent installed on the physical or virtual host. This is the base level of monitoring and is used to determine if there are any issues with the physical infrastructure. Its use is much like checking the temperature of a patient. If the temperature or CPU is high, it is used as an indicator that something is amiss. That is typically the extent of the information it can provide.

In an API or integration environment, the next level of monitoring is service or endpoint monitoring, as shown in Figure 10-12. This is sometimes referred to as synthetic monitoring. Periodic probes test the availability of a service. Our team generally includes an *isUp* operation which simply returns a HTTP 200. False positives may be eliminated by defining rules for alert activation, such as three consecutive failures. As the request generally traverses the full network infrastructure route to the endpoint, a problem with a load balancer or firewall configuration can also be identified which may not be reported in the infrastructure monitoring dashboard.

Figure 10-12. *Service monitoring*

Due to a complex network environment, there have been instances of changes or updates to external systems which have impacted our service availability. The periodic, scheduled execution can be used as indisputable evidence of when the issue occurred, and a further benefit is that it can alert the team of an issue before it is found and reported by an external consumer. If this was the triage of a patient, this would be checking blood pressure or oxygen saturation levels. Lower flow rates could indicate a potential block in the system. On its own, it does not indicate the cause – but helps to narrow down the areas which require further investigation.

Application Performance Monitoring

From my first encounter of Application Performance Monitoring (APM) many years ago, I have been extremely impressed with this feat of software engineering. The APM consultant instrumented our application's Java Virtual Machine, and with the magic of byte-code injection, we were able to view transactions flowing through our platform. At first sight, this was the Holy Grail of transaction tracing that I had sought after for so long. After more exposure and examination, I discovered that APM has a specific role in the software development lifecycle, and my quest for albeit a slightly "Holier Grail" was not over.

Although APM can be used daily in an operational environment, the insights it provides, as shown in Figure 10-13, are generally considered during load testing and performance engineering. Like a dye injected into a patient's bloodstream, it shows the exact path a request follows to reach its destination. Some APM products also surface the exact database request which surfaces unindexed, poor performing queries.

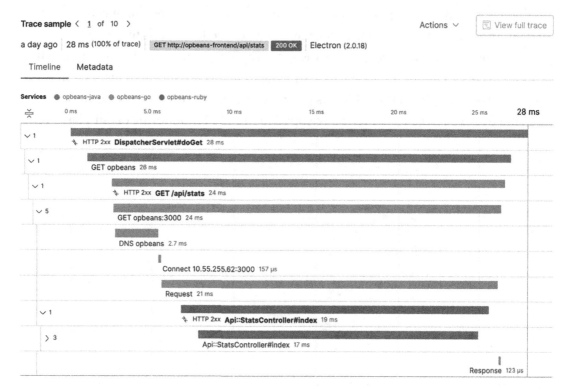

Figure 10-13. *APM transaction tracing*

An APM resolution path can be used to optimize the solution by identifying areas of high-latency and potential bottlenecks in the system architecture. In complete honesty, this could very well be the Holy Grail which operations personnel can use as the single oracle of information for transaction execution. At this time, however, based on my personal experience and observation of our current operational processes and procedures, we have not yet reached this conclusion.

Functional Monitoring

The objective of Functional Monitoring is to probe deeper than simply verifying the availability of an API endpoint but to test and confirm its full operation. One of my favorite interview questions to prospective technical team members is to ask which stream of the project they would lean toward – project management, design, development, testing, or support. Just for reference – project management was a "loaded" option and for the unfortunate few who selected this, it was the end of the line. As many would love to write code, the most popular response is development, with almost no votes for support. Evidence of my belief that it is possible to write a significant amount of code in an operational role is presented in Figure 10-14 – an application, nicknamed *"Homer Knows"* which I developed for internal monitoring of our platform.

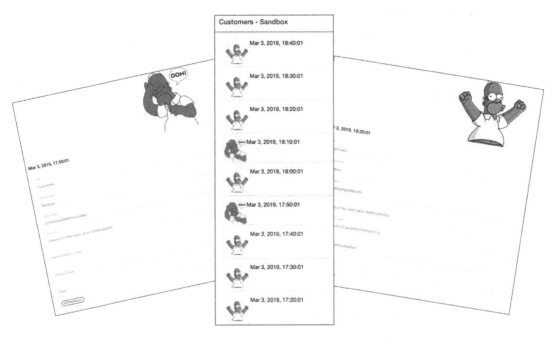

Figure 10-14. *Homer Knows*

A key element of our Marketplace is the OAuth process flow. This is made up of a sequence of API calls, with redirects to a web user interface (UI) prompting the user to authenticate and authorize the request. We were able to verify only the early API calls, but only discovered issues with the UI and later calls when third parties indicated an outage. From an operational perspective, it troubled me that our approach was *reactive,* and I used this as motivation to build a custom application, accessible via desktop or mobile, which simulated a user (Homer Simpson) running through the flow on a regular schedule triggered by a simple *cron* script. If the process succeeded or failed, *Homer* would *know*. In addition to learning a new mobile application framework, this exercise afforded me the opportunity to consume the API in much the same way that a third party would. Continuing our medical analogy, it allows the operations team to observe a patient *during* a potential incident which could reveal the root cause in real-time.

Telemetry

A dimension of Monitoring which particularly appeals to me is Telemetry. I first came across this concept from watching Formula One (F1) racing. As the car moved around the circuit, the race engineers were able to get detailed information about every facet of the machine. This possibly afforded the pit crew incredible insight into the operation of the car and if used correctly, could be used strategically for an extra ounce of competitive advantage which would ultimately win the race.

Leading on from this revelation is firstly the amount of data which is constantly pouring in – from tire pressure levels and temperature to remaining fuel to oil temperatures to airflow, there are possibly tens if not hundreds or thousands of metrics to be scoured through. The true beauty of telemetry is that it affords remote control of the source. Present F1 regulation may not allow, but in previous years, the race engineers were able to change the configuration of the car remotely. For example, if they found that engine temperatures were dangerously high, the race engineer (in consultation with the driver) could lower the maximum revolutions per gear to preserve the engine until the end of the race.

From a software engineering perspective, this is extremely exciting as it allows the operations team to make "runtime" configuration changes to the solution for optimized performance or possibly to preserve application availability. Examples of changes include adding more replicas or instances of a container to handle anticipated traffic, dynamically changing endpoint configuration using an environment variable strategy or displaying and removing maintenance pages during change windows. It should be noted that the objective of telemetry is not to make massive changes to the operational domain but affords the ability for "remote control" to make subtle course corrections or updates. In an operational environment which cannot afford downtime, this is certainly an extremely versatile weapon to have in your arsenal.

Alerting

A key lesson learnt is that a poor alerting strategy can quickly result in operational process failure. As the platform experienced an increase in volume, the number of alerts sent out overwhelmed the support team. Detailed investigation revealed that most alerts were due to data issues or downstream problems, which the Marketplace support team could do little to remediate. Within the mass of unactionable items (noise) were real system issues, which were increasingly missed, causing unnecessary delays in issue resolution.

The approach we have since adopted for real-time alerting, in anticipation of high traffic volumes, is that alerts are not sent on the "noise" but via a classification of the errors found. Initially all new errors are alerted on. Upon consultation, the errors are reclassified for alerting, if there is no immediate action that can be taken by the team. The errors are still logged and tracked in the operational service desk, to allow data to be rectified or downstream systems to make changes. In addition, all errors are also reported in operational dashboards, and a daily report of all errors is sent to key stakeholders, which assists with tracking volumes related to downstream systems.

In keeping with our strategy to leverage enterprise services where possible, the platform was initially configured to leverage the alerting capability of the organization which allowed alerts to be sent to standby engineers via various channels such as email and text message (SMS). A challenge with emails, even to a distribution group, is that important alerts were missed in a slew of messages, replies regarding investigation or resolution on a specific thread caused even more messages and finding or tracing through previous incidents meant having to rummage through an email archive. The drawback of using SMS is the cost due to mobile network charges. It soon became apparent that a traditional mechanism would not be an ideal fit and an alternative approach would be needed.

An alluring solution was integration to popular communications platforms like Slack, which other teams in the digital space were using. This had the potential to propel our alerting to the other end of the capability spectrum. Upon deeper reflection regarding this approach, we identified a few potential drawbacks. Using a non-enterprise standard would result in significant divergence from the organization strategy, integration connectivity challenges to the Slack service, and the requirement that every member of the team would need to have additional software installed and configured – sometimes on a personal device, not to mention the overhead of administering the service.

An awesome middle ground which we found was to use the organizational communication software standard, Microsoft Teams. Teams has a great "channel" feature where alerts are routed to as messages. Support engineers can start a thread on a specific message, which developers can follow and reply on if called upon to assist. As an organization standard, we also leverage the security capability and distribution policy of the mobile app. The major benefit is that we are once again in alignment with our strategy of leveraging the capability and might of the organization by consuming enterprise services.

Support

In this section, we discuss the "human" element of our support capability. The best solutions are built with consideration and awareness of *people, process, and technology*. As the *people* element, the members of the support team draw on the *technology* such as logging and monitoring and *processes*, such as Incident Management, to maintain the health and stability of the Marketplace. With the Marketplace requiring 24x7 attention, a significant debt of gratitude is owed to these support engineers in our team. We delve into more detail by discussing the structure of the support team, our approach to transition solutions from development to operations, and our internal and external communications strategy.

Roles

A foundational principle of our organization's digital playbook is the practice of *"you build it, you run it."* At first glance, this may appear to be an unforgiving "tough love" approach to agile solution delivery. From first-hand observation, this is possibly one of the greatest enablers to building responsible and reliable solutions. From prior project experience, I have observed a clear demarcation between solution delivery and operations – with the split spanning departments and divisions, each with its own staff and organizational structure. Although the delineation allows clear focus, separation of concerns and defined areas of responsibility, it inevitably results in an *"us-and-them"* culture. Development teams may callously deploy solutions to production, and operational teams may be reluctant to accept ownership unless onerous conditions have been met.

The full-stack squad, discussed in the chapter detailing Development, also includes support personnel who are responsible for the day-to-day operation of a solution. This approach ensures that responsibility and accountability for an API product, from inception to retirement, remains with the squad. If the solution has been poorly designed or does not have the requisite amount of logging or error handling, for example, the loop between operations and development is short and closed quickly. It is also a standing rule that the developers of a solution will be responsible for post-rollout support for 30 days. During this time, the developer will perform Level 1 support while shadowed by operations personnel. Knowledge sharing sessions will also be scheduled during this time to provide the support team with the information and skills to operate and manage the solution. For more complex solution delivery, members of the operational team may be assigned to the project team to allow more insight into the internal execution and a seamless transition to support.

The following list details the roles within the support team:

- **Operations lead**: First point of responsibility for the overall health of the platform and coordinates the activities of the team – from the scheduling of support staff to standby rosters. Requires sufficient technical acumen to understand an issue and resulting impacts, possibly the ability to dive into the detail but also the restraint to determine when to enter the battlefield and when to direct the troops. Unfortunately, technically minded folk enjoy the detail far more than process. The benefit is that the Lead can help with issue resolution. The risk, which I can attest to personally, is that the individual takes on too much, becomes a single point of failure and possibly the largest threat, does not have time to put in or support the necessary processes and procedures to *manage* the team. It is for this reason that this role is best staffed by a balanced technology and process-oriented individual.

- **Level 1/2 support**: As mentioned above, this role is generally filled by developers during post-rollout support. Based on the nature of your Marketplace, the platform requires 24x7 support, and this group of engineers stand on the front line to identify and triage issues and maintain the integrity of the API products. Well-defined dashboards and alerting mechanisms, discussed later in this chapter, are key to assisting this team with identifying issues. Triage is an extremely important function for a support engineer, and the ability to determine the root cause of an issue is a key trait that we seek to instill. The engineer maintains ownership of an issue until resolved or mitigated, even if it falls outside the boundaries of the platform. If additional assistance is required, a support request detailing the issue, impacted domains, analysis, logs, and possible area of suspicion is created. This is then assigned to the next level of support for investigation.

- **Level 3 (Development) support**: With a smaller team, issues which cannot be resolved by Level 1/2 are routed directly through to developers for assistance. The benefit is that it allows a shorter loop between issue detection and resolution. The drawback is that it could impact precious development time. In keeping with the *"you build it, you run it"* ethos of the team, it keeps developers accountable regarding their delivery. Essentially, well-written code and attention to solution knowledge sharing with the operations team will minimize interruptions to future development. If necessary, a code update may be required. Based on the severity of the issue, this may be included in the next release or fast-tracked through the process for immediate deployment.

Transition

Given the pace of delivery, API products within the Marketplace from multiple streams are constantly delivered and updated to keep up with Product Owner requirements and consumer demands. The operations capability is run as a shared service for maximum efficiency. That is, a single team supports all API products, across various streams. This allows the team to have one support engineer on Level 1/2 support, typically on a 24x7 schedule, which also reduces costs.

With new updates to the production environment, the delivery team is primarily responsible for post-rollout support for a specified period. During this time, the members of the operations team will provide shadow support to observe issues which may arise and how it may be remediated. This may be viewed as "on-the-job training" or implicit knowledge sharing. The delivery team also runs knowledge sharing sessions, the number of which is proportional to the complexity of the release. The delivery team views this period of transition in a *"let me help you help me"* light. That is – the probability of support requests escalated for development support is inversely proportional to the knowledge and skill of the support engineer. Simply put – an empowered support engineer may be able to resolve an operational issue without requiring assistance from a developer.

From personal experience, I have found that having to field support queries midway through development requires context switching which seriously impacts my delivery capability. Apart from the feeling of pride of having a solid, reliable solution in production, this is more than enough reason for any developer to ensure the operations team is suitably empowered to support their solution.

Communication Strategy

A key element of any Operational capability is an effective communications strategy. With a high number of integration points inside and outside the organization, keeping alignment across all stakeholders is no mean feat. The following is a sample of our current mechanisms:

- **Periodic updates**: Updates are sent every 2 hours, via WhatsApp, by the support engineer on standby detailing: i) stability of the production Live and Sandbox environment; ii) commercial statistics of internal consuming applications, such as visitors and sign-ups; and iii) analysis of API calls in the form of a comparison of current traffic to a week ago.

- **Third-party communication**: Notice to third party of planned maintenance which would impact the availability of API products. This is generally done as soon as the Marketplace team receives notice from a supporting enterprise system or downstream service provider of a planned update. As we have a well-governed organizational change management process, this is typically done at a minimum 3 days before the event. Notice of incidents and emergency outages are also sent to third-party operations team in the event of an internal or downstream system failure. Due to the vast number of platforms and systems in the enterprise, it did take time to register our platform as an "affected/interested" party for systems we did not directly integrate to. As an example, the Marketplace does not integrate directly to the mainframe – but would be significantly impacted in the event of an outage.

- **War room**: This measure is generally activated for a serious outage within the enterprise. It is typically triggered by a standby support engineer who observes a number of failed requests exceeding a defined threshold within a period of time for critical API products which are revenue linked. Feedback from supporting teams, be it enterprise service support or downstream providers, is relayed to the greater Marketplace team.

- **Focus call**: With a prolonged outage, a focus call will be convened with mandatory participation from all supporting teams. As this may result in participation from many engineers and system owners, the intention is to have all stakeholders available to resolve the issue as quickly as possible.

Process

To allow a uniform approach to the handling of operational incidents, a lightweight process flow, shown in Figure 10-15, is the primary reference for the Marketplace support team. It provides different routes for issue remediation – if necessary, an "Incident" is raised which is the organizational standard for communicating issues across systems. As the reader will note, the process clearly defines a notification strategy to keep all stakeholders aligned.

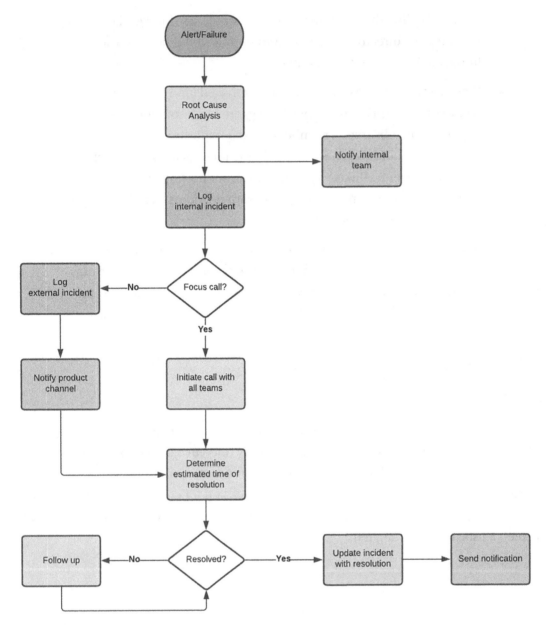

Figure 10-15. *Incident management process*

Issue Tracking and Reporting

At the launch of our Marketplace, there were few API products and even less consumers. Much like a small-town sheriff maintaining law and order, our approach was very much off the cuff. Issues were tracked on the back of a napkin and resolved just in time.

In the same way a small town sees an explosion in growth with the discovery of gold, the Platform grew with the addition of new API products built by many delivery streams working concurrently, with railways being built to new backend providers and third-party providers flocking in to consume the APIs. Issues piled up and the gun-slinging sheriff approach of maintaining the environment quickly became a single point of failure.

A key element to supporting the environment has been the implementation of a service desk to log, track, and report on issues. Support engineers were given clear instructions that requests which required more than a few minutes to resolve were to be logged diligently. The time taken to capture the issue, even as trivial as fielding a development query from a third-party provider, has proven to be invaluable as it affords the team a well-defined timeline and record of events. As visibility regarding the operational environment has improved, it allows the operations management team a clear view of the battlefield. Troops can be diverted to the most critical issues and items which are not progressing increase in visibility with time.

In much the same way that the development team has a daily standup call to discuss the tasks for the current sprint, the operations team also has a daily call. This has been strategically scheduled just before the standup of the platform team as it allows any items, which require more technical support, to be discussed with a larger audience. Issues, outages, errors, and remediation activities from the previous 24-hours are discussed in this session. With representation from the senior members of the team, this provides insight into stability of the platform, guidance regarding handling of similar circumstances in the future, decisions for the next steps to resolve outstanding items, and an opportunity for the operations team to request additional assistance by way of development support, time for further investigation, or escalation to persuade an external dependency to respond.

A further objective of the daily session is to reciprocate the gift of visibility and give the support team a view into upcoming releases across delivery streams. As the development sprint nears completion, some elements may not be released due to delays in testing or external dependencies. Keeping the support engineers updated of the release schedule allows the team adequate time to prepare, potentially alert the delivery leads of planned maintenance or potential stability issues of external systems which are key to the release and more importantly, is a clear signal of appreciation and respect to the operational team for keeping the platform running smoothly.

With a technically minded team, and an affinity for APIs, we have assimilated the interfaces provided by the service desk software, and it has become one of the key sources of data which is programmatically mined daily. In-flight issues in various lifecycle phases are aggregated and displayed on a custom dashboard which is used to quickly identify hotspots in the platform. For example, a high number of third-party provider support requests reporting intermittent network issues could highlight a problem with the firewall which can be addressed pro-actively. Historical items are also of importance and are used for reporting to external stakeholders at periodic review sessions as shown in Figures 10-16-1 and 10-16-2. These reports provide insight into the stability of the platform, mean time to resolve issues, and traffic volumes which may be used to motivate for funding for additional infrastructure and personnel for the platform. It provides clear, unambiguous, and data-backed evidence regarding key support focus areas to be addressed to afford the platform greater stability.

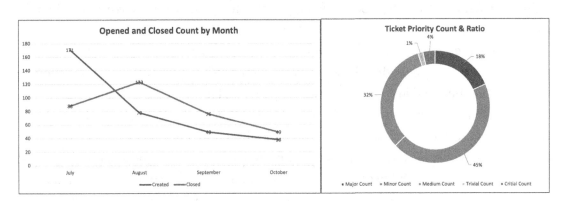

Figure 10-16-1. *Reporting – ticket trend and severity analysis*

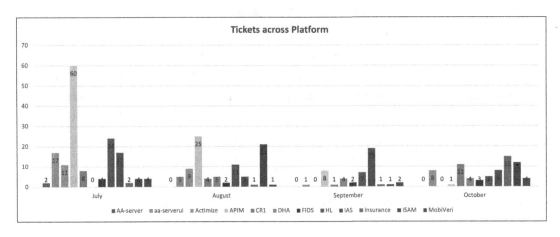

Figure 10-16-2. *Reporting of tickets by application domain*

Service-Level Agreements

Incidents are classified by support engineers in different categories based on the severity and priority of the issue. The definition and the severity mapping follows the matrix defined in Table 10-1.

Table 10-1. *Severity-response mapping*

Severity classification	Severity tag	Standard response time
Functionality completely blocked (All users affected)	Critical (showstopper)	< 30 minutes
Partial functionality blocked (Many users affected)	High	< 2 hours
Partial functionality affected (Workaround available)	Medium	< 24 hours
Section of functionality affected (Low user count)	Low	< 48 hours
Support team is blocked (Backend dependency)	Blocked	Tracked in Service Desk

Supporting Systems

Our Platform has two major dependencies – one internal and the other external. Internal components which are the assembly blocks of the Marketplace, discussed in the chapter detailing our platform architecture. An issue with an internal component could potentially result in the entire platform being rendered unavailable. External elements are backend systems which are service providers for the API products. One or more API products could be impacted based on the nature of the provider interface. In the sections below, I discuss the internal and external supporting elements in more detail.

Platform As a Service Strategy

As discussed in the chapter detailing the platform architecture and illustrated in Figure 10-17, the strategy is to leverage enterprise capabilities as much as possible. We have realized and accepted, almost from inception of the Marketplace, that the organization has highly skilled, focused, and dedicated personnel, often with years of operational experience managing a specific system. With this in mind, we have adopted a strategy to leverage enterprise capability as far as possible.

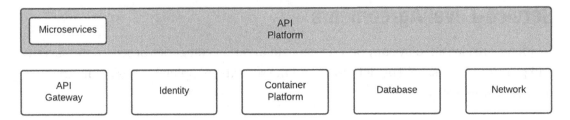

Figure 10-17. *Managed platform services*

The outsourced, "managed service" approach has its drawbacks as it tightly couples us to the enterprise, and we might have to wait longer for system upgrades and must share resources with other tenants. However, we have found that the benefits of accelerated platform maturity, dedicated technical support, and significantly lower operational expenditure budgets make this an appealing option.

Should an issue arise in a supporting system, the Marketplace support engineer will follow the incident management process by contacting their counterparts who manage that system. If direct contact cannot be established, assistance is required from the operations command center which will initiate a defined escalation process to track down the relevant system owners. Ownership of the issue still resides with the API Marketplace support team until the outage has been resolved. As each system has its own dependencies, the root cause could be further down the stack. As an example, a database outage could be caused by a loss of connectivity to the Storage Area Network (SAN) which was the result of an update to a firewall rule. From years of experience of supporting complex, interdependent systems, our organization takes a no-nonsense approach and for high-severity, service affecting outages, a "focus call" is quickly convened with mandatory participation from all supporting teams. This approach results in speedy identification of the root cause and remediation. It is at these times, when observing the full might of the enterprise brought to bear to resolve an outage, that we are thankful for our platform-as-a-service strategy.

Backend Dependencies

As illustrated in Figure 10-18, an API Marketplace has a number of consumers, each using one or more APIs, and an API integrates into one or more provider systems. Working our way back up the tree, it can be observed that a failure of a single provider could potentially impact one or more APIs with the ripple effect of impacting one or more consumers.

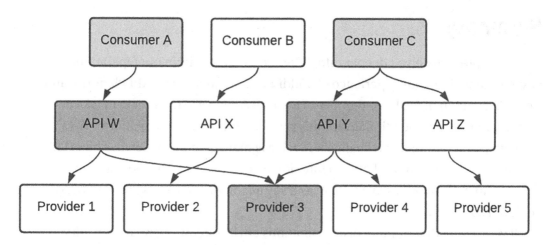

Figure 10-18. *Consumer, API, provider link*

Our approach to managing this complex network of consumers, APIs, and providers is as follows:

- Have a clear view of which backend systems are **providers** for each API product. This is a "living" view as each release might see new connections between product and backend.

- From the nature of the API, determine the **criticality** of the backend. As an example, if a security service provider is unavailable, it impacts authentication, and users will not be able to sign in; if a reference data provider is unavailable, cached data may be used temporarily.

- The API Gateway can be used to determine the API products that consumers have subscribed to.

- Draw up a service matrix to allow the operations team to quickly determine the impact of a loss of a backend provider interface. Consuming applications may also require additional measures such as displaying maintenance pages or cordoning off specific functionality for a critical provider dependency.

- An important item on our platform backlog is to publish the status of our APIs. Availability of provider systems will be a key input to this view.

Summary

In this chapter, we delved deeper into different domains within our Operational environment. From our experience of building and launching an API Platform, and from observation of the large number of areas to consider, a key lesson to take away is to have a view on operationalization early in the lifecycle of the platform. We also highlighted our approach to change and release management, which has been tailored, and importantly accommodated, to function in an already established organization. Once again, a DevOps *practice* is seen as a key enabler which allows agile delivery to be achieved consistently and reliably.

It is essential that running of an operations environment always be considered from a *people, process,* and *technology* perspective. As much as this may sound to be stereotypical, these elements are intrinsically intertwined, support each other, and result in a far more efficient and reliable platform. The logging and monitoring approaches discussed provide the *technology* capability and allow insight into solution execution. The support team roles, empowerment, and communications strategies highlighted show how the *people* element fits in. A well-defined *process* is key to a well-run, predictable, and stable Marketplace.

Our Marketplace, and likely yours too, is dependent on many internal supporting elements and backend service providers. Finally, we delved into our approach to leveraging enterprise managed services and efficiently working with provider systems. In all honesty, this chapter turned out to be longer and far more detailed than anticipated. I attribute this to the vastness of the operational landscape and to the simple fact that a solution will spend the greater part of its lifetime within an execution context.

CHAPTER 11

Conclusion

We are now in our fifth year of our API Marketplace implementation. It is remarkable that the pace and energy of the platform is more vibrant and stronger today than it has ever been. I honestly believe that the platform is now a living, breathing, *almost* self-sustaining entity. As I glance at my to-do list, there are still several areas that I have identified for optimization. One of the factors which this could be attributed to is technology options that were previously not available. We are on a constant quest to streamline performance and execution – possibly a perpetual one as new avenues and approaches appear with each iteration of the platform. Another significant factor is that backend product teams are now extremely keen to publish their service for external consumption, and we have a growing list of APIs scheduled for delivery.

In all honesty, while writing this book, I have questioned the time that I could have spent nurturing the platform. The reason which anchored me to the book was to attempt to capture our formula for success by sharing my experience from the last four years – to bootstrap other implementations. As indicated on a number of occasions, each Marketplace implementation will be unique, tailored to the needs and identity of the host organization. It is highly unlikely that the Marketplace you will build or are currently building will adopt every concept or approach outlined – from Platform Architecture to Operations. However, it is a fervent hope that while reading this book, the solutions outlined will provide a foundation, catalyst, or trigger for innovations in your platform.

With the benefit of hindsight, and from keen observation of many recurring themes, I am of the firm belief that there have been key ingredients to our formula that were essential to the success of our implementation. Although many are not technical, they are essential to the engineering spirit of this initiative.

© Rennay Dorasamy 2022
R. Dorasamy, *API Marketplace Engineering*, https://doi.org/10.1007/978-1-4842-7313-5_11

Team Dynamic

In Chapter 1, I highlighted the key roles to pilot the Marketplace star ship into new and unchartered territory. As much as these can be filled with talented individuals, it is essential that the roles function as a single unit. With any long-term project, human resource changes are inevitable. Ours has been no different and we have had several changes, with just myself and one or two other team members, the only constants.

This has afforded me a unique vantage point to observe several permutations, some successful, some not. The reason that our current configuration has been the most successful can be simply attributed to a fantastic team dynamic and culture. The various personalities, very much like the crew of Star Trek, complement and importantly balance one another. There are many occasions when there are more differences in opinion than universal agreement. Oddly enough, this is possibly the reason for a successful team culture. By considering a number of perspectives through active, healthy discussion and debate, we generally find the most balanced solution. Reciprocally, if everyone was similar, the end result would be heavily weighted in a specific way.

In every discussion, all viewpoints are heard and considered. This can be attributed to great facilitation by the ship's captain. If consensus cannot be reached, the captain adjudicates, taking all inputs into consideration. Although a team member's solution may not have been selected, they feel placated as they had the opportunity to share their view. With a solution or target identified, all members of the team pull in that direction.

The whole is greater than the sum of its parts (Aristotle).

Organizational Support

I am also of the firm conviction that we would not have been able to sustain full operational capability, let alone establish an API Marketplace, without a strong enterprise service foundation. This was not always my view. In the early stages of building the Minimum Viable Product (MVP), we viewed the rest of the enterprise as an impediment to our success. The concept of third-party developers leveraging organizational capability combined with our radical technology selection was years ahead of standard practices. In hindsight and introspection, the petulant mindset and impatience of our project team several years ago was relatively immature. Given that we were attempting to build a new digital channel into the organization, we should have proceeded with far more care and caution. The proximity of an API Marketplace at the outskirts of the traditional enterprise to bridge third-party access was most likely the contributing factor for both the project team's selection of bleeding-edge technology and the organization's cause for concern.

The mindset shift from annoyance to appreciation from the project team and suspicion to trust from the rest of the organization occurred during the process of operationalizing the platform. By leveraging enterprise capability, we inherited the experience and expertise of seasoned veterans, which helped fast-track the maturity of a platform from running under controlled laboratory conditions to reliably servicing real-world workloads. By demonstrating more patience and resilience, we were also able to evangelize the benefits that the capability and reach that an API Marketplace could afford the greater organization and lobby support from various enterprise domains.

A key lesson that I have learnt, both personally and professionally, is that it takes far more time and energy attempting to skirt around process and governance. Rather afford the organization the necessary respect by learning how to navigate existing process and more importantly, understanding its function and purpose. Odds are – you will discover that it serves to protect the organization and its users. Once you have a firm grasp of the process and function, then try to optimize for agility.

Seek first to understand.

Agility to Pivot

There were a few occasions when our mission of establishing the platform faced significant challenges, sometimes threatening the very existence of the initiative. Standout examples include a key backend provider for our first API product withdrawing at the last-minute due to regulatory requirements and a high-profile third-party consumer likely to miss a key annual target due to trouble consuming a new API.

The speedboat operating model, discussed in Chapter 1, allowed the project to pivot on a dime and change direction quickly. Interestingly, to mitigate the loss of the key backend, a system of far less importance and visibility in the organization was selected as a replacement as it provided similar, but lesser used functionality. At first, the project team was disappointed that we were not launching with more fanfare that the higher profile backend would have afforded. Over time, this fast changed to relief, as we observed the challenges of supporting a live API and how ill-prepared we were to transition from prototype to execution. In all honesty, had we launched with the higher-profile API, we would not have had sufficient time to stabilize our operational platform.

Apart from the learning that our APIs should be designed to be far simpler and the need for active third-party developer engagement, the potential bombshell of missing a key milestone date resulted in the creation of a new integration model. This allowed the platform to absorb complexity where possible to fast-track API adoption. This pattern has since become a cornerstone of our Marketplace and is actively used for future product design. The silver lining from this encounter is that an API Marketplace implementation is not strictly black-or-white. In true start-up mindset, the team and platform should do everything possible to create and sustain third-party adoption. If that means handing out T-shirts and mugs at developer meetups to spur interest or building a user interface to support an API,

Do what needs to be done.

Developer Centricity

As discussed in the chapter on monetization, the key element powering the Marketplace is the third-party developer. I can unreservedly say that everything exists for third-party consumption. Although your Marketplace may have the widest range of API products and built on a superb ground-breaking technology platform – without *active* third-party participation, the initiative is lost.

APIs should be conceptualized and crafted with third-party needs, interest, and aptitude in mind. Technical teams may become enamored with the cool factor and bragging rights of integrating into a legacy mainframe using a morse-code protocol developed by the founders of the Unix operating system. If the functionality it exposes is of no interest or little use to consumers outside your organization, the effort is wasted. Product owners have the unenviable task of bridging the digital divide between semi-delusional backend providers who believe their legacy system has ground-breaking capability and flighty third-party consumers looking to build the next killer-app.

The Sandbox concept, discussed in great detail, is a tool which can and must be used to facilitate this interaction. It is not simply a mechanism to support third-party testing. It can be used to gauge third-party interest and demand, shape an API definition and most importantly as a buffer between super-agile external consumers and a more stoic, well-governed, traditional enterprise ecosystem.

Finally, and possibly most importantly, the developer portal is your Marketplace shopfront and represents the first interaction between a third party and your platform. The next time you stand in front of a physical store or land on a new ecommerce portal, consider the decision-making process that would result in further engagement. With that in mind, launch your developer portal and consider it from the perspective of a third-party consumer. This should constantly and honestly be done by everyone in the team, even friends, family, and colleagues from other teams to get as much feedback and review as possible.

Engage your third-party community as quickly as possible to solicit feedback and understand your market. The developers or third parties in your territory may need assistance and support to use your platform. Be sure to keep this in mind.

The Developer is the center of your universe.

Where to Start

By now, the task of building an API Marketplace may seem to be incredibly difficult. After all, you are establishing a new digital channel into your organization, and such a capability needs to be underpinned by a planet-scale platform architecture. Not to mention APIs which must be superbly designed, developed according to agile principles with enterprise-level support.

At this point, I would like to share with you my number one coding principle:

Build simple and iteratively.

The principles, platform architectures, approaches to design, agile development, and operational procedures shared throughout this book have evolved over *years* and are still evolving. Our implementation started with a single API product to demonstrate an MVP. If I had to do it over, I would drastically reduce even this humble scope. It is possible, even advisable to start a sustainable API Marketplace with a handful of API products. The products could serve a niche function, and the platform can most certainly operate on a legacy architecture – as long as it is stable. Limit the number of initial API products – I would suggest a maximum of two to start. Resist the temptation of having a developer portal (shopfront) full of products. In the humble opinion of a developer, having one fully functioning API is far more impressive than ten "coming soon" indefinitely.

It is also easier to retrofit fewer products – for improved performance, monitoring, and operational visibility. A key lesson throughout this book, and one I have learnt through many years of integration experience, is that the interface serves to support the greater solution. As long as it is stable, predictable, and reliable, consumers are not really concerned if it uses the power core harvested from an advanced alien spacecraft which crashed to earth or archaic processes which were used to build the pyramids. Allow your platform architecture to evolve over time – in line with the needs and requirements of the Marketplace. Again, restraint is advised as this is an opportunity to use the latest and shiniest technology.

Set a timeframe, possibly as short as three months, not longer than six, to publish your first API and iterate from there.

Keep in Touch

In writing this book, I have drawn on years of experience, predominantly integration, across a wide range of projects and contexts. One of the marvels of working in technology is that there are many, possibly infinite ways to solve a problem. This is the reason I can't wait to open my notebook everyday as I get a new problem to solve – in *my* way. I would be especially keen to learn of your API Marketplace journey and the approaches that you and your team adopted to solve challenges – maybe in the same way we did, maybe (and very possibly) in a completely different way. Please feel free to stay in touch and let me know if you have any thoughts, suggestions, feedback, even counter-arguments, or criticism to any of the content throughout the book.

I believe that we can only go forward if we share and work collaboratively. I look forward to hearing from you.

Index

A

© Rennay Dorasamy 2022
R. Dorasamy, *API Marketplace Engineering*, https://doi.org/10.1007/978-1-4842-7313-5

T, U, V, W X

Y, Z

Printed in the United States
by Baker & Taylor Publisher Services